BEHIND THE LENS

th

FORTY YEARS

Behind the Lens

AT RTÉ

GODFREY GRAHAM

ashfield
PRESS

ASHFIELD PRESS • DUBLIN • IRELAND

ISBN: 1 901658 55 4

Typeset by Ashfield Press in 11.5 on 14.5 point Dante
Designed by
SUSAN WAINE

Printed in Ireland by
ßETAPRINT LIMITED, DUBLIN

FRONTISPIECE
Brian Cleeve, Simon Weafer, Colette Kavanagh, Godfrey Graham and Odran Walsh filming in Bavaria

OPPOSITE PAGE
James Plunkett and Godfrey Graham. (Photograph: Robin Boyd)

Paris 1962 … the young girl looking at the painter is my wife.
This book is dedicated to Sheila.

CONTENTS

ACKNOWLEDGEMENTS

The author is most grateful to the following for their help and guidance while writing this book: Her Excellency Mary McAleese; George Waters; Louis McRedmond; Don O'Farrell; Cathal Goan; Jim Mulkerns; Colm O'Laoghaire; Michael Monaghan; Charles Byrne; Declan Kiberd; Steward Pollock; Charles Scott; Bill Harpur; Adrian Moynes; Máirtín Mac Coniomaire; Bobby Lamb; Judith Elmes; Joe Barry; Eibhlin ni Oisin and Michael Talty, RTÉ Reference Library; Garech de Brun; Pat Johns; Claire McEnery, Shannon Airport; Kenny's Bookshop, Galway; Pat Dineen; Hélène de St Pierre; Maureen Hurley; Martha at Switch Secretarial Services; Niall Toibín; Gabrielle Brocklesby; Sheamus Smith; Orla Murray, Susan Kennedy at Lensmen; Peter Thursfield; John Hedgecoe; *Queen* Magazine; Camera Press; Dermot O'Shea; Cyril Irwin; Michael Moriarty; Robert Monks; John Bowman; *The Irish Examiner*; *The Irish Times*; Michael Colgan of the Gate Theatre; The Behan Estate; Random House; Maurice Craig; John Daly at Trinity College Library; John Kinsella; Alan Smale and Eamonn Lawlor.

FOREWORD

T HE ONLY WAY TO INTENSIFY personality is to multiply it; and that is precisely what Godfrey Graham has done through a lifetime which has seen him dance, act, bowl leg-breaks for the national cricket team, serve as a photographer's apprentice, and become a major recorder of the face and mind of contemporary Ireland.

In this vivid memoir, which is itself a cinematic sequence of exemplary scenes, he records how a career as a movie-actor might have beckoned, but that, all things considered, being behind the lens of a camera is perhaps a safer place to be. Not always, however – for on occasion this intrepid camera-man has had to record an interview on top of a church steeple or to brave the angry waves of the Atlantic in order to secure his necessary footage. He has witnessed violent unrest in eastern Europe under the communists and in Africa under local tyrants. He has been threatened by those very Orangemen whose opinions he was trying faithfully to record and professed his relief – despite his proper pride in our all-Ireland cricket team – in returning safely across the border to the reassuring sight of green post-boxes.

Many shy persons, who would never dream of being movers and shakers, are drawn to a career 'behind the lens': but Godfrey Graham is so sociable and so urbane that, had his life turned out differently, he might well have made a major impact on the playing field as a sports professional or in the debating chambers of the Dáil. He is both gentle and generous, but he has also a forcefulness which goes with great ability. He has, of course, the cameraman's quiet shrewdness too, the capacity to size up very rapidly the salient elements in a given situation, whether he is recording Edna O'Brien's return to her parental home or Seán O'Faoláin's musings on national identity.

His own imagination catches fire most often in the presence of artists, from David Lean to Mary Lavin, from Austin Clarke to James Plunkett, from James Joyce to Pat O'Connor – but that is because there is a touch of the artist about his own work too. In that work, imaginative audacity is tempered only by a strong sense of the material realities of the world in which people are asked to live their lives. He has the gift of empathy with his chosen subjects, often learning how to see them as they would see themselves. It is, you feel, the poetic streak in a Kavanagh or a Plunkett which brings out an answering lyricism in Graham's own composition of the pictorial record, whether it be of Clarke as surrogate priest in black hat and coat or of Kavanagh cradling a wounded kingfisher. Such moments have an element of chance and good fortune about them, but it takes a true artist to identify the moment when a man or woman is revealed in all their fullness.

All autobiographies are in some sense triumphs of the human spirit, as it learns to put order on the chaos of a life; but this book is a very special kind of victory. In it, a distinguished Irish lighting cameraman recalls the dyslexic boy he once was, struggling with an undiagnosed problem and fearful of his future. There is a poignant sense of roads not taken when he leaves his good friends in mid-stream at Blackrock College. Yet his imaginative and astute mother has already divined her boy's real destiny – and so he goes on to a great career in which he learns how to use the images of a changing world in order to explore his innermost self. In that sense, the work of Godfrey Graham is not only his major legacy but also his truest autobiography, yet the present reconstruction in words of his progress from North Great George's Street through Blackrock and into the world is itself a work of which the troubled teenager might never have dreamed himself capable. It stands as a monument to the making of a man who, whether he works in word or in image, has the gift of explanation without simplification.

What is most notable all through is the author's magnanimity and kindness. Many of his subjects, in the presence of a less sensitive man, might never have relaxed sufficiently to reveal their authentic personalities. You get the sense that it took a rare kind of trust for a soul, in all the vulnerability of its self-making, to risk an encounter with what for most people in the 1960s and 1970s was a strange new medium. Yet Godfrey Graham not only set his subjects at ease but also, in recording those decades of change from 1960 to the present, helped Irish people to know and understand themselves.

Reading these lucid pages, one feels nostalgic for a time when the

1982 Jacobs Award winners: Back: Godfrey Graham, Ian McGarry, Bernard McLaverty, Forbes McFall, Harry Bradshaw, Andy O'Mahony, John Bowman, Pat Kenny.
Seated: Twink, Leo O'Donnell, Minister John Wilson, Senator Gordon Lambert, Trish Barry.

national television service took the trouble to record all major authors and artists, as well as the daily realities of ordinary life. There is a youthful enthusiasm and openness about the approaches to topics by teams of people who came together for short periods of shared creativity – and who were forever willing to be taken by surprise. They were the lucky ones, fortunate enough to share in the glory days of the new medium, before national form gave way to cosmopolitan formula; and they were blessed to have Godfrey Graham among their number. He indeed has the versatility of the true Celt.

DECLAN KIBERD

Small boy playing in St. Stephen's Green

THE EARLY YEARS

IN 1898, MY GRANDFATHER 'Professor' Dickie Graham bought 35, North Great George's Street, a property that had been built in 1784 for Lord Valentine Brown, Earl of Kenmare. My grandfather had one or two other houses nearby which he must have sold in order to acquire No. 35. He was a good businessman, who always liked music and dance.

Some five years later, Denis J. Maginni, the dancing master, came to him to ask if he could rent a room in which he could run his dancing academy. My grandfather agreed. Maginni conducted his dancing school for some years with great success. Sadly, Maginni's wife and their six children succumbed to the dreaded consumption in 1906. He was distraught and seems to have disappeared off the scene. Maginni would later be immortalised by James Joyce in his novel *Ulysses*.

Apparently, my grandmother, Nana decided that it was a pity to let the dancing academy go to waste and suggested to my grandfather that they should run it themselves. Grandad had applied for a singing and dancing licence before this when he lived at 26 Temple Street so he had this kind of idea in his head. My grandparents would become extremely well-known teachers of dancing over the next 40 years.

Later, Richard Graham ran into trouble with the authorities for running his dancing school without a licence. On May 18 1927, he appeared before Mr. Collins at the Dublin District Court. *The Irish Times* reported at that time: 'A great deal of merriment accompanied the hearing of four summonses at the instance of Inspector McGloin against Mr. Richard Graham who carries out a Dancing Academy in 35 North Great George's Street, for permitting his premises to be used for dancing without being duly licensed. Inspector McGloin gave evidence of having visited the place and observed

'Professor' Dickie
Graham when he met
Peadar O'Donnell and
Seán MacBride. (Portrait
by Harry Kernoff)

dancers dancing there and carrying on. He had previously warned the defendant.'

It seems my grandfather defended himself by explaining that he was the first man to introduce the Charleston to Dublin. He told the court he taught jigs, waltzes and reels and that jazz was played in the premises. He explained that his dancing activities were run in a very responsible manner, adding, 'My hall and house are closed at 11 p.m. sharp every evening'.

The most revealing comment from Inspector McGloin in the newspaper's report of the case was that it was 'cheap skate dancing' that was carried on there and that numerous complaints were made to the police about the conduct of the persons leaving the house. Presumably this meant that the ordinary people were able to go to my grandfather's Dancing Academy, which the authorities resented.

When Dickie Graham protested that he had been in the house for over twenty years, the Judge asked whether it was the place where Denis J. Maginni ran his academy. According to the newspaper report, my grandfather responded: 'Ah, he's dead this long time and all belonging to him. I made a small fortune from the place. I have bought six houses there.' The judge ruled that my grandfather could not conduct his dancing academy without a licence and fined him £20. Granddad gave notice to appeal.

The court case tells so much about Dickie Graham, who must have been quite a dynamic businessman. He paid the licence in due course.

My father told me that my grandfather could not run his dancing classes or private lessons during Lent. The Church did not approve. So he needed another way of making a living. In 1911, he went to London and bought two 35mm projectors and opened two cinemas, one in Capel Street, the other in Redmond's Hill.

In 1909, James Joyce opened the first movie house in Dublin, the Volta, which he managed.

The Sinn Fein paper of October 19, 1912 announced:

IRISHMEN, WOMEN, AND CHILDREN
Support the ONLY Picture House in Dublin
Owned by an Irishman
THE NEW IRISH CINEMA
Capel Street [Next Trades' Hall]
NOW OPEN! NOW OPEN! NOW OPEN !
Continuous Performances Daily 2 to 10.30.
Change of Pictures Mon., Thurs, and Sunday.
Prices: 3d., 4d., 5d. Children 2d. up to 6pm.

Over the next year, the cinema also received notices in the *Bioscope* magazine in London:

'That progressive little house in Capel Street is owned and managed – in the most capable way – by Mr. R H Graham. Some recent improvements have been made, noticeably the installing of a new Kemm Projector, and the raising of the screen. The outside of the hall is prettily decorated, and the floor is amply sufficient to allow everyone to see plainly.

'A picture depicting the adventures of the great *Buffalo Bill* was shown last night for the first time in Dublin. Mr Graham is determined to make the theatre a bigger success in the future, and it would look as if he were

Projector in my grandfather's cinema

going the right way about this. Here's luck – the best to him.' (3.10.1912)

'The Irish Cinema, Capel Street, Dublin, the proprietor of which is that well known gentleman Mr. R Graham is doing fine business. In fact Mr. Graham was commenting to me the other evening on his lack of room. At the same time he informed me that he had received six offers to purchase the place. This speaks volumes doesn't it? On Sundays it is packed to over-flowing'. (26.2.1913)

'The Irish Cinema in Capel Street Dublin continues to merit the approval of all its numerous patrons. On Sundays it is difficult to keep the crowd from bursting in oblivious of pay box and attendants, to see more quickly the good fare provided by the proprietor Mr. R H Graham'. (17.4.1913)

Earlier, there had been a devastating fire at the cinema at Redmond's Hill. *The Freeman's Journal* noted:

SERIOUS FIRE IN DUBLIN – PICTURE THEATRE GUTTED
'At about 3 o'clock yesterday afternoon, an alarming fire occurred on

Redmond's Hill at the premises No. 16, which are used as an animated picture theatre.

About 5 o'clock Captain Purcell and his men had entirely extinguished a fire, which at one period threatened to be of considerable magnitude. Mr. Graham is, it is said, the proprietor of the cinematograph exhibition'.

All films at the time were printed on highly flammable nitrate material.

The newspaper reported that 'the flames were so fierce as to damage the signboards and blister the painting on houses in the immediate vicinity of the fire, whilst on all sides the crackling and breaking of windows was heard'.

There was no screening in progress thanks to Providence.

My grandmother told me stories of how, during the troubled time coming up to 1916, British soldiers raided the house when there was a dance on, looking for revolutionaries. They would brush by my grandmother at the door, looking for people on the run. When the dancers heard the soldiers, the men who were dancing would pass a weapon or papers they might be carrying to the women with whom they were dancing.

The British never searched any of the women. Grandmother told me that, as they departed, the officer in charge, would say, 'Sorry for this disruption, Mrs Graham, but we are after these bloody revolutionaries.' The soldiers would return to the dances on other occasions with their own girlfriends.

There was a huge big kitchen with a black range in the basement. The old IRA had a munitions store there, but they did not tell Nana. In the huge pantry, my grandmother would reach in for an egg underneath the hams hanging from the ceiling and on a number of occasions came out with something much bigger than an egg – a mills bomb!

I used to wander in Nana's domain and into the three arched pantries. As a five-year-old, I was frightened on occasions to look up and see a pheasant or pigeon hanging upside down, seeming to be looking straight into my face.

Nana was a great storyteller, *Cinderella*, *Red Riding Hood* and *Hansel and Gretel* were told with the greatest detail. My brother Roger and I never tired of listening to the stories. Nana was a Wicklow woman, whose maiden name was Brown.

She grew sad when she told me about her brother Harry who was in the Royal Dublin Fusiliers and, like so many other Irishmen, was at the Somme. When home on leave, he was walking down Westland Row and was shot by a group of marauding Black and Tans. Imagine dying like that, in your own city, having survived the Somme.

When the GPO was shelled on Easter Sunday 1916, my grandmother put my father Tommy and his brothers, Richard and Jimmy, into the pram and had to evacuate the house. She pushed them all the away to a bungalow that they had on the city outskirts, near Rathfarnham, very near St. Enda's where the Pearse brothers had their school. It was quite a long way, right up to the Yellow House on that road and left of the Tuning Fork. Our family knew Padraig and Willy Pearse quite well.

Today, the house is still there and the old faded brass nameplate still remains – 'Rose Villa'. A lovely rambling cottage, it stood on a couple of acres, with a stream running through the garden and a big chestnut tree with a swing. The same family who moved into the house after my family left is there still.

My grandfather decided that, if he could set up his projectors at 'Rose Villa', he could show movies there in the evening. But he never managed to do this because he had difficulty powering the machines. However, he did run afternoon tea dances there, with the idea that as the light faded he could show some movies. He was ahead of the drive-in movie concept in the U.S. It must have been an idyllic lifestyle.

Some days after the fighting had finished, my grandmother returned to the city centre and life continued on. In the War of Independence, it seems that my family were more sympathetic with the Anti-Treaty faction because a platoon of men from that side were billeted in the house at 35 North Great George's Street. De Valera came to the house in disguise dressed as a woman for secret meetings. An American-based Professor has since told us that he came across details of the James Joyce Centre at No. 35 on the Internet. His own father had been billeted in the house on the Anti Treaty side. They were attacked and one man was shot dead, others were injured.

My father told me that when he was 13 he took messages for De Valera on his bike, across the Three Rock Mountain and the Featherbed. This is certainly plausible because he lived in Rathfarnham, at the foot of the mountains, during his summer holidays from Synge Street CBS. It would have been relatively easy for him to get involved in this type of activity.

In 1931, Peadar O'Donnell and Seán MacBride were trying to found the new society, Saor Eire. They went to see Lady Gregory at the Abbey Theatre to ask if they could hold their inaugural meeting in the theatre. Lady

Gregory's heart was in the right place with regard to the struggle but she wasn't very happy. In front of her were two of the most famous Irish socialists of that day and she apologised, saying that she couldn't give them permission to use the National theatre for this meeting. So they left disappointed.

Seán and Peadar came to see Dickie Graham at 35 North Great George's Street. I should love to have been a fly on the wall to watch the interaction between those very different characters. MacBride born in Paris, with a sense of European culture and history, fluent in Irish, English and French. Peadar rooted in his Donegal background, Irish to the core. Standing in the little ballroom talking together with my grandfather, they must have been dwarfed by the cameos on the wall ... those pictures of Spanish, German, French and Italian figures dancing, musicians with instruments, and not forgetting another little cameo of two children, my father Tommy, age seven years, and his five-year-old sister, Rosaleen, about to do an Irish jig. Dickie Graham had commissioned these paintings in 1916. He gave Seán and Peadar the room they needed for that meeting and others over the year that followed.

Those cameos have been restored and are still in the ballroom. They are modest paintings and not great works of art. However, as social history, they are of huge interest.

NORTH GREAT GEORGE'S STREET

'That most superb of streets', as historian Maurice Craig calls her, 'it is slanted through Joyce's *Nighttown* along a steep access from his college, Belvedere, down Monto to a view of the Custom House and the River Liffey'. The street where Sir John Pentland Mahaffy, Provost of Trinity College, and Sir Samuel Ferguson, lived. How it had fallen from its great elegance by the 1930s.

I was born in 1936, when my parents were living in 35 North Great George's Street. At four, I went to the Loreto Convent, which was about ten doors up the street from where I lived.

Nana was a very strict Catholic. She would attend Mass every day at the Pro-Cathedral or with the Jesuits at Gardiner Street. She knew Matt Talbot and said he was a gentle character, seated on the church steps, bound with chains and other uncomfortable things wrapped around him. Even when her hip became unbearably painful, Nana would traipse up and down North

Great George's Street to Mass in all weathers. She advised me that I should seriously consider the priesthood and, at that time, during the 1940s, I was a child seriously committed to the church and I did consider it for a few weeks. Nana's only daughter Rosaleen had her wedding reception in No 35. It went on for several days and nights.

Opposite No 35 was a small garage. Behind that garage was a laneway that came out at Grooms Hotel, across the road from the Gate Theatre. Down by the side of No 35 was a similar lane. Apparently it was possible for people who were on the run in O' Connell Street or Parnell Square to get as far as Fairview using this maze of lanes at the back of the big houses. This was used frequently during the troubled times.

We didn't have a big grassy garden at the back of 35 North Great George's Street and I used to be taken for walks to Mountjoy Square by Mary where I would play on the grass. I was also told that I threw the odd tantrum, holding onto the railings for dear life and screaming.

In those days, there was a lot of poverty on the street and in Dublin's inner city. Most people did not have very much. We were slightly better off because of the Dancing Academy and my grandfather's properties. Some of the houses in the street had ten, fifteen, twenty people living in them. Some were really tenements. I remember many of the children were barefoot. The rag and bone man used to come along once or twice a week and you could hear him calling from quite far off. On other days, a fishmonger would be along with a small cart, ringing a hand bell. There were few cars. I remember it as a rather rough part of the city and my mother saying that she would have to get her family out of there. We were living rent-free at the time and had the third floor to ourselves, but she said that we needed to start somewhere else.

My grandmother's house was such a vast place for a little boy to grow up in. The staircase was very steep and seemed endless and sometimes frightening. From my bedroom I could see the boys passing to and from Belvedere College, at the top of the street. There were high ceilings in the house with Greek warriors riding in chariots. I would lie on the floor and look up at them. Another room had strange sea creatures. It was years later that I realised they were the signs of the zodiac. They had been created by Stapleton & Thorp, possibly the best of their period. The Earl of Kenmare, Valentine Brown recognised who were the best artists when it came to plaster work.

I remember my mother taking Roger and myself on the train to

Family homes in North Great George's Street, now the James Joyce Centre, and later, Blackrock House in Blackrock, Co. Dublin

Blackrock. After you passed Lansdowne Road and Sydney Parade, you were in a dark piece of track. Then suddenly Merrion Gates, a burst of light. All the children sang out 'the sea, the sea', running to the windows of the carriage. I didn't realise at that time that we would soon move to the seaside.

Back in the old house, if we were very good, from time to time my grandmother would give us little trinkets from a press in the front room. They had been bought for spot prizes to be given out at dances long ago. The press is still there in the bookshop at No 35, now the James Joyce Centre.

BLACKROCK HOUSE

I was about seven when the family left North Great George's Street and moved about six miles south of the city centre to Blackrock, near the sea, where we were to start our real growing up in a very different environment on Dublin Bay. Nana, Jimmy and Richard remained at No 35.

We lived in an immense apartment on the top floor of Blackrock House. There was a baby grand piano in one corner of the living room and I grew up listening to my father, who had studied with Professor Larchet at the Royal Irish Academy, playing the works of the great composers Beethoven, Rachmaninoff and Stravinsky while, at the same time, the modern music of George Shearing, Count Basie, George Gershwin, and, of course, Jerome Kern and Richard Rodgers. My father was a contemporary dance teacher in the 1920s, '30s and '40s and he used this music when teaching his clients.

Madame Toto Cogley was a friend of my parents. A Parisian, she had married Fred Cogley, Senior who had been in the *Irish Independent*. She had come from Paris in the 1920s, which was the heart of European culture at the time. For instance, she had seen the ballet, 'Parade', which was inspired by Colteau. The decor was by Picasso; the choreography was by Léonide Massine. This amazing work was produced by Diaghilev's Ballet Russes. What a stunning production this must have been. Toto brought these experiences from her own native city, the Paris of Jean Paul Sartre and Simone de Beauvoir. It must have been a wonderfully interesting range of memories and experiences that Toto brought with her to Dublin at that time.

Fred Cogley, Senior, had met Toto on a visit to Wexford. He had worked in the *Freeman's Journal* and when the *Independent* was set up, he transferred to that organisation. Toto had come from Paris to Dublin and set up a small theatre workshop. Later on, when Micheál MacLiammóir and Hilton Edwards came to the city, they were advised to contact Toto because she knew all the literati at the time – actors, producers and other theatrical people. Toto Cogley was one of the founder members of the Gate Theatre. She had been in the Paris Conservatoire before coming to Dublin. Toto's mother did not think that Fred Cogley, Senior, was good enough for her daughter so the couple, who were madly in love at the time, eloped … not to Gretna Green or some similarly romantic place, but to Santiago in Chile, where they were married.

Toto came to my parents' parties at Blackrock House where she met painters, writers, poets and musicians, including Harry Kernoff, Harry Dineen and his wife Maureen, the journalist Seamus Kelly, painters Muiris MacConghail and Seán O'Sullivan, and the dancing teacher Evelyn Birchall. These were the friends of my parents, with the result that my development in the appreciation of music and the arts was a very rich one.

Getting back to Miss Birchall. Michael Powell, the film director, had made a film called *The Red Shoes*. I was the only boy in Miss Evelyn Birchall's ballet school when the film was released. Miss Birchall insisted that we must all see this film, myself included. However, she told us not to worry when Moira Shearer danced over the balcony to her death at Monte Carlo, landing on the train track in front of a train, reassuring us that, when the film cut to the close up, the blood over her feet, dress and legs was only Heinz tomato sauce. The class felt much better after this and soldiered on.

The film is exquisitely photographed by Jack Cardiff who is still alive and well, I am glad to see. Powell's film is a masterpiece. I recently obtained a beautiful DVD copy in London, which is quite rare. Powell captures exactly the nuances of ballet, the high art, the athleticism, the sheer fitness the dancers have to attain, the injuries and the pain that they have to go through and simply dance on. This film also exposes the battles of the egos and the eccentricities of the main players, artistic director, choreographer, designer, musical director. Director Martin Scorsese says this is one of his favourite movies of all time. As a young dancer of ten, my hero was Léonide Massine in the role of the ballet master. He also danced in the *Red Shoes* ballet within the film, playing the part of the cobbler who made the red shoes that were possessed and finally never stopped dancing, exhausting the ballerina and driving her out of her mind. Léonide Massine's skills were breathtaking as a character dancer.

Every year, Evelyn Birchall had a production in the Gaiety Theatre. She cleverly choreographed a 30-minute ballet that she called 'The Red Shoes' as part of the programme. I danced the Massine role of the cobbler, thereby linking me with my hero (at the time). In ballet for me, it has always been the music that captivated me first, then the story. I was fascinated much more by those in the character roles than the classical dancers. To me, they were like actors who could also dance. In Miss Birchall's school, I was eventually overwhelmed by being surrounded by too many women. I did have a strong attraction to the opposite sex but this was like blanket bombing on a large scale. However, I had lasted for four very enjoyable years that left me with an abiding interest in and excitement for dance of all kinds.

Madame Toto Cogley's European influences were stimulating for a city cut off from the artistic activities of the outside world. Things of the mind were the only escape from the grey, dull existence of Dublin in the 1920s and '30s. For example, in 1934, Dublin Corporation met to discuss banning jazz from Radio Éireann. The young Gaels of County Meath were angered by jazz, stating that they didn't want any kind of African stuff like that in Ireland.

Toto Cogley adored ballet, painting and sculpture. She was petite in a bird-like way and she was my godmother. Toto had extensive knowledge of Paris, the city where James Joyce lived and was beginning to establish himself and where his book *Ulysses* was published in 1922 on his 40th birthday. She must have been a breath of fresh air from continental Europe to the grim Dublin of the 1930s, just a few years before the horror of war struck Europe and the world again. Dublin was also suffering from the treatment of our leading writers, whose books were being banned at that time, with the result that there was a continued depression, like a black cloud, over much of Irish society.

In 1943, if you looked out the windows of our apartment in Blackrock House, you could see the necklace of the lights around Dublin Bay stretch from the Bailey Lighthouse to the city. Those were great days. Kernoff had painted my grandfather and my mother. I still treasure these canvasses.

My mother and father had two dance studios at that time. One was on the top floor of the Bank of Ireland building, overlooking Capel Street Bridge. It was a lovely location. When you looked out of those windows down to the bridge at night, you could see the Liffey drift lazily by. It was almost Parisian in a way. The horse-drawn cabs seemed to glide over the surface of the bridge. The lamps shimmered in the water. The other studio was on St. Stephen's Green, where Eircom is today. Waiting for Dad to finish teaching, I would play in the Green before heading for the tram with him, home to Blackrock.

Behind Blackrock House was Maretimo Gardens East. All the residents had access to a private beach, reached by a bridge that spanned the railway and a private gate for which there was a key. There were three sandy coves with a high outcrop of rocks and two bathing pools, one slightly larger than the other, filled to a depth of about four metres when the tide was in. There was a little bathing pavilion for changing and a lovely boathouse, with some fine sailboats. It was quite obvious that this whole beach area was from another era when life was more elegant for some, and one family might have had this entire land running down to the sea. It was a magic place to grow up. We played, swam, canoed and fished.

When the tide went out, a vast lagoon of four acres of water remained. Plaice or flat fish would remain 'til they were bigger and then would go out to the open sea. With the help of some older fishermen, we learned a tech-

Maretimo Beach behind Blackrock House

nique of spearing the fish, wading in up to our knees and prodding the sand.

It was fantastic to meet all the other families who were living in the flats in Blackrock House and in Maretimo Gardens, the semi-detached houses nearby. It was 1943. On the corner of Seapoint Avenue, near Blackrock House, was Meany's shop. The Meany family ran a great business from the 1930s into the 1990s. Every summer, the outside of the shop was bedecked with rubber swimming rings, little coloured windmills and floating ducks. We could walk along the path from Blackrock House on the same side of the road in safety near the tram tracks to buy our sweets and ice creams.

My brother Roger, Ray Dineen and some of the O'Brien children would meet up along the way. I remember a gang of us so often, our two or three pennies clutched in our hot little hands and our faces looking just over the edge of the counter, watching the ritual as Mary would take the box with the new block of ice cream out of the fridge, an ancient deed chest. She

Godfrey Graham, Ray Dineen, Neil og O'Brien, Niamh O'Brien, Roger Graham and Terry O'Brien in Blackrock House, 1943. Photograph – Dalton.

Godfrey Graham at Willow Park

would then take a big carving knife from a jar and open the box. Then a silver metal frame would be pressed down on the block of ice cream to mark the cutting point. A two-penny ice, the smallest you could have, was all I was ever able to afford. I never saw any child get more than a two-penny ice cream and I never saw my mum or any other mother buy a whole block of ice cream in this era.

The summers were long; they seemed to go on forever. The steam train would pound through on the track just behind the big grassy bank. The steam would plume up into the sky. The bank, which was about 30 metres high, was made from the soil that had to be dug out when they were making the tunnel for the railway.

I remember Pat and Brian Pearce's father being on the beach with us one day in the early 1940s and we spotted aircraft flying over Howth. He pointed out immediately that it was a German Messerschmitt being chased by a Spitfire or a Hurricane … something we were to see from time to time. Brian and Pat's father knew about these things because he was in the Irish Naval Service. He was an officer on one of the corvettes during the War. We all had gas masks at the time. My Dad was in the Blackrock branch of the Local Defence Force at the time, ready with others to defend us should Mr Hitler arrive unexpectedly.

I had joined the Brendan Smith Academy of Acting. I think my mother and father were eager to have me go on the stage as an actor or dancer. I was there for the best part of a year during which time the film *The Blue Lagoon* was going to be made by Frank Launder with Jean Simmons and Noel Purcell. I went to an audition at the Gresham Hotel and was picked to go to England for a screen test at Pinewood Studios. Before I set off for London, Noel Purcell, who was a good friend of my Uncle Jimmy, patted me on the back saying, 'I'll see you in the south sea islands'.

It was a terribly exciting adventure. It was 1947 and post-war Britain seemed all grey. It was my first flight in an aeroplane, a Dakota. We were there for about a week trying to learn the lines and so on. The producer, Frank Launder, had made another film in Wicklow already with Deborah Kerr. He had also tried to help the fledgling film industry in Ireland in the 1940s, and had written the introduction to Liam O Laoghaire's gem of a book, *Invitation to the Film*.

I didn't get the part, and when I was older, eventually ended up working behind a film camera, which is probably a safer place to be.

SCHOOL AND CRICKET DAYS

When we moved to Blackrock, I went to Willow Park School. I remember settling in very well there. There were plenty of sports – rugby, cricket, tennis, croquet, a little hurling and some Gaelic football were played. There was a good atmosphere in the place. Fr. Stanley was a great personality, a warm and friendly man. He seemed to have great drive. I played half a dozen rugby games at full back. I was a bit spindly at the time and I was given a dispensation, which was a bit unusual. I played tennis and cricket. The War was still on at the time but I do remember these years being very happy ones. I went to Willow Park every day on the tram from Blackrock. There was a lay teacher, Mr. Billy O'Byrne, whom I found to be strict but, even at nine, I realised that he was a real teacher. My slow reading speed and spelling meant, unfortunately, that I dropped out of his class. None of the other teachers, some of whom were studying for the priesthood at the time, spotted that I could not spell or read.

My cricket was improving. I had devised the leg break that spun prodigiously. I was getting wickets at levels above my age group. I was twelve years old when I played against St. Mary's. Fred Cogley was a demon fast bowler who hit me on the head with the ball. Some people say this may explain a lot about my behaviour from then on. So be it. I worked with Fred at RTÉ over the years and we joked about our first meeting on the field of play. He was one of the best schoolboy fast bowlers I have ever seen. Life is funny. Fred is related to Toto Cogley, my godmother.

Seán Piggott was a pal of mine at Willow Park. His father, Joe, played senior cricket for Phoenix and Pembroke and was a terrific coach. Joe Byrne was with us, too. I was lucky enough to be included in a little club, called St. John's, that was being coached for several summers. We practised in Castle Park School in Dalkey, thanks to the kindness of the headmaster. I seemed to take to bowling

I used to play French cricket with my brother Roger – a game which involved using a tennis racquet to defend your feet and legs as your opponent tried to hit them with the ball and thus regain control of the racquet. One day it occurred to me that I might win more games if I could spin the tennis ball so that it would turn from right to left. Having Joe Piggott as a coach was one of the best things that ever happened to me. He knew so much about the game. I tried to bowl over arm, the spin ball that I had devised when playing French cricket with Roger. It seemed to cause the batsmen a lot of problems, bowling them out, sometimes even bowling them behind their legs and hitting the stumps. So I practised as hard as I could. In January and February, I would go into the big handball alley in Blackrock College, use some tape to shape the wickets on the end wall, and bowl for hours, managing to spin the cricket ball on the concrete. As a result, I was bowling very well, with both my line and length under control, by the time the cricket season began in April.

When I was 13, I moved to Blackrock College. My studies were in more difficulty there. I did enjoy history and religion because they were taught by people who had good imaginations and imparted the meaning of the stories that appealed to me. Mathematics, French, Latin and English were beyond me because of my chronic inability to spell and read at the normal speed. In first, second and third years at Blackrock College, I was beginning to get extremely worried about my future. Would I get a job? What would become of me? I was agonising about these things all by myself, there did not seem to be the same concern from my teachers, who were just not aware of my

Blackrock College senior cricket team in 1953. Donie Grehan, Peter McCormack, Cyril Irwin, Godfrey Graham, Willie McCormack, Tony Fallon, Gerry de Brit, Paddy Dempsey (capt), Paul McQuaid and Simon Kenny

situation. I know there must have been some good teachers in 'Rock but I didn't have them for classes. By then I was dropping into the D grade. I got a lot of caning in those years because my preparation was bad and a lot of the time my work was incorrect. Somehow I never felt any resentment for the punishment that was inflicted on me. It was the natural order of things in those days. Our parents, even the boys, really never discussed it. While I worried so much about my future, there was one thing that kept me going at the time – nobody could play my leg breaks. In 'Rock, I was playing on the senior team and was three years younger than most of my cricket contemporaries. I joined Pembroke Cricket Club, playing with men's teams while only a teenager.

I must have been 15 when I was selected to play cricket for the Leinster Schools' Senior Team. This was my first representative game. We were to play Munster at the Mardyke in Cork. What excitement. My Dad said he would take me to town from Blackrock House by bus. He suggested we attend Mass at Clarendon Street on our way. I had never been in that church.

I was impressed with the interior. There is something about an Order Church. Then on to Kingsbridge Station, or Heuston as it is today.

The rest of the squad was there, with the officials. Our captain was Joe Hopkins. Joe was a few years older than some of us, a real father figure, and a great wicket keeper and fine batsman. We boarded the Enterprise, its massive steam engine exploded into action. We were on our way to Cork. I had never gone anywhere in Ireland. Most of us had no idea how far away Cork was. It was lunchtime when we arrived.

As soon as we got out of the station and saw Cork, I could not believe how different it was from my city. The river was divided into three or four tributaries. The houses in tiers, rising up, the hills surrounding us. The sounds of snatches of conversation. They were so high in pitch, not like that flatter Dublin sound I was familiar with.

Our bus wound its way to the Mardyke. More delights. The cricket ground must be set in one of the prettiest locations imaginable. A great monastic church overlooked the cricket ground. Beautiful gardens, some with orchards, looked on to the River Lee. Fitzgerald's Park nearby. A little fairground was close to the field of play. One of Cork's most prestigious tennis clubs nestles between the river and the cricket ground. I had a good game and got some wickets. There was a great welcome from the Corkonians.

I would return to play in a senior Inter-Pro against Munster many years after this, opening the batting with the great Stanley Bergin. We put on 59 for the first wicket. Later I met and played against Noel 'Skippy' Cantwell who was a useful middle order batsman and kept wicket. At the time he was captain of Manchester United and Ireland.

Some years later, I was walking over O'Connell Bridge and spotted Skippy Cantwell walking towards me. He seemed to be preoccupied. 'Great to see you, Godfrey. I am hamstrung. Can you help me? I have to get nine pounds of Hafners sausages urgently. I can't find the shop anywhere'. I turned him around and took him to Henry Street, just around the corner from the G.P.O., beside the entrance to Radio Éireann. Noel was delighted to be back on the train back to Cork that same day. His purchases were for a party in the cricket pavilion at the Mardyke. Imagine coming all the way to Dublin. He must have had another reason to be in Dublin, but perhaps not, who knows? Hafners sausages were something special.

I was getting many wickets on both the Junior and Senior Sides at Blackrock College. Paddy Dempsey captained our team.

Cricket saved me in a sense. Imagine how I felt. I had not even taken the Intermediate Exam. My loving parents, because of their lifestyle, had never given me sufficient supervision in my early years at school. I simply slipped through the net. I was dyslexic. I simply could not remember what a word looked like even a few seconds after seeing it, with the result that I just could not spell. If you can't spell, you can't read either.

In all the time at Willow Park and Blackrock College, no prefect or priest ever made me feel that I was a failure in any real sense. They looked to a student's strengths despite other difficulties. I left with glowing references that talked about my personality and my ability to get on with people, that they felt I would do well in whatever career I would choose. There was not one reference to my academic record. There was really nothing to say.

I did regret at the time losing contact with my contemporaries, I lost those years in fourth, fifth and six year. However, if I had been at 'Rock until sixth year, I would have gone into banking or insurance, maybe, or auctioneering, or worked in the civil service. I would never have had the opportunities and the career that ultimately came my way in broadcasting.

I had met priests at Blackrock College, some of whom were eminent scholars and theologians and who were experts in the classics. My brief exposure to French and Latin was stimulating. These people fired my curiosity in things spiritual, something that has stayed with me to this day. I left at 16 with the realisation that fascinating, unexplored subjects were out of my reach at the time. I would return to study social ethics, moral theology and communism in adult life.

In the early 1950s, my father brought a girl from Sadler's Wells in London, a dancer who had grown too tall so had to become a teacher, to head the ballet school in Dalkey. Things went fairly well for a few months but the '50s were not the best time to launch such a venture. Dad was ten years before his time.

He had approached the President of Blackrock College, the Rev. Vincent J. Dinan some years earlier and suggested that the boys at the college were well known for their achievements on the rugby field. However, when it came to socialising on the dance floor, they might need some help. The college president agreed so the sixth year 'Rock boys had ballroom dancing lessons on Sundays in the Castle. This went down very well but, of course the lads had to dance with each other which wasn't ideal – it would have been bad if word got out that the 'Rock boys had gone namby-pamby!

The matter was discussed following suggestions from some of the boys that they needed the real thing, namely girls, if only for technical reasons. Apparently the authorities in 'Rock wrote a letter to the Reverend Mothers in Sion Hill and the Sacred Heart, Monkstown, cordially inviting an appropriate number of sixth form girls to join the classes. After a considerable delay, the idea was rejected. The boys were not to get the opportunity to learn to dance with real girls yet!

Father Joseph Corless was going to produce *The Gondoliers* that season. The Dalkey Dance Studio's days were numbered. Dad knew that there was a dance called the *Cachucha* in this Gilbert & Sullivan operetta and suggested to Father Corless that his choreographer Stephanie from Sadler's Wells might help out. He agreed.

I was in the chorus of that production, one of eight boys who were to dance. Some of us had done Irish dancing, such as The Walls of Limerick, most had never danced at all. I had some ballet training. I was chosen to be one of the four girls to dance the cachucha, complete with castanets! It was probably more to do with my alto voice than anything else. The group included Frank Kelly, who went on to greater things as a comic actor in such programmes as *Hall's Pictorial Weekly*, *Father Ted* and many more.

Stephanie rehearsed us for six weeks. Some of the lads who played on the rugby teams said she was tougher than their coaches. There was much agonising about the fact that those boys who were dressed as girls should not look too feminine. Stephanie disagreed, saying that the dance would look as real as she could make it. However, the 'girl dancers' did wear rugby shorts under their skirts so that, as they spun out high around them, the 'Rock rugby tradition was still clearly in evidence. Our performance went down so well with the audience that there were at least three encores!

The 1950s, our time, were full of excitement. We felt the hand of authority on our shoulder but it did not stop us discovering life as we emerged into adulthood … a little brake was a useful discipline.

Around that time, my father started to run teenage 'hops' at the Christian Institute, next to the Adelphi Cinema in Dun Laoghaire. The hall was a badminton court and there was a small stage. I was 16 and all my friends from Blackrock College attended regularly. Dad would play all the latest records on a gramophone, including Nat King Cole, Johnny Ray, Joe Stafford, Frankie Laine and, of course, Frank Sinatra. Admission to the 'hops' was half a crown and we got a chance to meet the girls from Sion Hill and the Sacred Heart in

Monkstown. Our first romances blossomed. Happy days!

Cricket was still an important part of my life. Having already joined Pembroke Cricket Club, I continued playing at that club after my school cricket. I had managed to go from the Under 19s, to the Second XI then to be selected for the First XI at Pembroke while still 16.

The Irish Cricket Union used to pick one or two players who showed promise and send them to Lords in England, to work out with the young professionals of Middlesex. I was sent there for part of two seasons, in 1952 and 1953. Stuart Pollock from Belfast, a cricket hero of mine, captained Ireland in those days. He was a fine batsman and a marvellous cover point.

My father had lost his dancing business and was short of money. The Irish Cricket Union and Stuart made it possible for me to go to Lords. On the first occasion, on board the boat from Dun Laoghaire, we had a very rough crossing before reaching Holyhead and finally getting the train to Euston. There were two young fellows in their early twenties travelling in the same compartment. They had old cases tied with string and bottles of Guinness with them. They offered me one. My cricket bag was on the rack over my head. As the night wore on and the lads got drunker, I worried that there might be a scuffle and my bowling arm or right hand might get damaged. I need not have worried.

Years later I realised they were emigrants, who were forced to leave Connemara, probably with no jobs to go to and deeply unhappy, like so many thousands of others. My Dad's brothers, Jimmy and Richard, were to follow my companions to the car factories in Birmingham and spend half their lifetime there. The 1950s were a desperate time. Nobody had a penny.

It was a fabulous experience to be coached at Lords and to bowl at some of the Middlesex players who were in the current side at the time. I was a leg spin bowler. They liked what I was doing, but they also worked hard to improve my batting and fielding.

I remember one day when I had been bowling in the nets from about 10 o'clock in the morning and saw Denis Compton come out and walk into my net. He and his brother, Lesley, played soccer for Arsenal. I spent about an hour and a half bowling to him and it was the great sporting experience of my life. This man had a wonderful eye but his feet were the thing. He was like a dancer. He moved his feet so well that he always gave you a problem because, just as you let the ball go, he moved his position, changing the equation of the line and the length. It was fascinating to bowl at him.

Now, when I go back to Lords as a member of Middlesex, I just walk around the ground and remember those days in the 1950s.

In 1954, I was 17 and was selected for the national side, playing for Ireland against Scotland. My captain was Stuart Pollock. I got two wickets and should have had a third. It was the last game the great off spinner Jimmy Boucher played for Ireland.

This was an exciting time in my life, being part of a great team at Pembroke with players like Stanley Bergin, Ciaran O'Malley, Mickey Williams, Bill and Ken Haughton, Harry Hill and, later at Phoenix, with Jimmy Boucher, all the Quinn brothers and Donald Pratt. I held the record as the youngest player to play cricket for Ireland for 49 years.

My mother took me out of Blackrock College when I was only 16. I had shown an interest in photography and had started an apprenticeship with James Mulvaney, the photographer. My journey had begun.

It was the early 1950s when I started work at Pollock's Opticians and Photographic Shop on Grafton Street, where I worked as a junior. I was fascinated with cameras. Grafton Street was still elegant. Opposite us was Tyson's, the men's shirt makers and outfitters, stocking the finest selection of top class men's clothes. I bought my first cricket sweater there. It cost me two weeks' salary. Tysons made the horse racing colours for the British Royal family at that time.

I had access to cameras, the Leica and all its systems, and was trained in Germany at the factory at Wetzel near Frankfurt, which was in the American zone. There was an eerie feeling in Germany so soon after the War. The people at Leits made gun sights, night binoculars and periscopes for submarines as part of the war effort. Two G.I. dentists on the course took me in their Porsche on a pub-crawl and to some of the nightclubs. It was quite an eye opener for a young chap. Dublin, it was not. I saw my first autobahn, this one had been used by Hitler's armies.

On returning, I started to shoot pictures of street atmosphere from the upstairs windows. In Grafton Street, people were more elegant. Couples were turned out so well, men linking arms with their partners as they strolled down the street. Hats and gloves were obligatory. Sybil Connolly's salon was nearby. Adrienne Ring and Winnie Butler were at their most elegant. Hilda Moriarty was a stunning young woman who was in Dublin then. Later, she became involved with Patrick Kavanagh and was the woman in his poem about Raglan Road.

Fergus Linehan and friends John Buckley, Frank Morris and Ian Duff (above). Shots taken by Godfrey Graham from the upstairs windows of Pollock's Opticians and Photographic Shop (of street atmosphere) of the elegant people on Grafton Street in the early 1950s

THE ARRIVAL OF IRISH TELEVISION

GETTING INTO FILM 1960

I MET SHEILA at a dance at Belvedere Rugby Club on Anglesea Road. Within six weeks of that first meeting, we were unofficially engaged and married 18 months later. I was now working with Lyle Smith in Terenure, selling cameras and representing his Agfa colour film laboratory.

One day, when walking past the College of Surgeons, I met Jim Mulkearns. He was Colm O Laoghaire's lighting cameraman at the time. He had a good command of Irish and cut and shot the Gael Linn newsreel in collaboration with O Laoghaire for years. Jim was a very good-looking guy, in an American kind of way, complete with a Clarke Gable-style moustache. He tended to dress in double-breasted suits in those days.

'Hi kid, what's cookin'?,' he asked. Jim knew that I had a background in still photography and, when I asked him would it ever be possible to work in film, in moving pictures, he replied, 'I begin to shoot a film next week in Ring in Waterford, in 35mm Eastman colour. You can be my assistant cameraman for two weeks at £10 a week.'

I said that I'd do it, but would have to speak to my wife first. Sheila and I had been married for about eighteen months at that time. The film work would mean giving up the job and the car that went with it. In addition, we had a mortgage to pay but, to her eternal credit, Sheila said that if I wanted to be a film cameraman to go for it.

Everything that I have ever achieved since meeting Sheila is because she believed in me. It is great to have that feeling, to have someone's love and support. Needless to say, she has her own mind on most things and has sorted me out when necessary … I'm a bit of a dreamer, I suppose!

I worked with Colm O Laoghaire on television commercials and a few Gael Linn newsreels a number of times over the next nine months, gaining experience that would be invaluable when Telefís Éireann was launched.

NEW YEAR'S EVE, 1961

On the opening night of Telefís Éireann, I wanted to be a part of it so much that I borrowed an Arriflex from Colm and filmed the exterior scenes in O'Connell Street in the snow, with Michael O'Hehir and Patrick O'Hagan.

I also filmed the orchestra in the ballroom of the Gresham Hotel as Charlie Roberts counted down to transmission. Standing in the snow-clad street, I got talking with a young man who told me he had come back from Canada to try to get into the new television service. It was Paddy Gallagher. We would work together many times, including a film about Franco's Spain, another on Arthur Power, Joyce's friend in Paris, a film about Ennis and other programmes.

I gave these rolls of the first night transmission to George Morrison, the film archivist. I suppose he still has them. Bill Harpur was head of film in those days. I think he saw my potential and gave me my first break.

I was lucky to get into Telefís Éireann, not as a cameraman initially but as a cutter joiner in the editing department. I purchased a Bolex camera and went to work every day hoping that someone would ask me to shoot something. In those days at RTÉ, we had four news cameramen and two programme cameramen. There was simply not enough and producers would ask me to film small sequences for them. I remember James Plunkett asked me to work with him on his famous *Mountain and Meadow* programme.

Telefís Éireann was only up and running a few months. I was working in the film editing department and I was surrounded by my colleagues there, Myles Merriman, Maureen Robbins, who had come home from the US where she had acquired valuable experience, Roy O'Farrell, Tom Clery, John Feeney. We were dotted around in little cutting rooms like a rabbit warren.

One day, our supervising film editor, ex-BBC, Roger Johnston was in the next cutting room and exploded in uncontrollable laughter. Then other voices joined in, including Frank Hall and Des Greally. I stopped what I was doing and stuck my head around the cutting room door. There was a group of people around an editing machine. It was Frank Hall and a bunch of his pals. In the film, Frank wore a white shirt and running singlet, was trying to run with a top athlete and carry out an interview as they ran. Frank was attached to a lead and carrying a ball and biscuit microphone. There were three factors, namely the tracking car, driven by Simon Weafer, the 16mm Auracon camera, operated by Stuart Hetherington and Frank himself. His lead stretched into the back of the car and was plugged into a sound box. The sound operator, Pat Hayes, was also in the car. The pace of the car and the runners had to be constant and at a speed that allowed Frank keep up with the athlete while conducting the interview.

The film team simply could not get the pacing right and although the athlete would run fast, Frank would try to keep up with him. When Frank was out of breath, Simon, watching in the mirror, would slow down. Frank was also trying to avoid being tripped up by the mike cable. The athlete would now slow also. Frank would be about to ask the next question when the runner, for some reason, would start to run faster. Again, Simon would drive faster. Frank was left two or three metres behind but still attached by the mike cable. By the time he caught up, he was so breathless he could not speak a word. It was hilarious. Unintentional, but the best piece of slap stick comedy you would see. We could never have staged it so well.

They were on the main road of the Phoenix Park. By now, Frank was totally out of it. He was desperately trying to make hand signals to the driver. Simon was confused and thought Frank meant him to increase speed, which he did. Frank held on for dear life to the mike lead for what seemed a long time and passed out the runner. By now, other people in the newsroom had come in to join the jollification – Pierce Kelly, Andy O'Mahony, Charles Mitchell. It was one of the funniest scenes I have ever seen.

For the next year or two, when the staff in the newsroom were down in the dumps about something or when a few of the journalists needed some-thing to cheer them up, somebody would suggest running the 'Frank Hall Olympics'. Like a bunch of kids mitching from class, they would open the old film cabinet where really rare and precious things were stored. I saw a baby Power in there once, an old copy of *Playboy*, a few Mars bars and there was always a large quantity of Tayto crisps for some reason. The rusty old battered film can with the 16mm negative and sound track were taken out. One of the band would volunteer to ask somebody working in a cutting room on another programme to spare the ten minutes 59 seconds to run this rare footage. They never refused because people knew about this film. It was legendary. So they would creep in, remove the programme they were working on from the editing machine, and lace up the 16mm film and sound track. The film sequence was historic. All over the building people who had never seen it on air knew of its existence but only a very privileged few ever saw it again.

We had two programme film cameramen at the start in Radio Telefís Éireann, Sheamus Smith and Michael Monaghan. These two men and their units had to do all the filming and documentary work all over the country, as there was no material emanating from the provinces at that stage. These two units, with Smith and Monaghan, worked in the four corners of the island. Other programmes came from the studio and newsroom. Directors with their production assistants led these teams at the time, with soundmen and electricians.

Michael Monaghan knew me from before I had joined RTÉ. He gave me great encouragement; perhaps he thought I had some possibilities. I used to understudy him on shoots, when he would let me operate the Auracon 600 camera. I watched him light and work with the electricians and saw how he interacted with the different directors. At the time, I was still working in film editing so I had to get permission every time I went on location with Mike and then get back to do the work I should have been doing. It was exhausting but worth it.

Mike was working with Ciarán MacMathuna, making some programmes on traditional music. We were filming with Willie Clancy, Seamus Ennis, Paddy Maloney and Seán Potts. Dolly Maloney, a beautiful young singer, was also involved in some of these programmes. One day I joined Mike, Simon Weafer, Pat Hayes and Seán Keville on their way to darkest Wicklow or so it seemed that evening. It was beginning to snow as our cars went down the very steep road towards Garech de Brún's house, 'Luggala', and Lough Tay, one of the steepest tracks in the Wicklow Mountains. It made us all feel as if we were falling like a stone, particularly in the dark with the added danger of snow on the road. Located at the foot of this saucer-like lake, 'Luggala' is like a Russian dacha or a residence of a Russian prince where he would entertain his guests, go fishing and shooting, or provide a roof under which a struggling composer could hide away as he toiled through his next symphony. To complete the scene, Lough Tay shimmered like a mirage in the moonlight. Roaring fires lit up the beautiful interiors.

That night, our musicians were some of the cream of the crop. We set up a group shot of about six musicians who tuned up very slowly, drifting into the melody as if in some sort of slow motion. I had never been exposed to anything quite like this in musical terms. It blew my mind in a way, for me, it was a long way from Rachmaninoff, Stravinsky and the ballet at Miss Evelyn Birchall's dancing school on Stephen's Green of the 1950s. The sound and the rhythms were extraordinary. I had never heard the bodhrán before. The uilleann pipes were also strange to me then, I had never seen or heard them. The pipes resembled an animal struggling to get free from a man trying to control them or a small octopus that couldn't find a comfortable place to rest. But, in the right hands, the uilleann pipes sounded wonderful, particularly when you heard Seamus Ennis play them. He had a beautiful tone. That night, the young Paddy Maloney was playing. Seán Potts was there and Éamon de Buitléar, too.

There were wonderful opportunities and possibilities for all of us at the start of the television service. Garech de Brún had founded Claddagh Records, which recorded albums with Patrick Kavanagh and Austin Clarke, as well as a beautiful album about Beckett's work. Jack MacGowran did the voiceover for this and it was quite superb. Leo Rosen and Seamus Ennis were both active. To work with such people was fascinating. The Chieftains came later, led by Paddy Maloney.

Working with traditional players, many of whom spoke Irish, I began to enjoy the sound of Gaelic spoken so naturally. My knowledge of the language was limited but it seemed to me that I could provide the image as part of the music and the speech, therefore I felt part of and linked to the whole. Certainly working with people who loved the language was inspiring. There were, of course, others in television who used their command of Irish in a cynical way to further their careers. Love of the language was the last thing on their minds.

I remember working on a number of programmes with Michael Monaghan during those days with traditional musicians. It gave me great confidence. When Mike became a producer a year after the station opened, I got his job. I was 25 and considered myself to be in the right place at the right time and extraordinarily fortunate. At that stage, I had had 24 transmissions of my footage from when I was working in the film editing department. Working with those traditional musicians in those days in the early 1960s, I would never have imagined in my wildest dreams that one day I would have the honour of photographing the film, *The Blue Note*, the production made by Seán Ó Mordha about the unique Seán Ó Riada.

Sheamus Smith gave me great help during that first year. He spent time with me working on technical aspects of the cameras. Like Mike, Sheamus went on to become a producer, before becoming editor of RTÉ's *Seven Days*, manager of Ardmore Film Studios and, eventually, Ireland's film censor.

IN THE BEGINNING

I have always believed in life. If you are ready and know what you want, whether it be a job, friendship, the love of a girl, you have to be ready to recognise it and reach out for it. Time is so fleeting. The night I first saw Sheila changed my life. The chance to play cricket that the Irish Cricket Union and Stewart Pollock gave me. The moment when I bumped into Jim Mulkerns on St. Stephen's Green and gave up my job and a car on the promise of just two weeks' work on a film.

I always wanted to try to be very good at something. I was prepared to make any sacrifice to attain it. Life is so strange.

Noel Purcell, the actor, knew my father's brother, Jimmy, who worked in the Theatre Royal as a carpenter and in set construction. He also knew Dick Forbes, the brilliant Cork humorist who, as I have mentioned elsewhere, wrote the sketches that were produced in the Theatre Royal for years.

At the beginning of his career, Noel Purcell worked as a callboy in the Gaiety Theatre before becoming a stagehand. He served his time as a carpenter or, as he would put it, in the wood-butchering business. Noel was a giant when it came to pantomime, both physically and as a character actor. He worked initially with Jimmy O'Dea and Harry O'Donovan before he eventually drifted into films in Britain. He was lucky enough to get into some major movies, including *Captain Boycott* and John Houston's *Moby Dick* with Gregory Peck. He was also in *Mutiny on the Bounty* and *Blue Lagoon* with Jean Simmons, in which I nearly got a part. He played in *The Seekers* with Jack Hawkins and many other character parts in British movies.

When I was in the cutting rooms at the beginning of Telefís Éireann, I had bought a 16mm Bolex camera that cost half the price of my house – the house that Sheila and I had bought by the skin of our teeth. It was an act of madness to go out and buy a camera that was so expensive but it was the only way I could prove that I could shoot film. I kept the camera under my rewind workbench in the cutting rooms.

Godfrey Graham with Noel Purcell.

One day on my lunch break, I was sitting in the nearby newsroom, listening to a programme on Radio Éireann. It was a sponsored show. They played the *Dublin Saunter*, sung by Noel Purcell, with the first verse that goes, 'Dublin can be heaven with coffee at eleven and a stroll in Stephen's Green'. The images were so vivid I decided to shoot the pictures described in the lyrics. After the record ended, I knew exactly what shots I would use to illustrate the piece. It has such Dublin character and also elegance about it. I had worked in Grafton Street since I was 16 – and seen it every day and smelled that coffee. On my first day off, I used my own film and shot 300 feet which good old Jack Doyle processed for me in the RTÉ lab. The next thing was to show the pictures to my boss, Roger Johnston, our supervising film editor at the time. He was ex-B.B.C. Roger viewed it and was impressed. He said right away he would cut a piece that was about three minutes 50 seconds long to the music and lyric. He did a marvellous job, using his vast experience to enhance my pictures. It was an education to me. I never forgot the contribution the film editor makes. The station transmitted my little effort.

Isn't life interesting? Noel Purcell, a friend of my family since the 1930s, had patted me on the back at Dublin Airport when I was on my way for a film test for the film *Blue Lagoon* to be made at Pinewood Studios in London in 1947. In 1961, his performance of the *Dublin Saunter* was the vehicle that gave me the break I needed into shooting something for Telefís Éireann. All I can say is, 'Thanks, Noel' and offer my advice to be always ready.

About a year after the Frank Hall 'Olympics', the producer Michael Johnston and Frank Hall got a message to me. Frank had a crazy idea. He wanted to interview a steeplejack. Fine, I thought! But more was to follow. Frank wanted to do it up at the top of a steeple. This is what surprised me. Nowadays this happens all the time but not in the early 1960s, when film cameras and sound equipment were much heavier and bulkier. The sound-

Godfrey Graham and Simon Weafer and the Aurocan camera, taken up to the top of the steeple – below

man was Pat Hayes, a friend of mine, and we had worked on many *Discovery* programmes with Charles Scott and Brian Cleeve. We did a recce. It was not the highest steeple I had ever seen but, looking up, I was somewhat nervous about going up to such a height with one hand holding equipment and the other on the rung of the ladder that went straight up.

The morning of the shoot was cold and clear and there was no wind, thank goodness. We assembled at St. Saviour's Church on Dominic Street and met our steeplejack, Jimmy, who said that he would look after us up there. He asked how were our heads for heights. We shrugged our shoulders. I suppose he thought RTÉ would not send a crew who were scared to go up. We said we were O.K. Michael's plan was to get us up as high as we could and shoot the interview with the cameraman, Frank and the steeplejack clinging to the ladders. Getting the cameras and equipment up was difficult. I had to lash the tripod to the ladder with the help of Simon Weafer who had been in the Irish Army Engineers and was an expert in this type of thing in difficult locations. We lifted the camera on a rope. Later on I went up further with a small hand camera, the Bolex, to shoot material looking back down past Frank and the steeplejack, for additional shots.

Pat Hayes was one of the most inventive of all soundmen I ever worked with. He decided there wasn't going to be enough space or ladders up there so he would be safe. The street was rather narrow. He went up to an adjoining building and slung a mike lead, like a lasso, across to the steeple, then attached his microphone and operated from the roof opposite. It was one of the riskiest shoots I ever did. The real danger in that sort of filming is that the cameraman can get a false sense of security looking through his camera viewfinder and just step off the ladder. You tend to concentrate much on the shot – most cameramen by nature are enthusiastic – that you can get carried away, literally. We got an amazing sequence. Frank Hall was the sort of guy for whom you would do anything. He had a marvellous sense of humour that carried the rest of the team with him in a sense. I suppose it is what some people call leadership, real leadership, he was like that. Michael Johnston was a good team motivator, too, which didn't surprise me, given his background and sporting interests.

We reassembled on the ground and thanked the steeplejack for all his care of us up above. There was a general sense of relief after the assignment. Frank said we all needed a really good lunch after that, on him. He said there was only one place to go, The Castle Hotel, where the food was genuinely

Frank Hall

old-fashioned country cooking and the roast beef probably the best in the country, if not the whole world. Nobody in our team had ever been there. It was in Gardiner Street, not far from my grandmother's old house in North Great George's Street. As we entered, I was suddenly aware that we had somehow stepped back in time and that we were somewhere in the Midlands, maybe Mullingar or Longford. The food smelled beautiful. As we entered the dining room, we were hit by a warmth that seemed to envelope us, like a hug from your granny. I noticed all the waitresses were dressed in black dresses, not too short, with sparkling white aprons and little bonnets. I could see there was a certain type of customer, mostly people who seemed to be up from the country, thick-set men used to eating good food since birth, the sort who unfortunately don't take much exercise. Eating for them is serious business. There was something of the French about them the way they seemed to attack the food.

Some of our team opted for the beef, others the lamb, the sweetest I have tasted. Plates arrived with ploughman size helpings, then the potatoes that were marvellous, also. The waitress told us they had come from the Aran Islands, floury, unforgettable. The other vegetables were also marvellous and the whole thing was rounded off with apple tart and cream. Nobody was drinking wine in those days in this type of hotel. It would be the exception.

People drank water, lemonade – that was more the norm. Drinking was a serious business but it happened in the bar and not when you were eating food. How different things are today. Nothing seemed to have changed in this dining room for 50 years. Frank made the observation that, when he wanted to, as it were, get back to the country but could not spare the time, this was where he would come. Frank Hall was an Ulsterman from Newry. The rest of us were all Dubliners. We had never been to The Castle Hotel. This lunch was just what was needed after our adventures up the steeple, on a cold morning.

Over lunch, we talked about jazz among other things. Frank was a double bass player in a small combo and we appreciated some of the same players, instrumentalists, George Shering, Dave Brubeck, Ella Fitzgerald, Oscar Peterson and our own Irish talent, Noel Kelihan, Peggy Dell, Jim Doherty and Ian Henry. Frank Hall was to go on to create, with others, *Hall's Pictorial Weekly* with the Minister of Hardship and talents like Frank Kelly, Eamon Morrissey, Paul Murphy and Pat Daly. It was produced by John Condon and Peter McEvoy. I wish we had them now. A broadcast organisation needs a good satirical team. It is great to see this series again and now available on DVD. The historian, John A. Murphy said the programme had probably contributed to the defeat of the Fine Gael/Labour Coalition in the General Election of 1977.

RTÉ hasn't had too good a record in the way it has handled some of the talent in comedy and satire over the last 20 years. It needs particular skill to both encourage and also insist on some disciplines but it is a difficult thing to administrate. Perhaps we don't need administrators making the decisions but creative programme people, people who make programmes with a passion.

Those were great days and some of RTÉ's finest hours. I worked with Frank Hall on occasions, there would be long gaps when we wouldn't work together at all. All you could do when you worked with people of such talent and who were so amusing, was to enjoy the time you spent with them and do your best to contribute to the programme. The nature of our job in broadcasting meant you came together briefly with a team and then you might not meet for a year.

Parallel with the film cutting rooms was the RTÉ newsroom, which was a large working area. Reporters and cameramen could have easy access to see their film footage. The news division had four film cameramen. Stuart

Hetherington I knew slightly as fellow cricketers at Phoenix, before he joined Ardmore Studios and worked on some major feature films in the camera department there. Stuart was one of the first cameramen employed by Radio Telefís Éireann and went with the Irish Army to the Congo when he was only 18, with soundman Bill O'Neill and reporter Seán Egan. Stuart sent back some superb footage from that assignment. Later, he joined me in Programmes and did definitive work in drama and documentary. Still later, he moved to management and co-ordinated all the RTÉ film units for many years.

Bill St. Ledger, a swash-buckling cameraman with real talent, had worked in the UK with Movietone News. On an assignment in Rome to cover the event when Pope John XXIII became Pope, Billy was late, unfortunately. The gates of Rome and St. Peter's Square were shut against him and standing at every quarter were the Swiss Guards preventing him from going any further. St. Ledger was racking his brains, what could he do? He had already shown his authorisation but to no avail. I can imagine what was going through his mind. Imagine missing an event of such importance. He would never live it down. An observer saw Billy go into a form of tantrum. The Swiss Guards, carrying their long spears, did not weaken in any way. Billy put his camera, tripod and other equipment down on the ground and, with a grand gesture reminiscent of a nobleman from Venice in the 16th century on a visit to Rome, brought from inside the pocket of his by then rather rumpled jacket an envelope with an official stamp. He handed it to the Officer in Command who opened the envelope, looked at it for some time and then gave it to another colleague to scrutinise. The other colleague handed it back to the first officer who carried the piece of paper to a table, stamped it with a red Papal insignia and gave it back to Billy. With the sweat running down St. Ledger's face, he put the unpaid E.S.B. bill back into his pocket and entered St. Peter's Square to shoot the Pope.

The other two newsroom cameramen were Seán Burke and Gay O'Brien. Seán was one of those true gentlemen and had tremendous integrity. Like Gay, he had come from the newspapers and both were established still cameramen. They knew all about covering photo assignments but moving pictures were something different. In a short time, they had grasped this difference and became excellent film cameramen. Seán did distinguished work in Northern Ireland and specialised in Michael O'Hehir's sports department, working on many major sports assignments at home and abroad. People may remember Seán's poignant pictures of the tragic events of the Stardust disaster.

Gay O'Brien was an inspiration. Nobody I ever met in RTÉ had quite the same commitment. He had the heart and the courage of a lion. There is the great quote from a reporter when Gay was driving down the avenue with him on his way to Derry. Gay said, 'And to think that we have this job to do, how marvellous, and they pay us for it, too. I'd do it for nothing.' Accompanied by soundman Eamon Hayes, Gay O'Brien shot the famous footage of the Civil Rights march in Derry and the events when hysterical RUC officers assaulted demonstrators. Their sound and pictures went all over the globe and had a political impact that helped to change things.

Later, Gay O'Brien covered the aftermath of the assassination of Robert Kennedy. He travelled on the train carrying his remains. His footage was stunning; the atmosphere of the train at night and then dawn was top-class. He shot pictures at the graveside, as well. Irish viewers were profoundly moved by this footage.

I had the honour of joining this tradition after a year in film editing, watching this kind of footage from these unique men. They laid the ground-work and the footprints for people like me to try to follow.

PRESIDENT JOHN F. KENNEDY'S VISIT – 1963

I was now a programme lighting cameraman and my first assignment was to be transferred to the newsroom to take part in the coverage of the John F. Kennedy visit to Ireland. This was the start of a great adventure. Simon Weafer was to drive the camera car and we had two 16mm Bolex cameras. No sound was required from our unit and we were to start filming the President as he crossed the city boundaries on the edge of Dublin on his way in from the Airport. I filmed him approaching as he went by at Drumcondra in the motorcade. I dropped the film to Val on a motorbike. This was at 8.15pm. Val got the film to Montrose where it was processed and on air for the 9 o'Clock News. There was no East Link Bridge in those days, so it was some achievement.

We drove straight on to New Ross. Our main assignment was to cover the presidential helicopters dropping out of the sky onto the GAA ground where several thousand children were waiting to see the President. I had a position on a camera tower right in the centre of the grounds and got some good shots of the President's arrival and his meeting the children.

President Kennedy sitting by the fireside in the homestead at Dunganstown, Co. Wexford, having a cup of tea with Mrs Ryan and her daughter Josephine Ryan, on the left. (Photograph: Pádraig MacBrian)

The only difficulty was that, having done those shots, I was to get onto a tracking lorry to travel in front of the presidential limo. Having got down from the camera tower carrying my camera and tripod, I had to get through several thousand people milling around the grounds to get into a position where I could get onto the tracking lorry about two hundred yards away. I had difficulty getting out of the grounds and then found myself running behind the presidential car, trying to get to the tracking vehicle ahead of the president. I ran as fast as I could, slowed by the security and crowds. I got behind the tracking lorry, with some 50 to 60 national and overseas movie and still cameramen on board. There was no way I could get up on this vehicle and I began to cause a problem as I was in their shot. The cameramen got angry, shouting to me to get out of their shot. I kept running, with the president's car just behind me. It was only a matter of time before the White House Secret Service men took me out of the way. I remember looking up

President Kennedy meeting President and Bean De Valera at Áras an Uachtaráin. On the left are Seán Lemass and Mrs Lemass. Second from right is Mrs Eunice Shriver. (Photograph by Andy Farren)

at one of the NBC cameramen. To my amazement, he stopped shooting, bent down and lifted me off my feet. I had the Bolex in one hand, my tripod in the other. He flung me behind him onto the tracking lorry. I got to my feet and began to photograph John F. Kennedy.

The motorcade arrived at the quays. The President stepped out. He began to address the very large crowd. It was possible for me to stand eight feet away and shoot without any interference from the guards or the White House Secret Service men. What different days they were! It was here that he made the famous speech in which he said that, if his people had not gone to America, he would probably be working at the Albatross factory across the river behind him. The people were overcome. What a brilliant piece of speechwriting.

I can now reveal a secret. The President was to travel on to Dunganstown where his relations lived but Telefís Éireann had no way of covering this journey. We had assistance from the BBC who provided one if not two Outside Broadcast Units, in addition to our own O.B. units. The technology had not been invented to cover a moving motorcade and transmit picture and sound live. Michael Monaghan, Simon and myself had travelled to New Ross some weeks earlier, and from a platform on our Mercedes film bus, filmed a low angle tracking shot on the same road at the same time of day. We hoped that, on the actual day of the President's visit, the weather and light would match. It did.

So, when JFK got into his limo and was swept away from the quays at New Ross, this was live but, at the same time in Montrose, a director cued the film I had shot two weeks earlier and, for five minutes and 30 seconds, the television audience watched what President Kennedy saw as he travelled to Dunganstown … a lovely country road with trees, cows in the fields, and bird song.

Back in Dublin a couple of days later, Des Greeley, the chief manager of the television news division at RTÉ said he wanted me to go to Áras an Uachtaráin where President Kennedy was meeting President and Bean De Valera. Special permission had been given for one White House cameraman, one still photographer and one RTÉ film cameraman to be there.

It was a private dinner and I was to be there by 7 p.m. I needed an electrician because we were shooting indoors but Des could not provide me with one. At Áras an Uachtaráin, we were ushered into an anteroom just beside the dining room. The White House cameraman was there, along with Andy. A few minutes later, the Presidential entourage came in, led by President De Valera, with Bean De Valera, Seán Lemass, Mrs Lemass, John F. Kennedy, Eunice Shriver and Frank Aiken.

I had a big problem because the small room was quite dark. I switched the speed of the camera from 24 to 12 frames per second so that I could get a picture, increasing the amount of light to hit the film. The image movement would be Chaplinesque but the party was standing still and posing for the still camera so the resulting film did not give away the fact that the camera was running at the wrong speed. I was very pleased with this film, which was syndicated all over the world.

Some weeks later, our Director General, Kevin McCourt received a letter from President Kennedy's office asking if would it be possible to film the

Army cadets who had officiated during his visit. He had been very impressed with their general demeanour and high standard of appearance at all the ceremonies in which they had participated.

Michael Monaghan, Simon Weafer and myself filmed the cadets forming a guard of honour at the 1916 memorial at Arbour Hill and going through their drill at a number of army barracks in Dublin. This 15-minute film was sent to the White House and is lodged today in the John F. Kennedy Library in Boston. The sad thing is that, just a matter of months later, some of those very cadets were sent to take part in J.F.K.'s state funeral in Washington.

FARMING

I worked with Michael Johnston on *On the Land*. It was where I cut my teeth in documentaries on farms all over the island. We met fine people in farming, working on everything from the little farms with only a few acres to the bigger enterprises. We filmed on a farm in County Meath owned by the Bruton family and met the two children, John and Richard, who would later make such an impact in politics.

It was an eye-opener for us. Paddy Jennings, Justin Keating, Joe Murray,

Jack Tobin, a typical small farmer of the 50's from Ring, Co. Waterford who went through bad times before the new dawn began in the late 60's

Paul Gleeson and SHeamus Smith all made a great contribution. Also Pauline Kelly and, later, Gerry O'Callaghan.

An extraordinary thing happened as the programmes were being transmitted. City dwellers became interested in their country cousins. There seemed to be a marvellous reaction to and interest in the series, which made quite an impact.

The Agricultural Advisor was so important in conveying modern methods of farming to the community. Television was a perfect medium and helped to transform the farming industry. It was a great achievement for Michael Johnston, who produced these programmes from the start.

EDNA O'BRIEN

One of the finest directors I was lucky enough to work with was Peter Kennerley. He had such a grasp of the picture and a wonderful ability when working with his editor to cut and shape the flow of the film, never losing the story. He made films in the *My Own Place* and *Discovery* series. A portrait of playwright Hugh Leonard in his native Dalkey that captured the essence of Leonard. Another about Edna O'Brien. She returned to Clare. The film showed her with her parents and portrayed a complex writer. It was great to photograph these subjects. Edna is a fascinating woman and it was intriguing to be with her in the old haunts that shaped her character and so many of her stories.

Edna O'Brien's first books, *The Country Girls* and *The Lonely Girl,* in 1962, caused quite a stir when they were published. Peter Kennerley was to shoot the documentary, for which Andy O'Mahony did the voiceover and co-wrote the script.

It was exciting to get a chance to work with Edna. Peter's idea was to take her back to her roots in Scarriff, County Clare and that county. The weather was mixed, full of wind and rain. We shot a sequence on the beach at Lahinch. Edna wore a long, elegant, black dress with a long crocheted coat that picked up the light beautifully. It was a russet brown colour. She walked on the sand, a lonely figure etched against the sky, merging into that natural environment very well. She talked with a local man, whom she hadn't met for years, as if she had only seen him the other week. The red berries on a bush displayed a sensual presence as she brushed by them.

The most intriguing moment came when Edna returned home to where her aged parents still lived. Andy observed that the house was substantial,

Edna O'Brien directed by Peter Kennerley, on Lahinch Strand in Co. Clare.
(Photograph: Ronan Lee)

with some acres surrounding it. Edna's mother and father had welcomed all our party earlier, including, of course, their daughter. As we broke the ice before filming, Peter asked her parents to go into the main living room where there was a good fire burning and explained that Edna would join them in a few minutes. We set up in the far corner of the room as unobtrusively as we could.

Mrs. O'Brien was on one side of the fire, her husband on the other. When Edna came into the room, she went to the side where her father was. There were three people in my shot but there could have been acres between them. The uneasiness was striking. I panned my camera from one to the other. The differences between daughter and parents, since Edna had left all those years before, were evident. We could see her mother's pride in all that she had achieved as an author. Her father was watchful, however, and apprehensive. Very little was said, if anything. No dialogue was needed; they conveyed everything in their body language.

Edna's ability to describe the elements that influence our lives is well known. I noticed how important simple things were to her – a footpath, an old handball alley, the old bench in the corner of the garden. The interaction between the physical and the spiritual. Above all, the mystery of the relationships between two people. These are the things that exercise her mind.

Edna spoke to us on camera in some detail about her work and her life and what it meant to her. With every year that passes, her status as a major author increases. It was a privilege to spend some time with her.

Recently, Ronnie Foreman and I invited Edna to give a talk about James Joyce at the Merrion Hotel on Bloomsday. Despite her busy schedule, she consented immediately. Her observations were fascinating and fresh. The same people repeat their observations on Joyce in all media ad nauseam. This was not like that, this was new. Her feminine insight captivated the invited audience at the Merrion for thirty minutes. It seemed as if she had also experienced rejection from Ireland and criticism that can be merciless to the artist. O'Brien's recent book on Joyce is a major contribution to the understanding of a genius.

HUGH LEONARD

Hugh Leonard had been working in the U.K. in the early 1960s for some years and writing for Granada Television. He had returned home to his native village of Dalkey, on the outskirts of Dublin.

Peter Kennerley wanted to shoot a programme on Leonard for his series, *My Own Place*. It was a pleasure for me to meet and work with such an author. Leonard had originally worked in the Civil Service. His first play, *The Big Birthday*, was produced by the Abbey; I think it was in 1956. A year later, they produced *Leap in the Dark* and, in March 1958, the Globe Theatre produced his delightful *Madigan's Lock*, which I seem to remember seeing years later at the Abbey Theatre. Watching his plays, *Da* particularly, working with him, and remembering *The Patrick Pearse Motel*, which captured perfectly the Swinging Sixties and the movers and shakers in politics, with his scalpel-like cuts at people in politics, was fascinating.

Hugh Leonard was a true Dalkeyite. I had lived in Coliemore Villas earlier so when our film team moved around the narrow streets of the village it was also familiar to me. Bernard Shaw had a cottage on Torca Road, between Dalkey and Killiney. Michael Yeats, son of W.B., still lives there.

Around the village, many of the house names are Italian – Sorrento, Villaggio, Mount Alto – giving the place a continental flavour. A village like Dalkey is unique on Dublin Bay, there is nowhere else quite like it. Dalkey is tiny in scale, almost Lilliputian, with its own little harbour. You can go down to Coliemore Harbour and take a boat to Dalkey Island, which has a Christian heritage going back to the 9th century. To think of Hugh Leonard walking in his old haunts in the warm sunshine of those summer days of the 1970s reminds me today of his story, *Home Before Night*, which was to come later.

Kennerley wanted to study the writer under close scrutiny. We worked with him late at night. Hugh, like so many writers, seemed to get the creative flow in the wee small hours. I liked the sequence that we did of him at his typewriter. I think we managed to capture the loneliness. We shot some aerial pictures approaching the coastline and finding Dalkey village in that way – seen from the air, it seemed to have added charm – but the sequence I liked best was when Peter took the unit to Dalkey Island and did some pictures looking back at Coliemore Harbour. That film about Hugh Leonard still stands up very well.

Nearby Bulloch Harbour is bigger than Coliemore and has its own charm. In the last few years, a number of seals have taken up residence just outside the harbour and enjoy contact with humans, always showing themselves when there are people about. If you happen to be walking in Dalkey today, you may see Hugh Leonard, a bit older now, popping into his favourite pub, The Club or a restaurant, or maybe browsing in the Exchange Bookshop. When Maureen Toal and Milo O'Shea lived in Dalkey, they loved The Club also and I remember my mother and father spent a lot of time there. U2's Bono lives five minutes away, whether by car or Harley Davidson. Author Maeve Binchy is just around the corner, Val Mulkerns a five-minute walk away. BBC newsman John Simpson and broadcaster Pat Kenny are also nearby. Film producer, Neil Jordan is within ten minutes of the main street, singer Lisa Stansfield is also a local, and the mysterious Enya lives not far away but is rarely seen.

The Celtic Tiger has catapulted Ireland into a new era of four-wheel drives, second homes, three continental holidays annually and a semi-detached house near Dalkey which sold for more than €1 million at a time when so many young couples find it almost impossible to buy their first house. This, we are told, is progress.

Main Street, Dalkey village, home of Hugh Leonard

ENTERTAINMENT

I first worked with Tom McGrath soon after the television service began. He was always easy-going, a Dubliner to his fingertips. He was the type of director who appeared to be relaxed but always wide-awake, especially when on the job. He did some big music shows with Dick Haynes and others. I think he was the first person to call me Godders and, if I said, 'Just a minute, Tom, we have to wait for light', he'd tell me to stop whingeing but always waited until I was happy.

When the Theatre Royal was to close, there was great gnashing of teeth in Dublin. The ordinary people resented that anyone could shut down their theatre. Generations of Dubliners felt it was their property. It had staged the great shows from the West End and, more recently in the 1950s, Danny Kaye, Nat King Cole, Bing Crosby, the Stan Kenton Band and Count Basie had performed there. Then there were our own Jimmy O'Dea, Noel Purcell, Danny Cummins and Maureen Potter.

Dick Forbes, a good friend of my Uncle Jimmy, did most of the writing for the sketches at the theatre. Tom McGrath said that we had to make a programme about the Theatre Royal, the fine old lady. I got to shoot the film. I remember shooting the Royalettes, a great dance troupe, on the night before the curtain came down for the last time. Jimmy Campbell conducted the orchestra. Tom was not given full co-operation, for some reason, and had to construct a major sequence from stills in Studio 1, at Montrose.

I suppose the closure of the Royal was one of the first examples of the developers moving in on an amenity that the people used on a regular basis. The ordinary man and woman in the street were not aware of those forces who wanted to change the city, but primarily to make money. For me, the eventual demolition of Hume Street, in spite of so many protests, was another example of this.

Tom brought a film crew to the *Rose of Tralee* festival. Mike Murphy was the presenter. I had worked with Mike and Twink on *The Live Mike*.

Tralee was a bundle of fun. In those days, the outside broadcast unit would cover the main event. Tom was shooting an anecdotal film to be broadcast on one of the evenings during the Roses week. We filmed the parade. I remember Mike and one of the Roses going on some of the carnival rides, with me hanging on for dear life with one hand and holding the faithful 16mm Bolex camera with the other.

In another programme, soon after the film *Lawrence of Arabia* was released, Tom wanted Mike Murphy to play an Arab sheik so we needed a bit of sand. Well, quite a lot of sand, actually. Tom decided on Dollymount Strand, stating that he wanted to see sand as far as the eye could see. When I tried to explain that Dollymount wasn't the Sahara, Tom told me to use filters, special effects and Vaseline. For the uninformed, Vaseline can be smeared on a clear filter to create an effect.

Mike emoted, gazing from his tent and staring into the distance, wondering if the figure of Omar Shariff would appear on a camel from behind a sand dune, while the Royal Dublin Golf Club shimmered in the background. Happy days. The props men, electricians, soundmen and PA all working hard. What an opportunity it was for us all.

Mike Murphy went on to greater achievements and, in my opinion, broke new ground in radio with the *Arts Show*. He is sorely missed by viewers and listeners and by his production colleagues. I always found him a marvellous guy to work with. Light-hearted, yet on the ball. He would try anything, sometimes at some risk to himself.

I still miss Tom, too. He was real showbiz. He just wanted to make the best show he could. They don't make them like Tom McGrath any more.

DISCOVERY DOCUMENTARIES

IN 1964, JACK WHITE decided that we needed a documentary film series. They called it Discovery. The series was directed by Charlie Scott who had come back from Canada. He had been a lighting director and was now a producer/director. Brian Cleeve was going to present the series and write the scripts. It was marvellous to be part of that team.

Each film was shot in four days on 16mm black and white film. It did not matter whether the location was in Kildare or Kerry, it had to be shot in the same time, including travelling. We spent a lot of time driving late at night. Sixty-eight documentaries were made between 1964 and 1967 by a whole range of producers. The film was processed in RTÉ. It was edited the following week. Sound dubbing was on Friday and the film was transmitted the following Monday. We were, of course, able to scrutinise the quality of the negative. The editor was handling the original negative at all times during the whole editing process so he or she saw no positive image. It was only when the telecine operator electronically reversed the negative image on the air that we saw the positive finished picture.

The telecine operator had control of how the film looked on transmission. The sound and picture were on two separate machines and had to be synchronised very accurately. It was an amazing, hazardous experience. When I think back, I am amazed at how it was done week after week, month after month, year after year.

Among the subjects we dealt with was the life of a lighthouse-keeper, a fish farm in County Kerry, and the River Shannon. None of us had seen this vast waterway and, when the documentary went out, viewers in other parts of the country were absolutely amazed. There was a film made about the development of forestry in Ireland. We were lucky enough, thanks to the Air Corps authorities, to get our hands on their first helicopter and got some marvellous aerial pictures, the first I shot myself.

Charlie Scott was great to work with. He was so confident and gave the cameraman lots of freedom. I remember filming with him in Connemara. He had heard that a woman who had gone to America 50 years ago was now coming back for the first time to spend the remainder of her life in Connemara in the cottage where she was born. We went to her little house and she told us the story of her times in America and how she didn't want to learn English. She was 87. She had been in service in Boston. Charlie handled the old lady, slipping into Irish with ease and drawing out her marvellous memories. I was learning all the time about the people of my country in all their diversity.

I remember Brian Cleeve as one of the best scriptwriters I ever worked with. He was sensitive to the image like no other writer-presenter. Brian was not a hard-nosed journalist with those particular skills and, as a result, was open to the creative possibilities of film for television. He went on to write novels and short stories.

In 1964, Charlie Scott was directing a film about some Danish people who had established the first fish farm in Kerry. Brian was also working on the documentary. We were staying at the Butler Arms Hotel in Waterville.

One evening at the hotel, I had a most surprising meeting with Charlie Chaplin. I was feeling very lonely, missing Sheila and the children, and went into the billiard room. Just the overhead light was on, illuminating the table. I started to strike a number of balls. I was concentrating. I began to sense I was not alone. A small figure moved at the other end of the full-size table. There was just the sound of a gale blowing off the Atlantic. The figure moved again. It was Chaplin. I did not move, nor did he. Neither of us spoke for what seemed a long time. I had the cube in my right hand. I straightened up, smiled and bowed to the master. Chaplin returned my bow, spun on the spot and was gone. Years late, I discovered that Charlie loved billiards. I wondered what it would have been like to play with him. Maybe he, like me, wanted to be on his own at that moment.

The brief meeting with Chaplin brought me back to the Blackrock House days, where one Christmas my Dad gave me a little Projector 9.5mm with the sprockets between each frame. There were two films, *Felix the Cat* and a Charlie Chaplin film about life behind bars, featuring Chaplin and a cellmate

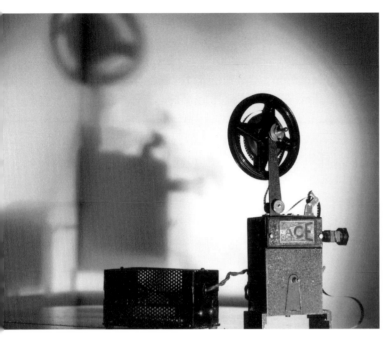

The Pathescope 9.5 Type projector Godfrey Graham's father gave him when he was ten, on which he saw his first Chaplin film

With a Charlie Chaplin look-alike in Hollywood

trying to escape. The projector was mains-operated but had a handle that you turned. I spent hours in a little cloakroom, seldom used, where I could get total darkness, even during the day. I knew every frame of both films.

At that time, my father had not told me about my grandfather's two Dublin cinemas in 1911 – 1913, where he had played piano. This was before he went to the Royal Irish Academy of Music to study under Professor Larchet. Dad would later perform on 2RN, Ireland's first radio station, a number of times.

That evening in the billiard room in the Butler Arms Hotel, I shared a silent movie moment again, not in that little cloakroom but in the living presence of that great comic genius.

When we were making the documentary about the Kerry fish farm, the farm director was very helpful to us in every way. It was, of course, in his interest to be so. Our team had worked very hard. Some of the Danish people had entertained us in their homes. Charlie Scott felt that some gesture from RTÉ would be appropriate and an invitation was extended to our Danish friends, about eight of them, to join us for dinner on our last night at the hotel.

That afternoon, we were filming in the high mountains and Charlie asked Brian to return to the hotel ahead of us to supervise the table layout and to discuss the menu with the chef. It was about 6.30 p.m. when Charlie and the team got back. We wandered into the dining room where a large table was already prepared. It looked like the Wedding Feast of Cana and Charlie commented to me that he hoped Cleeve had not gone over the top. On the table were bottles of red and white wine, the latter carefully chilled, along with fruit cordials in very elaborate receptacles that resembled something in a scientific laboratory. The table was close to where members of the Chaplin family usually sat.

We freshened up. Our guests began to arrive in the foyer of the hotel at about 7.30. Eddie Bolger and Bob Finlay, part of our team, were floating around in readiness for the event. The chef had excelled himself with wonderful scallops, prawns and salmon from the open sea. The Danes wanted fillet steak and milk-fed chicken. I suppose that, having spent all day looking at fish, they didn't particularly want to eat it every evening. Brian was Master of Ceremonies and did a superb job. His touch was on the table and the party went well, continuing into the early morning hours with some singing and dancing.

Our team surfaced next morning. We had no shooting that day, just the long journey back to Montrose. After breakfast, I bumped into Charlie coming from reception. He was as white as a sheet. I took him into an adjoining room and asked him was he all right. He had a bill in his hand and told me we had been charged £125 for the dinner for 16 people, including all the wine and soft drinks. Charlie said it was a very large sum of money and that Cleeve had gone over the top. I pointed out that he had asked Cleeve to supervise a very special dinner, which was exactly what he had done. Charlie retorted that he hadn't wanted him to put on the Lord Mayor's Show. This was 1964, when the average industrial wage was approximately £4.50 a week. and RTÉ's twenty-four-hour expenses allowance, which paid for everything, including B&B and all meals, was about £4.20. When Charlie submitted his expenses bill on his return to Dublin, it landed on Jack White's desk. Jack White hit the roof, asking how he could justify spending this amount of money on entertainment. Charlie pointed out that the Danes had given us full co-operation and looked after us very well.

Looking back now, when the euro equivalent of £120 old pounds would scarcely pay for a fair meal for four people with a few bottles of wine, it seems ridiculous that Jack White should get so upset about Charlie's expenses, particularly when Charlie never abused his expenses in any way. However, it is a graphic illustration of the early 1960s when people were quite poor, although Seán Lemass had started the industrialisation of Ireland and the country was beginning to move forward.

Charlie Scott had also taken the *Discovery* film crew on other adventures. Scott made that film about the lonely life of the lighthouse-keeper, with a superb script by Brian Cleeve, taking the keeper 'off the light' as the Irish Lights people put it. It was a lighthouse to us. Getting their man on to the lighthouse in summer was easy. It was a totally different matter in winter, when a gale or just a heavy sea running, with massive swells, makes it extremely difficult.

Scott got total co-operation from the Irish Lights people. They brought out our crew, which consisted of Simon Weafer, Des Troy, Pat Hayes and me, with production assistant Maura Lee, Cleeve and Scott, of course. We were on the 'Ierine', one of the Irish Lights tenders. It carried the navigational buoys positioned in the ocean around Ireland to mark hazardous dangers for sailors and seamen. The steamer also brought supplies for the keeper, after many weeks in solitude, and put the replacement keeper on safely.

We boarded the 'Ierine' at Castletownbere Haven, that marvellous natural harbour on the County Cork coast. Our team did not know quite what to expect. We steamed along for some hours towards the Great Skellig. This was the summer of 1964, before Irish Lights had a helicopter in service. There was a Force Five wind blowing, however, with a heavy swell running. The keeper had to be taken off in all weathers, using a special method – the steamer dropped anchor about 3,000 metres from the lighthouse and a cutter, with a powerful inboard engine and three men on board, was launched alongside the 'Ierine'. Then a longboat, with six oarsmen and a man at the tiller, was also lowered into the Atlantic. Our crew travelled in the cutter. The cutter crew fed a rope to the longboat and towed it, at high speed, towards the lighthouse. Pat Hayes and I were shooting. There was an opportunity for great shots and sound. Looking back at the longboat, we saw the crew members completely disappear behind 15 foot waves, then suddenly reappear holding their oars inboard. As we negotiated the high seas, the officer with us in the cutter explained that no boat with an engine could manoeuvre sufficiently well and hold position under the rock on which the lighthouse stood, because the propeller was exposed as the massive seas rose and fell. In a sense, the cutter would lose traction and could not operate in such conditions.

Our two small craft were at this stage some 100 metres from the lighthouse. The officer gave orders for the towrope to be released, setting free the longboat with its six oarsmen, replacement lighthouse-keeper and the fresh stores. Their boat moved closer to the lighthouse. I swung my camera to catch as much action as possible. I was shooting with a 16mm Bolex that ran for just 25 seconds before it had to be quickly rewound by hand.

I had never been in such frightening seas. A maelstrom of broken white water engulfed the men and their small boat. The main danger was the sudden rise of the water, up to 50 feet, for a few seconds. Then it fell away, causing the longboat to drop as the men fought to control the balance of the flimsy craft with their oars. Their skill was breathtaking. Only sailors of the highest skills could safely manoeuvre in such conditions; they reminded me of the men in the Melville classic, *Moby Dick*. As we watched and filmed, a large wooden arm was swung from the lighthouse. It was attached to a manually operated crane. There was a ring at the end of the wooden arm through which a rope, with a piece of wood attached, was dropped. You couldn't call it a seat but it was all that the replacement keeper would have to sit on.

As we filmed, our cutter rose and fell in the swell. The keeper waited for the right moment. The seas rose again. The seat was dropped into the long boat as the six oarsmen held the boat as steady as they could. It was not the right moment. The long boat fell away about 40 feet or so. Everyone waited for the next sudden rise of the swell. When it came, they were all lifted again and, in an instant, the replacement keeper was gone, picked up like an ant from a tiny piece of matchwood. I tried to shoot as much as I could as he swung on the end of the rope about 50 feet above the Atlantic swell, while Pat was recording on his L2 quarter-inch tape machine.

I hadn't considered what would happen next until I saw the look in Charlie Scott's eye as he shouted to the bosun above the noise of the sea to ask if we could follow. He replied that it was up to us. The longboat was returning to join our cutter. It had been laid off, waiting for the next piece of action. We all wanted to go on the lighthouse and nobody, especially Maura Lee, was going to admit to being afraid, so we transferred to the longboat. The oarsmen, the tiller man and all our equipment moved closer

Hoisting the crew (Maura Lee) onto the Great Skellig.

underneath the lighthouse again. We were able to shoot the men with the oars in close-up for the first time. I kept it close-up so Charlie could inter-cut these pictures with the film that we had shot earlier.

We got our lighthouse-keeper safely onto the rock. Brian Cleeve was to go on next, because he was the man telling the story on camera and in the voiceover so it was important to see him making the move to get on to the lighthouse. Brian was sitting in the longboat, waiting for the piece of wood at the end of the rope to drop into our boat. Suddenly he was gone, swinging over the water high over our heads. I was shooting as the crane operator swung Brian over some jagged rocks onto a flat landing area. He was safe.

I was next. Charlie wanted me to shoot from above the landing area, looking down into the longboat but I did one better. I shot with the Bolex as I was lifted out of our boat so I got footage as I was swung over the waves. This could be inserted to show what Brian had seen as he was lifted earlier. A cameraman has to think how his footage will cut with shots made earlier or even shots he may have to photograph. Maura Lee came next and showed great courage. Maura was a typical example of the breed of production assistants at the beginning of the television service who made a tremendous contribution to a programme and even carried a small number of producers who were not up to scratch. I can assure you that, being under the Fastnet Rock in a tiny boat, landing on the Bull Rock, arriving at the magic Skelligs and being plucked out of the sea, were experiences that none of us will ever forget.

Safely on the Great Skellig, we talked to the lighthouse-keeper about his life. He talked of the ancient monastic settlement that the monks had built on the summit centuries before. The island stretches jagged fingers of rock up to the sky in some kind of primitive gesture; it is one of the most exciting places that I have ever visited.

Charlie Scott knew about the beehive settlements. After mugs of scalding hot, sweet tea and home-made scones, a speciality of this particular lighthouse-keeper, we started up the thousands of steps hewn out of the rock by our ancient forbearers who had devoted their lives to prayer and the worship of God in this remote place, with only the gannets, gulls, puffins, majestic seals and porpoises for company. When we reached the summit, there were the five beehive-shaped stone dwellings. One of them had only its gable end still standing, with a beautifully delicate window facing east. I suppose this was their little oratory. The buildings nestled together as if they were afraid of the next storm.

We photographed this in great detail. As we observed the scene, I was struck by the simplicity and beauty. It had an order about it, a sanctity. These

Bee-hive settlements on Great Skellig, Co. Kerry. (Photograph: Don Macmonagle)

monks believed in their rock-steady faith. This, of course, gave the individual a confidence, which is good for the psyche.

Meeting and working with these Irish Lights seamen and lighthouse-keepers, surrounded by the natural beauty of the Atlantic with all its dangers, and ending up at the top of this majestic island with the spirit of Christianity which these monks embraced …what a wonderful experience and an amazing few days these were for us all. It remains in my memory as vividly as if it happened last week.

Thrown into a documentary film like this, you cannot know exactly what is going to happen. The presence of your companions and your friends makes a huge difference. The multi-skills of a team like this give you a sense of being really alive. It was a privilege for all of us to be involved with programmes like this and it helped us to understand so many elements of our fellow men and their tasks. It was so exciting to be part of the public broad-

RTÉ Irish Lights crew: Godfrey Graham, Charlie Scott, Maura Lee (PA), Brian Cleeve and Pat Hayes (sound recordist)

casting service, where our role was to hold up a giant mirror on Irish society, to bring the people to the people.

Another wonderful memory of working with Brian Cleeve concerns Odran Walsh's film about the poet Francis Ledwidge. Brian's narrative was interwoven with a picture as if the two elements were joined together. He enhanced my pictures like no other scriptwriter I ever worked with. It was a pity he left television far too soon. Internal pressure, not of his own making. The Ledwidge film would later win major awards at the Prague Film Festival.

Of all the locations I have visited as a cameraman, Matty Maguna's cottage near Navan, County Meath, must be the most nostalgic. It was late September, a warm sun glanced across the little orchard where the apples were fully ripe, the sweetness of the fruit trees pervading everything. We were greeted by Winnie Maguna, Mattie's sister. There was a turf fire. We sat and were offered some elderberry wine.

As I looked around, my eyes became accustomed to the low light. I noticed all the books filling the shelves. Text books on music, many on poetry, mostly by English writers. I moved my position in the room slightly and accidentally nudged a fiddle with my foot. A note sounded. I picked up the old instrument. Winnie said that Matty used to play it in the evenings when Francis would walk over from Slane. Francis Ledwidge and Matty Maguna were great friends. Matty was a printer by trade and a good fiddler, as well. When the evenings were closing in, they would talk of everything from the political situation in Ireland of the day to the darkening clouds in Europe which were to lead to the Great War and, above all, about poetry, Francis's latest offering.

Matty Maguna encouraged Francis in every way, as did Lord Dunsany. Matty saw his vision, his inner eye. Ledwidge was a trade union activist for the workers in a little lead mine near Navan, trying to get better working conditions.

Sitting in Matty Maguna's cottage with Winnie in the 1960s, listening to her speak of those days and nights of poetry and music, is something that I will never forget. That November, we travelled to Belgium, to Ypres, to shoot the images of the trenches that were left just as they were at the end of the Great War, that terrible horror.

Nearby, we filmed a little forest, with the late autumn colour. Francis must have been taken back to his beloved Slane and to Matty Maguna's cottage. The trees were the same but what a contrast in every other way to the peace of County Meath. Francis never came home.

When we get one of those late autumn golden days, my thoughts return to the orchard and to Matty Maguna's cottage. I have always wondered what became of the little place. Was it pulled down, in the name of progress? What became of Matty's fiddle or is it preserved in time, with all the bits and pieces of that cottage intact, just as I remember? I have wanted to go back but am afraid that my memories will be shattered, – so I prefer to let it rest – the orchard alive with bird song, and a purring cat sunning herself in her favourite corner, as if nothing had changed since the days when Francis Ledwidge came to call.

FURTHER AFIELD

SIR ANTHONY O'REILLY

In the early 1960s, Sheamus Smith went on to be a producer/director. One of the first programmes on which I worked with him, was *On the Land*, about the launching of Kerrygold butter. Tony O'Reilly, now Sir Anthony, was in charge of Bord Bainne in those days, and it was decided that the British launch would take place in sunny Manchester, presumably because of the large Irish population.

We flew on an Aer Lingus Viscount. When we were airborne and were at our cruising altitude, the air hostesses emerged and were as charming as ever. Tony and Sheamus were sitting together. Sheamus enquired whether this was an 'international flight'. Indeed it was, he was told, as it was travelling on to Paris. Sheamus replied, 'Good, our party will have champagne, please!' In a few moments, the champagne arrived, nicely chilled, so we celebrated Kerrygold's launch before we even touched down in Manchester. Fintan Ryan and I declined the champagne … we were young and thought it might affect our sound and vision for later in the day! Paddy Jennings was the reporter.

I had known Tony in a sporting context. Although I had not played rugby at Blackrock College, the great rivalry between 'Rock and Old Belvedere, particularly in the O'Reilly years, reached fever pitch. 'Rock seemed to have the edge in rugger but Belvedere blew us away when it came to cricket. I remember Tony O'Reilly, David Piggott and I playing for the Leprechauns Cricket Club against Galway Grammar School many years before. Tony was keeping wicket as I bowled my leg breaks. A dominant figure behind the stumps, he was also a very useful middle-order batsman, both at school and senior club level. Playing in a team game is a marvellous opportunity to interact with your fellow team members, all with the common purpose of beating the opposition. The qualities Tony showed in sport stood him in great stead in his later career.

In 'Rock, I loved the schools rugby competitions and followed every match, although I didn't play the game. I can still remember the great year when we beat Belvedere College in the final. O'Reilly was in the three-quarters and the Blackrock centre, Tom Cleary, intercepted a pass and ran from halfway to score. 'Rock won the cup again.

THE SEVEN SIGNATORIES

In 1964, Aindreas Ó Gallchóir embarked on research to find out if any close relatives of the men who signed the Irish Proclamation were still alive. I was fortunate enough to photograph the series.

As I have said, it was fascinating to be involved from the very beginning in the Irish television service. Many of the people who had won our Independence or helped to do so, were still around – De Valera, Frank Aiken, people like Ernest Blythe and Bulmer Hobson. Others who had passed on but whose influence was very real. W.T. Cosgrave, Kevin O'Higgins, Michael Collins. T. J. Whittaker. Seán Lemass had started the industrialisation of the Republic in the mid-1960s. He, of course, was Taoiseach and leader of the government that set up the television service.

As we began to meet the close relatives for the *Seven Signatories* programme, it was fascinating to discover what they felt about their family members who had put their names to the Irish Constitution. At that time, there was absolutely no certainty what the Irish people would get as a result of these men's efforts in their latest Uprising after so many earlier failed attempts. Most Dubliners in 1916 considered it another mistake by a bunch of hotheads and dreamers. One by one, we met the relatives of these amazing people. As I looked through my lens, I realised that it was a fascinating programme to be working on. They spoke of the family members who had been wrenched from them suddenly in some noble but lost cause; it was such a gamble.

This film series is safe in the RTÉ archives, along with thousands of other programmes. In recent years, RTÉ has spent millions on the facilities at Montrose and other sites so that the unique record of the Irish people is preserved for the generations to come. Many dedicated people in the library and archives have spent their working lives protecting this precious programme material.

NORRIS DAVIDSON IN DONEGAL

I got a message from my boss that I would be working with Norris Davidson the next week in Donegal. Sheila, who was expecting our daughter Lisa, decided to come with me in our first car, an old mini. We had no idea what the road conditions were like although we did know that it was a long journey. We were exhausted when we arrived at about 4p.m. and drove straight to the National Hotel.

I had never met Norris Davidson. There was a tall man aged about fifty in the foyer. This had to be him. I stretched out my hand and introduced Sheila. He smiled, said that we must be famished, welcomed us to Donegal and suggested a cup of tea. We met the charming Mrs Thomas and booked in.

Thirty minutes later, Norris said he would like me to look at a location for the next day's shooting, adding it wasn't that far away. I looked at my young wife. Norris suggested that Sheila should come along. We got into Norris's Triumph Herald with the hood down and drove for about 35 miles to a remote part of Donegal to look at a coastal area where we would be filming the next day. The journey was the last thing that Sheila needed.

The film told the story of a pilgrimage organised by the Church of Ireland in honour of St. Columba. Part of the assignment was to visit Iona later on, where I shot with Aindreas Ó Gallchóir and Chris Fitzsimons.

My next assignment with Norris was the series *The Changing Face of Ireland*. We were filming in County Wicklow quite near Norris's home outside Donard in west Wicklow, in November in heavy snow in the mountains. Norris was trying to illustrate how, in the days gone by, it was necessary to carry all the water if you did not have a well close to your home.

There was an old woman living in an isolated cottage across a number of fields and she still had to carry her water from a well some distance away. So we shot a sequence in some detail of her carrying the water four or five hundred yards to her cottage.

Norris's approach to shooting was extremely professional. In 1931 on a break from his studies at Cambridge, he made his first film about a suicide, entitled *By Accident*. After college, he spent six years working for John

Godfrey Graham with Norris Davidson (Photograph: Don Macmonagle)

Grierson in the Empire Marketing Board Film Unit and was widely experienced. During this period, Norris wrote two novels, *Galore Park* and *The Steam Yacht 'Soft Impeachable'*. Returning to Ireland, he made films for the Great Southern Railway and the Irish Tourist Board. During World War II, he served on coastal patrol with the Irish Navy. On the long spells of watch, he wrote scripts for Radio Éireann. In 1947, he joined the radio station as an official scriptwriter along with Prionsias O Conluain and P. P. Maguire. During the 1950s, he wrote, produced and presented dozens of radio features and documentaries. In 1962, his radio documentary *From the Ground Up* celebrated the start-up of the television service that he would join some seven years later. Then nearly 60, Norris was once again able to use all those latent skills of the filmmaker that he had put aside in the 1940s. Over the next quarter century, he would produce a set of television documentaries that were diverse and skilfully made.

Filming that day in west Wicklow, we did a sequence of the woman arriving at the cottage. We noticed a baby in the cottage in a cradle. The old woman said that it was her daughter's child. The baby started to cry. We were shooting the fireplace and other things in the room, trying to illustrate the period of the 1920s or 1930s. Norris needed the sound of the crackling fire, not the baby crying. The production assistant, Maureen Hurley, sat on a stool beside the cradle and sang a lullaby to the infant. Soon it stopped crying and the filming began, the baby's face lit by the firelight. I remember it as if it were yesterday. Maureen was also a fine harpist and had toured America and Scandinavia.

I was beginning to realise what an extraordinary director Norris Davidson was. He had taken Robert Flaherty to the Aran Islands to show him a possible location for the major film that Flaherty would eventually make about man's struggle against the elements, *Man of Aran*. Those of us who were working in the 1960s in RTÉ's television documentary department had the wonderful experience of working with people like Norris, who was definitely a unique talent.

Norris Davidson was also an expert when it came to opera and radio broadcasting. He was to make a film about Joan Denise Moriarty and her ballet company in Cork for which we filmed a performance at the Opera House. It was a highly successful documentary. Norris was a supporter of the little ballet company since it began. He would appear out of the blue in remote locations around Ireland and would go backstage with bottles of champagne and chocolates for the company. They loved him.

Norris Davidson had a particular skill for filming a major project from beginning to end. One example of this was his film on the building of the great organ for the National Concert Hall. Another was his film on the building of the *Asgard II*, from the felling of the trees, to the shaping of the ship's line, to its trials and, finally, to see it under full sail. I was involved in both these films.

During the film about the great organ built by Kenneth Jones, I went to Cambridge with Norris to see a beautiful organ that had also been built by Jones who was building the new instrument for the National Concert Hall. One day, having shot the sequence of the organ in the Cambridge church, Norris and the rest of the team were de-rigging for the day. As we were passing a particular building, Norris pointed to it and told me that he and Alastair Cooke used to go up and down that drainpipe to their rooms after hours when they were students and, once or twice, the drainpipe had almost come off the building.

On another occasion, when a colleague of mine was filming with him at Cambridge again, Norris announced that he had to leave a book back to the library. When they went in, Norris approached the young lady and placed a book on the counter. She noticed that the number did not tally with the records. She looked at her computer and asked him if he had borrowed the book from this library. He replied that he had and she inquired when this was. 'Over 56 years ago', he replied. 'I thought you might like to have it back.' That was the kind of man he was.

I asked him if he had seen the *Michael Collins* film by Neil Jordan, knowing he had been around then. He said that he hadn't but would catch up with it. There was a long pause, then Norris said, 'I used to dine fairly regularly with the Laverys in London in those days. Lady Lavery came to see my rushes on a number of occasions.' That was typical of Norris, you never knew what he would come up with next.

In about 1994, Norris was going to make a film about the Rotunda Hospital because it was shortly to be the 250th anniversary of that great institution. By this time in RTÉ television, we were mostly using electronic cameras, and film not used to the same extent at all. However, Norris insisted that this documentary would be shot on Super 16mm film. We did this over six months. The documentary was detailed.

My camera operator was Paul Daniels and Eddie Bolger was the electrician. It was an interesting documentary to make. Norris and our team were amazed at the premature babies, at how small they were and the highly specialist care needed to keep them alive. You cannot appreciate the miracles that the medical staff perform until you see at close range the care and scientific know-how that they lavish on the little ones.

Norris was now in his mid-80s and it was felt that this might be his last film. We felt this the previous year, too, when we made a film about Killarney and had presented a clapperboard to him at a dinner.

After the Rotunda documentary, Norris said that he would stop filming when he was 90. But the Birr telescope was to be his next project. He had been researching the project for years. I was one of a number of cameramen who shot the film about the unique Rosse family. William, the 3rd Earl of Rosse, designed and built the magnificent telescope in the mid-19th century. He was the President of the Royal Society at the time and made a huge impact on the international world of astronomy. In 1836, he married a Yorkshire woman, Mary Field. She brought with her a considerable fortune and, in due course, became very interested in photography. She was the first woman to win the Photography Society of Ireland's silver medal in 1859 for the excellence of work. Norris directed the film but, sadly, died before he could complete the editing. At my suggestion, Mike McCarthy saved it and it has since been shown on RTÉ, with a script and voiceover by John O'Donoghue.

I was working with Seán Ó Mordha on a film about the composer Séan Ó Riada. We were going to Paris to do some sequences. There was just the possibility that Samuel Beckett might give us an interview. Ó Mordha had already met Beckett on a number of occasions and felt there was quite a good chance, if he popped the question, that we might get an interview.

Some weeks before going, I was working with Norris and mentioned in passing that I would be in Paris and hoped to get to Beckett. Norris swung around and said, 'If you happen to meet that man, tell him I want my bat back.' Beckett was a good cricketer at Royal Portora, Enniskillen. Norris, who was in the same year as Beckett, had been given a new cricket bat by his uncle, bought in Elverys for the vast sum of ten shillings and six pence. Beckett put his eye on it and never returned it. Norris did not play cricket.

Regarding that interview in Paris, Beckett said no, so I never got a chance to ask him about the cricket bat. It might have been nice to meet him and talk cricket. We did have one thing in common as we both played cricket for Ireland. Beckett loved rugby and never missed an international on TV when Ireland was playing.

ARAN ISLANDS

My mother and father had honeymooned in the West of Ireland in 1934 and took the Dun Angus ferry to the Aran Islands. Years later, they told me that I would have to see the Aran Islands some day. When Louis Lentin brought a team to make a film on the islands in 1964, the Dun Angus was still in service. The soundman, Bill O'Neill had been a chief sound supervisor at Ardmore Studios when they began. Some years after he joined RTÉ and ran the dubbing and sound department and supervised the sound recordist at that time.

I knew Robert Flaherty's film, *Man of Aran* and had seen it a number of times. We had the pleasure of filming in one of the cottages used by

Threshing corn on the Aran Islands, unchanged since J.M. Synge's time there

Flaherty. It still had the thatched roof into which a glass section had been added to give more light for shooting indoors. Robert Flaherty shot the bulk of the film and processed the black and white negative on the Island. This was some job. He had a small number of helpers but it must have been a Herculean task. The storm sequence is breath taking. David Lean had so much admiration for *Man of Aran* and that sequence in particular, that he viewed it again before he embarked on his own storm sequence for his film, *Ryan's Daughter*.

We disembarked from the steamer at Inisheer into currachs, as there was no harbour on the island. Lentin wanted coverage of that sequence. There were six or seven curraghs. There was a heavy swell as people stepped into the flimsy crafts. Cows were also being lowered by rope into the water, then towed with a rope around their neck to the beach. There was a lot of confusion. Some of these cows had never swum and they were terror-struck. I was filming and Louis was calling the shots.

I looked up at the doorway at the side of the steamer, where some men were standing around a figure dressed in a black shawl. There was a flash of bright red from her skirt. It was a beautiful young woman holding a tiny baby in a white Aran shawl. Great skill was taken to get the precious cargo into the currach. A tall young man, the father it seemed, stretched his arms out to take the baby when the swell lifted the currach up to the correct height and then suddenly dropped again about four feet. Then the mother was gripped around her waist and safely reunited with her precious bundle.

As I shot all this sequence, I could not help noticing angry looks from some of the men but I continued filming. A little bit later, there was no denying the anger. There were four men in the currach with the mother and baby. Our currach was about four metres away. A man, who was not rowing, stood up and shook his fist at us. I looked at Louis. He told me to keep rolling. It was clear that the family was offended and felt we were invading their privacy in some way. I felt that I should cut the camera. As I watched the scene through my viewfinder, I saw a large piece of wood coming towards me. It missed my head by about a metre. The missile was about half a metre long and very heavy as it splashed into the sea behind us. I switched off the camera and we made our way to the beach, which I remember being very, very beautiful, with much activity. We shot more footage as we landed.

The islanders did not like to be photographed in those days. It appears that in the folk memory there were mixed feelings about the film *Man Of Aran*. Some people had done very well and were rewarded, others were forgotten. We tried to respect the sensitivity of the islanders in this respect but Louis had a film to shoot so we had to get on with it. We filmed on some of the other islands and I have to say their rugged beauty really took my breath away.

Twenty years later, I was to return to Aran with James Plunkett to film a feature on John Millington Synge. This time, we flew in two Aer Arran islander aircraft with Niall Buggy and the rest of the cast and crew. We shot in the cottage where Synge stayed during his period in Aran. Yeats had persuaded Synge to go on a voyage of discovery to the Aran Islands and Synge never forgot the debt he owed to Yeats for this. The striking beauty and primitive nature of the islands never left Synge and his experiences on Aran greatly influenced *Riders To The Sea* and other work. He took some excellent photographs, which were published in book form.

If you think about it, Robert Flaherty's *Man Of Aran* film and the storm sequence fascinated David Lean, yet Lean never quite matched it in his own film, *Ryan's Daughter*. The haunting power of the Aran Islands can also be seen in the work of James Plunkett, who needed to walk in the footsteps of Synge, a writer for whom he had so much regard. Plunkett made a film on his life.

I returned to the islands in the 1990s with Mike P. Ó Conghaile to discover that the islands were as captivating as ever. We did sequences with fishermen, using huge long lines dropped over sheer cliffs hundreds of metres into the sea. We came across two men working in a tiny stone field with sheaves of corn, threshing them in the traditional manner that had not changed since Synge's days or earlier. I hope the islands continue to progress, while retaining their unique natural beauty both for their own people and for the many from all over the world who will always make that voyage of discovery to these wonderful places.

TEA AND SCONES WITH THE PRESIDENT

Seán Ó Mordha and a small film team had got clearance to film in the gardens of Áras an Uachtaráin for a programme on a different subject, which had nothing to do with Cathal O Dalaigh, who was President at that time.

After an hour or so, a figure appeared through the great French windows. It was the President. 'Sorry to interrupt the work,' he said. 'When you have finished, please join me for tea and scones.' Seán thanked him.

Twenty minutes later, we entered the lovely reception room and within a few moments, President O Dalaigh joined us. He invited us to follow him to his private quarters where we would be more comfortable. As we sat on a comfortable couch and a number of easy chairs, silver trays arrived with tea. When the two attendants withdrew, the President explained that when he arrived at the Áras, the kitchen staff and chefs were excellent but, for some reason, there was no home baking. He quickly encouraged the baking of brown bread and a wide range of pastries and scones. He wanted us to enjoy this homely aspect of his residence.

We had a most pleasant hour or so and it struck me that here was a man who had achieved so much at all levels of the legal profession, including as a judge at the European Court, but had not forgotten the simple things of life.

I saw him during his period in office at small theatres up and down the country, supporting people who were committed to the arts. I always felt he gave great support to a profession that had been so neglected especially by State agencies over the years. Things have improved somewhat since then.

My grandparents had a rambling cottage in Rathfarnham, close to St. Enda's. My father had carried messages for de Valera on his bike over the Feather Bed Mountains during the War of Independence when he was 13 as I have mentioned.

I remember photographing President de Valera giving a Christmas message at Áras an Uachtaráin. As I watched him in my view-finder, my mind went back to the days when Dev came to secret meetings at my grandparents' main house in 35 North Great George's Street, disguised as a woman, wearing an elegant skirt, with high-buttoned boots and hat and gloves. What a vision! A voice in my head said watch the composition, is the focus sharp, how is the President lit? Most important of all, can I see his eyes clearly, especially with his spectacles on, are there reflections in the glass? I think I did a good job as far as I can remember. How strange it was to find myself with the President after all those family memories from my father. We found de Valera pleasant and warm and most hospitable. We enjoyed the Irish whiskey he shared with us. We spent over an hour in his company, before we felt it was time to take our leave of the great man. He showed no impatience. I felt we could have remained much longer.

MOVING INTO FEATURES

PATRICK KAVANAGH

IN THE SUMMER OF 1966, Adrian Cronin was asked by the Head of Features, James Plunkett, to make a programme on Patrick Kavanagh. I was lucky to be involved.

We first went to Kavanagh's home village, Inniskeen in County Monaghan. He seemed pleased that the State television was acknowledging his importance as a poet, having already experienced such a struggle for recognition in Dublin. I found him easy to get on with and he quickly became one of our team. He brought us to his old haunts, where he seemed to relive his childhood and young adolescence. Memories were flooding through his mind and he told us about them. Adrian had a good eye and we tried to capture on film the atmosphere of the little haunts and the nooks and crannies in his home village and the nearby townland at Mucker. Just to wander round with him was great.

One day, we arranged a picnic lunch from the hotel and picked up some beers and soft drinks in a local pub in Inniskeen. We shot film that morning and about 1.30 p.m. we found ourselves at a small stream where we stopped for lunch, flopping down with our equipment all around us. We spread out the Foxford rug that I had picked up some months earlier in that village in County Mayo. It was one of the hottest days, I remember. The sandwiches were good. Fintan Ryan, Simon and the rest of our team just relaxed in the ambience of the day, with the sound of the stream in our ears. There was a lot of birdsong.

Simon suddenly spotted a kingfisher. We all turned to look but could not see it. In a moment, Simon was on his feet, bent down and approached the

Patrick Kavanagh and the kingfisher

stream as if he were stalking some kind of prey. Kavanagh commented, 'The man is mad, imagine trying to catch a wild kingfisher on foot!' When I said Simon was a Ringsend man, Kavanagh said that explained everything, they were all half mad down there and spent half their lives at sea.

We resumed our conversation. Suddenly, there was a shout from Simon. 'The bird has a wounded wing. I've got him.' He carried the wild creature back to our picnic circle and asked the poet whether he would like to hold it. Kavanagh quickly said he would and stretched out his big hands. Simon placed the radiant creature so gently into the cupped hands, almost as if it were a piece of stardust that might blow away if he were not careful. We could not believe the moment. I reached back behind me for my Arriflex camera and framed a big close-up of the bird in the poet's hands. The strange thing was that the little creature, injured and obviously in shock, continued to move its head in a circle, not making any attempt to fly away. My next shot was a close-up of Kavanagh looking down at the new arrival. His eyes were full of tears, his face drawn as if he was about to break down. He was conscious of the miracle that had just happened – as we all were. The chance of holding a wild kingfisher in your hand is so remote but here he was, in an instant, part of this magic moment.

We picked up our bits and pieces. Simon took the bird to the film bus. He made a little nest out of one of our sweaters. We were then returning to Mucker to the house and where Kavanagh's sisters, Annie and Mary, greeted us. Patrick told them we had a kingfisher and needed a little box for him. Our team did some more shots around the cottage. It was Friday, time for us to return to Dublin.

The following Monday, as arranged, we met Kavanagh in Dublin at the Canal. When we arrived, he was walking along the towpath towards us. Greetings were exchanged but the first thing Simon asked was how the kingfisher was. Kavanagh recounted how they had looked after him, putting him beside the fire and feeding him with some home-made brown bread and milk, and that he gave the bird a sardine thought he might like. I found this very amusing. Kavanagh continued his story. 'Before I went to the station to get the train, I went out into the yard and launched the kingfisher back into the sky. He flew perfectly into a tree, with his back to me, then turned around and looked at me, as if to say thanks.'

We shot the memorable sequence at the Canal bank that morning, which turned out to be something of a classic montage and has now been seen so many times on television. For the rest of that week, we continued working with Kavanagh, paying particular attention to his memories of Dublin, which, as we know now, were from time to time very unhappy. Rejection is one of the most damaging things that can happen to anybody. It can destroy the personality of the strongest character. For the artist it is soul-destroying. Some individuals survive and find a kind of strength but many go under as a result. It was obvious that Kavanagh had been damaged by his experiences but he struggled on to create some wonderful poetry and prose. It was amazing to spend those three weeks with him. We were all young and the memories affected us and will remain with us for a very long time.

The director Tom McArdle made a film about Kavanagh some 25 years after the poet's death, called *The Gentle Tiger*. It was a joy for me to revisit the work of Kavanagh. McArdle wanted to re-assess Patrick Kavanagh after the lapse of those 25 years.

Hilda Moriarty was the girl in Kavanagh's poem, *Raglan Road*. They met in the autumn of 1943. Hilda, from Dingle, Co. Kerry, was a stunningly attractive young woman studying to be a doctor in Dublin. McArdle found Hilda Moriarty, still an elegant woman in her late fifties, living in Limerick. We all had the pleasure of meeting her. She reminisced about how Patrick was so sincere about his feelings for her, if a bit lacking in the more sophisticated nuances of courtship.

To watch Hilda in my viewfinder was fascinating, as she talked about the Dublin of the late 1940s and 1950s, Kavanagh's chronic shortage of money and his efforts to gain recognition for his poetry. A country man, trying to convince people he had the creative vision as the Dublin literati looked down their noses at him. Hilda Moriarty went on to marry Donogh O'Malley, who later became the Minister of Education and introduced free secondary education to Ireland. Patrick Kavanagh and Hilda would never have suited each other really. Life is strange. We are attracted to beauty that we can never have. We reach out only to be shattered by rejection. Like ships in the night, we drift in the hope that we will find the perfect partner. Kavanagh was a romantic. The most vulnerable of all but, if his nature had not been as it was, we would never have had *Raglan Road* and so many other beautiful poems.

The centenary of the birth of Patrick Kavanagh was on October 21, 2004. I had the pleasure of being the National Concert Hall for a major tribute. Brendan Kennelly, Tom Hickey, Ronnie Drew, the Cullen Harpers and Zoë Conway and others contributed to a wonderful evening. I introduced eleven minutes of the film that RTÉ had made in 1966, directed by Adrian Cronin. It was marvellous to screen the footage of Kavanagh walking through his village of Inniskeen again. His encounter with the kingfisher captivated the audience. Noel O'Grady made all this possible. His own singing of *Raglan Road* was a beautiful insight into the poet's lyrical ideas expressed in that poem. Seamus Hosey brought the sell-out audience through Kavanagh's life in a most enchanting way.

PAUL DURCAN

Durcan's voiceover for Kavanagh's poem *Lough Derg* was hauntingly grim and had a most powerful empathy with the ideas . I thought Paul's memories expressed in Tom McArdle's film *The Gentle Tiger,* made in 1987, were deeply moving. Durcan's reading of the *Canal Bank Walk* was so graceful in style, floating Kavanagh's words together with the imagery on the Canal.

When we were with Paul Durcan in his little house in Ringsend, he talked of his memories of calling to visit Patrick and his wife in the small ground floor flat in Waterloo Road and how Patrick looked out, in response to Paul's knock, in a protective way as if defending the privacy which, at last he possessed, unlike all the rest of his life. The struggle to be accepted by the so-called Dublin literati had left its mark.

After meeting Paul, it became clear to me that he had been inspired by the Monaghan poet in a very profound way, especially when Paul was trying to get a foothold himself in what must be the toughest form of writing. Paul Durcan is now such an important poet. He seems to capture the immediacy

Paul
Durcan

of life around him, whether he is castigating a politician or a stuffy academic. Like Kavanagh, Paul sees things, the human and the inhuman, the shallowness of life all around us, but also the good, which he observes with great compassion and tenderness.

AUSTIN CLARKE 1967

Austin Clarke had a house in Clonskeagh, beside the River Dodder, in Dublin. He had observed in a poem that the housing estates seemed to be drifting out from the city engulfing the country areas, and the sound of the church bell grew nearer and nearer as new churches were built. Austin's garden had high poplar trees. It was possible to get quite lost in that garden. The director was Adrian Cronin, the script was written by Augustine Martin. Adrian wanted a hand held shot moving behind Austin as he strolled in the garden. RTÉ had just received a new film camera, the Éclair NPR, a state-of-the art instrument and very suitable for shooting cinema verité-style.

Inside his house, in the library, we were surrounded by hundreds of books. Clarke loved his pipe and immediately lit up, creating plumes of smoke that were picked up by our backlight, and created a wonderful mood. Our team visited his other home, where he was born, in the shadow of the Black Church, at Mountjoy Street. Just around the corner was Paradise Place. He showed us the little back yard where he had played as a child and told us of the memory he had of looking into a little puddle after a rain shower and noticing the spire of the Black Church next door reflected in the water, but glinting in a way he had never seen. He brought us to the little streetscapes nearby where he had darted in and out with his schoolmates. Looking at the doors and windows of the little cottages now, he was amazed at how small everything was, as if they must have been occupied by much smaller people. We were only a stone's throw away from where another Dublin author, Dean Swift, described a whole city as a kingdom of the little people. The Lilliputians of *Gulliver's Travels*. Austin Clarke took us to Grafton Street where he said he loved to looked at the style and was strongly considering writing a poem about the mini-skirt. He wore a long black overcoat and formal black hat and explained that he was frequently saluted by passers-by who thought he was a priest. He would respond in a suitable manner so as not to disillusion them.

My favourite poem of his is *The Straying Student*. Adrian cast a beautiful

Austin Clarke (above), born in the shadow of the Black Church, Mountjoy Street, Dublin (left)

golden-haired Swedish girl, a model with Sybil Connelly's salon, as the fantasy woman in the poet's imagination. She was tall and very striking. On a beautiful April day with sharp light, we went to the Phoenix Park, where there was a blasted tree on a dramatic hillock. We shot Austin and the girl separately, and together, with the tree separating them, a symbol of the poet's struggle. At that time the poet was older, the woman younger. It was the memory of the old man's thoughts and how he remembered the way he felt as a callow youth, the power of the desire that haunted him. We visited Cashel of the Kings, which we knew would be stimulating because Austin had been drawn to our Celtic past. As I looked out over the central plain from that high vantage point of the Rock of Cashel, it struck me how lucky we were to be involved in such programme-making with a great living poet.

A year later, after the film had been transmitted, I was walking up Grafton Street, past the lady playing a concert harp in Wicklow Street. I could not decide whether to have a coffee in Bewleys, the Monument Creamery or Robert Roberts but, eventually, decided Roberts was the place. I was pleased to see Austin Clarke sitting in the corner of the restaurant. He waved, beckoned me over to join him and began to reminisce about our weeks together and how much he had enjoyed it. He added that people came up to him, having seen the film. The music was quite loud because Roberts had a string trio of fiddle, viola and cello, which added to the atmosphere. Bay Jellett, Mainie's sister, was the fiddle player and led the group. We ordered more coffee and sat and enjoyed the ambience as the big log fire crackled in the corner. He asked about Adrian Cronin, Fintan Ryan and Joe Kennelly, and talked about our filming in his garden, remembering the problem that we had in executing a particular shot because of light changes and movement of the camera. He had later written a few lines about this, stating, 'Godfrey Graham had some difficulties and challenges but, when I saw the preview, I discovered that he had overcome all these difficulties. In particular, a shot of the Celestial City of which I had a glimpse in childhood'.

In our conversations in Robert Roberts, Clarke had mentioned he knew James Joyce. Some years after this meeting, I came across his memories of those encounters in Paris in the 1920s. They are most revealing. I quote:

'Indeed in depressing moments I can still remember the drabness of the place, it was like a little laneway lit by gas and overshadowed by a blank wall of St. Sulpice. I think Joyce chose that gloomy side street because it reminded him of Dublin. It was always at about 6 o'clock he was there before me, a tall melancholy bearded figure in black. Fretting impatiently standing striding up and down before the wall or standing despondently at the kerb. We went into the same cheap little café, which was usually empty, and sat there in strange silence. What could I say to him, what could anybody say to him? I felt like a small boy in the presence of a kind but dejected schoolmaster and he sat there gazing abstractly through the thick lenses of his spectacles and sighing to himself. I was oppressed by the silence that I dare not break and by his misery. He was testing his own amazing memory. He and I knew it gave him pleasure to use me as a kind of walking directory but when I told him of premises in Dublin that had changed hands or buildings that had vanished he would sigh to himself and relapse into silence. That dream city, that vision of Dublin in which he was absorbed was static to him and I could feel how deeply the sense of change and of the new generations affected him and during those long intervals of silence I was back there myself in Dublin, back again in school and could hear the murmurs of the class, the chalk on the blackboard and I could see the brass candlesticks in the school chapel which had reminded Joyce of the battered mail of the fallen angels.' (Austin Clarke.)

INTO EUROPE

IN 1965, there was much talk about the possibility of Ireland joining the Common Market. Jack White, senior programme administrator, and producers Lelia Doolan and Odran Walsh, felt that a major film series was needed to try to explain the huge implications for the population of Ireland if we were to become part of that Common Market.

My son, Ian was born and, five days after Sheila and he came home, I left to go on the *Into Europe* series. I missed him, Sheila and my daughter, Lisa, so much. It was a decision that Sheila and I made at the time, but we did have some regrets about it then, and much later, too.

Odran a producer from Tuam, County Galway, with wide international experience, appointed executive producer of the series. The producers included Michael Johnston, Lelia Doolan, Pat Kearney and Dick Hill. The films were to be shot in Germany, Belgium, France, Holland and Italy. RTÉ television had never taken on anything this big. The research was extensive, as the programmes would examine the political, social and religious conditions in these countries, as well as the attitude of existing members to new countries, like Ireland.

Two film units, each incorporating a lighting cameraman, assistant cameraman, driver, sound recordist, electrician, presenter, director and production assistant, were on the road for three months. The directors and P.A.s linked with the crews, worked for about a week, flew to the next film team in another country and worked there for another week, before heading off again. Some of the films linked stories about people and countries, which continued from one location to another.

Michael Johnston was filming with Stuart Hetherington's unit in the south of Italy, telling the story of a father and son who were going to Cologne to work as road-sweepers. The father and son travelled by train.

Bob Finlay, Dermot O'Grady, Godfrey Graham, Dick Hill and Deirdre Murphy.
(Photograph: Colm O'Byrne)

Michael flew on ahead to Cologne with his production assistant, Joan Caffrey and, when the Italian party got off the train, he was there with Colm O'Byrne, Dermot O'Grady, Bob Finlay and myself to continue their story. We shot a sequence in the workers' hostel, where the father and son were going to stay in Cologne. I remember the Italians and the Irish had a marvellous party that night. They had brought wine from the little vineyard on their small farm and we brought some Jameson. We saw the father and son working on the streets of Cologne in sweltering heat.

As we went from country to country, we realised the great disadvantage we were under because some of us did not have the language of the country, although a few producers and P.A.s had some French and German. I remember filming with Lelia Doolan in Belgium. After a week of hard work, she said, 'All the best folks, see you in about seven days time.' She was flying to Moscow to research a film she was going to make there. We met a week later in Amsterdam. Of all the countries in which my team filmed,

Holland was the easiest from the point of view of the welcome. Most people spoke English.

Shooting the canals in the centre of Amsterdam was a real treat. There was a style and sophistication about the place. I remember filming with Dick Hill in Louvain University. John Horgan was the reporter. As we sat there in a street café between sequences, I was struck by the amazing link with the Irish college in Louvain. Now was a film unit from Ireland continuing that tradition, using the new medium of television to tell the continuing story as it entered a new phase.

We went to an area called Friesland, where they had their own language, and spent some days with them. It reminded us of our own Gaelteacht areas, which they knew about. There were many parallels and, of course, Friesian cattle come from there.

We filmed a Jesuit priest in Amsterdam who said it made sense for a couple to live together for some months before getting married to see if they were compatible. When we transmitted this in Ireland in 1965, it caused more than a few raised eyebrows.

Justin Keating was a reporter on the unit and I was with him in Belgium and Holland; his particular interest was the trade union movement and farming. Keating went on to become Minister of Industry and Commerce, a great communicator in the new medium.

Irish film crews did not travel a great deal and we were viewed with suspicion by border officials. There were long delays at innumerable border posts. There was still an echo of the war years when boundaries were rigidly adhered to. We had difficulties at times and were refused entry, waiting for hours. We were carrying the new carnet document which some border guards had never seen. How things have changed since.

After three months, the thought of coming home to see Sheila, Lisa my new son, Ian, was a wonderful prospect. We had to drive across the continent and get to the ferries. Today, many people in RTÉ would be amazed by the size of this assignment, but major projects were not uncommon in those days. We appreciated that this was an assignment of immense importance and that we were privileged to be on it. Of course, we were filming in 16mm black and white. It was long before RTÉ television had gone into colour but I was shooting with a 8mm camera in colour, so there is a colour record of the background to the series.

Thinking back to those days, we could never imagine the transformation of our country that occurred as a direct result of joining the Common Market.

LISNASKEA BYE-ELECTION

I think it was the following year, 1966, when John Williams took a film team to Lisnaskea to cover the bye-election. We travelled up in the morning, because clearance had been given to visit Lord and Lady Brookborough at their home just outside the village. Arriving in the early afternoon, we were received with a friendliness that surprised me and led into an elegant large room, comfortable and homely. Sitting at a table was Lady Brookborough. She stood and shook our hands. ' Welcome to Ulster,' she said, 'my husband will be here in a moment.' We were invited to sit and relax. There were some fine paintings and glass ornaments on a number of antique tables. A young man came into the room. It was Captain John Brookborough. He was less formal and we got talking about his passion, which was show-jumping and cross-country. He said he would never miss the Dublin Horse Show and that he had friends in the South whom he enjoyed meeting. Lord Brookborough joined us, again hand-shakes all round. 'Let's rustle up some tea,' he said. John Williams engaged the master of the house in some talk, carefully avoiding politics. Two waiters arrived with one of the finest afternoon teas I have ever had.

Two hours later, we took our leave of the Brookboroughs. They invited us to come to the Orange Hall at 7.30 that evening for a meeting and nominations. We rigged our camera, sound and lights about five rows back from the stage at the side, not to be in the way of the audience, who numbered 300 approximately.

On the platform were Lady Brookborough, Lord Brookborough and Captain John Brookborough, John Taylor, Minister of Home Affairs, the nominees and local officials.

I was fully aware of the delicacy of our situation, as were my colleagues. We had all observed our usual courtesy to all around us. The meeting began after the chairman dealt with the official business of the nominations. The winning candidate was duly chosen unanimously. I had been shooting the proceedings. John Taylor had not spoken up to that point. He rose to speak. To our utter amazement, he unleashed an attack on our State, speaking of the Republic's utter poverty, high unemployment, priest-ridden society, which shocked out team. My camera still rolled non–stop. I knew this was historic footage.

A number of other speakers echoed his sentiments. I reloaded my camera with another roll of 600 feet and continued. I also watched John Williams in case he wanted to convey new instructions. He signalled to continue. The next speaker rounded on us, referring to people of the Free State, pointing at us saying, 'go back where you came from', and inferring we were lesser beings, inhabiting some subculture.

That was the last straw. John indicated that we should get out of there, using the age-old hand signal in the film business of drawing his finger across his neck. We de-rigged slowly, with as much dignity as we could manage.

It was midnight when we came to the border. RUC and some B-Specials checked us out. It was a nice feeling when we saw the first green letter box in the van lights.

I had some good friends in Ulster in those days, mainly in cricket, and still have. I played with Ulster, Munster and Leinster men, wearing the shamrock of Ireland, with mutual respect on the one team. Within a few years, the Government of Northern Ireland was replaced by direct rule from Westminster. From this distance, the suffering endured in Ulster over the last 30 years saddens all right-thinking people. I think all children in Ulster should be educated together.

DOCUMENTING THE ARTS IN
THE MID-1960S

SÉAMUS MURPHY

MÁIGHREAD AND SÉAMUS MURPHY lived at 6 Wellesley Terrace in Cork, a place visited by people interested in the arts. Nancy McCarthy told me that, for the 30 or so years before I met Séamus in the mid-1960s, people with a love for music, painting and the arts gravitated naturally to that lovely house.

Séamus had been taught at school by Daniel Corkery. Seán O'Faolain had been in the same class. Seán Hendreke was a regular visitor, as were the poet, Seán Ó Riordain, John A. Murphy and William Harrington, who illustrated *Stone Mad*. Other friends included Louis Marcus and filmmaker Aindreas Ó Gallchóir, when he was working with Radio Éireann in Cork. Geraldine Neeson said Séamus had a mind like quick silver and that he simply loved life.

Another Cork haunt of this diverse group was The Palace Bar, part of a little cinema complex close to the Metropole Hotel on MacCurtain Street.

Séamus had created many marvellous pieces of sculpture. His bronzes of Eric Cross and Frederick May, whom my father remembered very vividly, are stunning. The pieces I liked most that Séamus created were the head of his father and a wonderfully simple statue of St. Gobnait in Ballyvourney. The little stone figure is in the village. St. Gobnait was said to love all wild things, particularly bees, so Séamus placed her on a beehive, with carved stone bees. He had also carved heads of Michael Collins and Countess Markievicz, which are in St. Stephen's Green.

In the mid-1960s, I heard Seán Ó Mordha was to make a documentary

The renowned stonecutter and sculptor, Séamus Murphy, at work. (Photograph: Eddie McEvoy)

about Séamus, whose sculpture I had admired for many years. The unique thing about Séamus was that he served his time as a stonecutter and had met a wide range of characters in the process. He could tell you about every piece of stone that appeared in a building in Cork city, its origins as to which quarry it had been carved out of and whether it was easy material to work with or what he called 'a bitch of a stone'. He told us so much about these things in his wonderful book, *Stone Mad*. He knew Frank O'Connor,

O'Faoláin and Daniel Corkery and, over a pint, would reminisce about the old days.

We spent many days in his studio watching him work and being watched by the many heads of famous people – Jack Lynch, Michael Collins, John Charles McQuaid and ordinary down-to-earth people from all walks of life. As the light began to change, as the days wore on, these characters seemed to change personality, the more we looked at them and the more they observed us. There was a fine head of Séamus's father, a train driver.

We drove out into the countryside to Kilcrea Abbey where Séamus pointed out some wonderful early stone carvings on graves and told us how he felt he was part of that heritage. We had an unexpected visit from Seán Ó Riordain, which was quite a treat. We made our way down the leafy lanes to a little pub, widely known by the stonecutters and Séamus pointed out that stonecutting, ' is a very thirsty business even when you are not stone-cutting at the time'.

As luck would have it, two of his old cronies were there and they shared some pints of Murphy's over an hour or two. I was struck by the difference in their accents – all Cork but with interesting nuances – and as the conversation ebbed and flowed about their childhood days in the stone yards it seemed like a beautiful piece of music to me, with its own internal rhythms, like a string quartet. Some months later I brought Sheila, Lisa and Ian to see Séamus in his studio and he was so welcoming to us all.

We shot a sequence near the River Lee, in Fitzgerald's Park. Séamus was walking under some dark trees in silhouette. The river behind him was bathed in sunshine. As he cleared the shadow area and our camera dollied back in front of him, Seán Ó Mordha called 'cut'. We were all happy with the sequence. We gathered our bits and pieces, before strolling through the park and bumped into Tom Barry, the man who had led the Cork brigade in the famous ambush! The extraordinary aspect about working in programmes in the early 1960s was that many amazing and important characters in the world of the arts and in the political sphere were still all around us, people who had shaped our nation in a very profound way. There were also people in RTÉ who were aware of the importance of that type of programming.

SEOSAMH MAC GRINNA

I had not heard of Seosamh MacGrinna. Deirdre Friel wanted to tell his story. MacGrinna was a Donegal man. Deirdre Friel also came from Donegal. MacGrinna was a teacher and spoke Irish. He wrote poetry and, like so many other poets, lived a hand-to-mouth existence. Seosamh had to seek work away from his native home place in the bad times of the 1940s and 1950s. He made his journey to Dublin, took a room in Gardiner Street near Mountjoy Square, nearly froze through his first winter, went through fits of depression and felt totally alone except for the occasional pigeon that flew into his room for shelter.

One January evening as it was getting dark, Seosamh returned to his lonely room. He had bought a small loaf of bread, a knob of butter at the Monument Creamery and a quarter pound of Hafners sausages. As he pushed the door open, a bird flew by his head. He dropped the loaf of bread as he reached to turn on the light. He could see the pigeon by now. It had perched on what remained of an old curtain rail. Seosamh would tell of those days.

Deirdre Friel wanted to create an echo of those hungry days in Dublin. Hungry for more than just necessities, with no friends, missing his people in Donegal. We got a room in a nearly derelict house. One of Deirdre's inspiring ideas was to obtain a pigeon that we'd lock in the room. The actor playing Seosamh climbed the dingy, rickety stairs and entered the room. Our unit was ready to shoot what happened next. The pigeon exploded, flying all around the room, close to the actor's face several times, before landing on the curtain rail. We had opened the top of the big window earlier. We had to move fast to shoot the pigeon in close-up. Photographer Eve Holmes was shooting a series of close-ups of the pigeon in various attitudes on her still Leica camera. My job was to establish where the pigeon landed. The bird was in flight again. I panned with it. Then, suddenly it was gone, flying out the top of the window in the centre of my frame. I was lucky.

We shot a sequence observing Seosamh, living through this sudden encounter. He says somewhere that the soul of the pigeon seemed to transfer to his soul. It was as if the wild thing, trapped in his room, was a signal. Shortly afterwards, Seosamh left that house and returned to Donegal. Interweaving Eve's set of beautiful still photographs of the pigeon with the sequence on film, Deirdre and her film editor produced a beautiful image which expressed very powerfully the struggle Seosamh was going through at that time.

We did extensive shooting in Donegal at the school where Seosamh taught, then some marvellous beach and seascapes and wonderful clouds so typical of the Donegal landscape where Seosamh had spent his boyhood years.

We met the Clannad group, the Brennan family. Deirdre and her husband, Barry Kelly, were good friends of the family. One evening, we needed a night exterior of a cottage, which we lit and photographed near their home. The family was all musical. We filmed them in a roadside pub where they were singing and heard, for the first time, Maire's beautiful voice. The group played locally then but I don't think they ever meant to make a career of it at that time, although I may be wrong about this! They were all so young, some of them still at school. Deirdre used some of their music in the film, which may have been their first professional gig. It was great to meet the family although I don't remember meeting Enya, who would have been only seven or eight years old then. What success Clannad and Enya have had. I have watched and listened to their music with great enjoyment ever since.

To get back to the film. Seosamh MacGrinna was still living in Donegal. By then, because of his depression and old age, he was living in some nice rooms in the psychiatric hospital in Letterkenny. We enquired if we might visit him if he was agreeable, and he gave his permission. We were all greeted. It was a sensitive moment, meeting the man whom we had been making the film about for all those weeks. Deirdre asked the doctor might we film Seosamh and he had no difficulty with that. When she asked Seosamh, he agreed. Deirdre stepped back and told me what she wanted. I moved in with the camera on the baby legs so I could see right into the poet's eyes. I did five or six shots of him as he worked on the piece of paper in front of him.

The shooting over, I went closer to Seosamh and thanked him for his assistance. I looked down at his desk where the piece of paper was. He had written down eight or nine lines. When I commented to him that he had written something, he looked at me and pointed out, with true Ulster directness, that we had asked him to write something so he did. I could see his fine handwriting in Irish script. The rest of the team had moved away to thank the doctor and the nurse. I picked up the piece of paper. I could not understand it because it was in Irish, but asked the poet if I could have it, as a reminder of our meeting. 'It is yours,' Seosamh replied.

We met Seosamh right at the end of our filming. By then, even before we met him, we felt we knew the man. I brought the single piece of paper to the RTÉ newsroom where a friend of mine in the Nuacht department translated what he had written. Deirdre would have translated it for me but I must confess that I wanted to have Seosamh's few lines for myself, because he had granted me his permission. I discovered that not only had Seosamh written something in those few short minutes as asked, but he expressed his sense of his entire life up to that moment. I was right. I sensed something deeper was going on when Seosamh began to write on the page.

Deirdre Friel's film is considered a modern classic. It will be shown on an ongoing basis. TG4 screened it about a year ago. For me, I was so lucky to be part of a team who worked on such programmes.

TO BUCHAREST AND BACK

WE HAD BEEN FILMING a documentary in Regensburg in Southern Germany for about three weeks and were quite tired. We were moving on to Munich, where German television was going to let us park our Mercedes film bus, and we wanted to borrow some boxes because we had a lot of equipment, nearly 40 pieces. They gave us eleven metal boxes, about the length of a rifle and some eight inches deep.

The express train pulled out of the station, the team settling down… sound recordist Denis O'Callaghan, electrician Mick Murray, assistant cameraman Simon Weafer and myself. We stretched out and got ready for the long journey to Bucharest that would take an overnight and most of the following day. It was the most comfortable carriage I had experienced in any train. The producer, Mike Monaghan, and Felicity Connolly, the production assistant, had flown into Bucharest about a week earlier.

It wasn't long before we crossed the border into Austria and then Hungary some hours later, at high speed. Simon was sitting with an old German couple. They discussed Simon's work at length and told him what they had gone through during the war years. They had seen people arrested by the Nazis whom they never saw again and told Simon how frightening it was.

We were delayed for some time for other bureaucratic reasons and then arrived in Czechoslovakia. Security guards with armed escorts seemed to be very vigilant and we could definitely sense that we were behind the Iron Curtain. Our passports and visas were required. There was a problem. The guard in control, who held all our papers in his hand, swung around and looked straight at us, pointing with his finger. 'You, you, you, you, out, out, out, out.' We couldn't believe it. They were throwing us off the train. We

Train station on the Hungarian-Czech border

had visas for Austria, Romania and Hungary but not for Czechoslovakia, due to a slip-up at Headquarters. We had been in Bavaria for three weeks so it certainly was not our fault, but we had to deal with the consequences.

As we were taken off the train, the old German woman reached out for Simon's hand. On the platform, we gathered our thoughts. I looked back at the window of our compartment and saw Simon's friend in tears, holding her husband's hands in a vice-like grip.

We jumped off the platform on o the track, pounding on the door of the goods wagon for what seemed a very long time. Eventually it slid back. Two men were inside. Not only was our equipment not there, the entire goods wagon was completely empty. Three armed guards had followed us. In a moment of madness, Denis lifted his Leica to his eye to take a shot of our escort. He was lucky they did not shoot him. They menaced him with their rifle butt. It was a frightening moment. We were taken back to the platform and our train pulled out to Bucharest. Standing on that platform on the Hungarian-Czech border without our camera, sound and lights was one of the lowest moments. Thirty minutes later, a train going west to Vienna stopped. We were instructed to board it and were now travelling in the wrong direction.

We made enquiries. A porter suggested that our gear might have been removed at the last Austrian border station. The obvious question was whether the train we were now on stopped there. He indicated that it did but only for three minutes. The four of us hit the platform before the train stopped. We fanned out. Mick Murray gave a shout to say he could see our equipment on a trolley. We flung ourselves on it, managing to throw it all on the train and jump on board. It was 11.30p.m. when we arrived in Vienna. I phoned the Irish Consul, who was most helpful. He said he would phone the Czech Embassy and that we should be there the next morning at 7 a.m. We managed to get a hotel for the night.

Early next day, we got a taxi to the Czech Embassy. Denis and I sat on the cases on the pavement outside, while the other two went in. We were tired, gazing into space, when suddenly Denis jumped to his feet. His passport was gone. He had it when he was in the taxi. He knew that he would never get a visa without his passport.

We were all in trouble. I put my head down, wondering what could be done. I turned my head to the right and noticed three men walking towards us, about 50 metres away. As they came closer I saw that one of them had a book in his hand. Denis had seen it, too. The man with the green book raised his hand. It was an Irish passport. The three men stopped and, in poor English, explained that they had found the Irish passport in the taxi. The driver told them that his last fare was Irish. The men from Vienna had got out of the taxi and walked back to the Embassy to return the valuable document. Denis and I could not believe the honesty. Passports were worth a lot of money in Eastern Europe in those days and still are. We thanked them and shook hands all round.

We were back on the train once more by 2.30p.m. with our Czech visas. When we finally got to the border, the same police came into our compartment and, without any sign of recognition, stamped our documents and were gone. With a great sense of relief, we stretched out in our seats,

Our team realised that things behind the Iron Curtain were going to be difficult but perhaps not quite how difficult. Before the train pulled out, I got up, walked to the dividing door. The next carriage was the freight car. I looked through the glass door and saw the eleven metal boxes the German television service had lent us. The mighty train gave a lurch and whistled.

We were moving. To my horror, the freight car became disconnected and remained where it was. In the darkening light, we had lost our equipment again, for the second time in two days. I rejoined the lads to tell them. Mike Murray proclaimed that we had done our best. He urged me to relax and have some more hock, which he said was very good. And it was.

Hours later, fast asleep, we were suddenly woken up by hammering on the compartment door. We had, of course, locked the door. I turned on a light. It was 2 a.m. The people on the other side sounded very angry. We didn't know who they were. The knocking got louder.

Simon grabbed a metal box to defend himself. He had visited many ports while at sea and knew how to look after himself. Denis, who had spent some time in South America, reached for his sound boom. Armed police and Customs officials entered the room. They searched the entire compartment and noted down everything. Before finally leaving, they listed who was wearing gold rings, as gold was all recorded in detail in Romania.

Finally, the train arrived in Bucharest. There was a big red star on the front of the steam engine and a plume of smoke rose from its funnel into the glass dome of the vast, old station. We got out and there were Michael Monaghan and Felicity to meet us. I didn't know what to say really after we greeted one another, so I explained that there was some bad news, we seemed to have lost the equipment. To his great credit, Mike said it wasn't a big problem; the main thing was that everybody was all right. We could get equipment from somewhere else. We really appreciated Mike at that moment.

Two days later, the equipment arrived. We went back to the station and had to pay £500 sterling before we could get it. It had all been searched but they did not open the film cans. Yes, things were going to be different in Nicolae Ceausescu's Romania. Bribery was the norm in Bucharest.

We were staying at the Athénée Palace Hotel, looking out on a vast square. To the left was the main concert hall, home to the Bucharest Orchestra Simfonica. The next day, Mike invited us to lunch at the Lido Hotel, just a ten-minute walk away. It had a pool and, unusually for the time, a wave-making machine, which meant that you heard the sound of the waves as you sipped your martini at a table.

After some time, a tall man approached our group. Introducing himself as Karl, he said that we must be the Irish. Only Romanian officials knew we were in Bucharest. Mike asked him to join us. He sounded American. He said he was in importing and exporting and would be happy to help us in any way. He mentioned an Irish grandmother. It seemed all so pat. He wanted to buy some sparkling Romanian wine but it was too early in the day. We had work to do. Then two officers from the secret police arrived and introduced themselves as brothers Babie and Georgio.

A young woman approached us and smiled. She was very dark and Turkish-looking. Karl introduced her as his fiancée, Magda. When she joined us, I couldn't help looking at her. She was amazingly beautiful, dark, but with a child-like face. She must have been 20 or so. A week later, she would invite us to her home for lunch with Karl and the two secret police colonels who were looking after us.

That afternoon, Karl told us that the Lido Hotel had been much used by the Gestapo who more or less billeted themselves in this hotel for most of their stay. All the architecture in the city was classic, some Greek influences and Romanesque. Looking out over the pool and hearing the sound of the waves, we could visualise how it must have been in the 1930s when the Nazis moved into Bucharest to get the oil and anything else they wanted.

We settled in well in the Athénée Palace and were working very hard for three or four twelve-hour days, shooting all over the city. Simon met the Iranian Ambassador in the hotel and had been invited to a party. Simon got on very well with everybody from whatever background. He asked if he could bring the Irish team with him. This was granted. There was quite a cosmopolitan community in Bucharest in 1968.

There were so few cars in the city and very few from the west. Apparently, Fiat had made an arrangement to have some of their cars assembled under the name of Seat and we had one of these for our use. When a car that wasn't commonly seen in the streets, dozens of people would crowd around, examining it in every detail. I asked Babie if there was much crime in Bucharest. Very little, he said. When I asked why, he said the penalties were so severe that nobody would chance it, particularly against a visitor.

The city's cinemas were very well supported. Just around the corner from our hotel, a cinema was running a Tarzan film, starring Johnny Weissmuller and Maureen O'Sullivan. Hundreds of people queued for this every day. It was a film from the West, several decades old and yet there was great interest in it. It showed us how cut off they were in Romania in 1968. I had seen it more than 20 years earlier at home in the Regent Cinema, Blackrock.

We had been away for almost four weeks and the trouble on the train had taken its toll. The filming in Ravensburg had also been hard work. In the sweltering August heat, we began to relax into the tempo of life of Eastern Europe. There were so many Turkish influences in the cuisine you could smell the Orient on the streets.

Peter McNiff had joined us in our first week in Bucharest. He was going to write the script and present the film. The city was beautiful. Wide thoroughfares, parks and flowers everywhere. In the evenings, there was music, dancing beside city lakes, in the balmy evening air. Summer makes life easier for the ordinary people.

Ceausescu was seen at that time as quite a good leader, like a Tito character. He was indulged by some of the Western leaders and received by the Queen of England. It was much later when he lost all feeling for his people, moving them from small farms into larger groups, destroying their individuality and dignity.

We were accepted by the Romanian government, not seen aligned too closely with either West or East. Coming from a small country, we could not do much damage and were invited to State functions. A visit to a collective farm was arranged.

One day, we were taken some distance outside Bucharest to see the biggest tractor factory in Romania. Mike and I were shooting a sequence in the cockpit of a huge crane that was tracking down the full length of the factory floor some 50 feet above the ground. It was driven and controlled by a beautiful girl with a bright red head scarf and a smile that would take your breath away. The man running the factory said that the girl showed much greater dexterity than the men and killed less people. That was why she had the job.

Karl told us that our secret police friends were carrying guns and would not hesitate to use them if necessary, warning us to be careful. Our escorts, Babie and Georgio, were becoming very friendly and would greet us in the mornings in the Romanian manner with a bear hug and a kiss on the cheek. They wanted to take us for a picnic to see their parents who were over 80 years of age and lived out in the country.

At 9 o' clock one Saturday morning, on our day off, they picked us up. There were six in our party. Karl and his fiancée, Magda, travelled with the detectives in their unmarked police car. We had our Seat. We drove out into the hills for what seemed like hours. At about midday, some of us began to

Michael Murray, Felicity Connolly, Denis O'Callaghan, Simon Weafer, Michael Monaghan, Romanian interpreter and the manager of the collective farm

worry about where they were taking us. Finally, we came to a small village. The two policemen got out and, after a while, returned with a large urn containing local red wine. Then the cars were off again for more miles. There was a huge mountain range up ahead. At about 2.30pm, we drove into a small village. We had arrived at our destination, after driving about 130 miles in the shade of the Carpathian Mountains.

We stopped in front of a tiny cottage with a red-tiled roof, a small veranda and steps. A very old woman stood there smiling, with outstretched arms. She hugged and welcomed her sons. Her husband was holding a rake, leaning over the gate of a tiny field full of sunflowers. They hadn't seen their sons for months and were like any small farmers in the West of Ireland, with all the same hopes and fears, overjoyed at the return of their sons from the city, with the big jobs.

Our team was introduced. We presented them with the Irish whiskey we had brought with us. We had chosen 'Paddy' because of the map of Ireland on the label. Most people in Romania didn't know where Dublin was and some hadn't even heard of Ireland. I noticed there was a fire burning just outside the cottage, with chickens on a spit. Nearby, on another fire, a stove bubbled with all sorts of vegetables. Our hosts pointed to the cottage and we entered.

A long table was set with food and salads and peppers of all colours. There were four bottles of Romanian Swica, a kind of spirit, a little bit stronger than vodka. We put our two bottles of Paddy on the table. At one side of the table there was a bench and on the other what seemed to be a double bed, where we sat.

Two chickens, dripping with garlic, were brought in from the yard but they were very undercooked. We ate some, not wishing to offend our hosts. The day wore on. People were relaxing. The red wine we had collected *en route* was going down very well. We did not understand anything the Romanians were saying and the locals had no English. We used body language to express ourselves. By now, we were having a very good time and Karl's fiancée interpreted as best she could.

The light fades in Eastern Europe much more quickly than in the West. It was twilight. The joint effect of the Romanian brew and the Paddy was

Romanian
peasant
women

disastrous. Simon, who was sitting on the bed, jumped up and shouted, 'Eureka' then fell down on his back onto the bed, out for the count. The party went on as if nothing had happened. He was quite safe there.

It became obvious that we were not going to get back to Bucharest that night. By then, I had a terrible headache. I put my head down on the table. Then I looked up into the face of the old man at the other end of the table. He got up from his seat and came over to me to show his concern. He lifted me up by the elbows and led me out of the room. Papa was over 80.

I could see the sunflowers backlit by a marvellous moon. The air was heavy. There wasn't a sound, except the voices in the cabin. He took me by the arm and led me through the little gate, into the field. The sunflowers were motionless. As we walked, I saw another identical tiny cottage in the distance. The family seemed to own it too. Still holding me firmly by the arm, the old man walked me up the three steps and pushed the door. The moonlight slid into the room. A little bed faced me.

I was a little apprehensive as to what was going to happen next. A broad smile shone out of the old man's face. He took the beautiful bedspread and pulled it back, revealing a spanking white sheet. He bowed most courteously and left, closing the door behind him. I looked around the little room. The wooden floor was spotless and polished. There were woodcuts, some little icons on the walls. There was no latch on the door.

Birdsong woke me. I had not moved one inch in the bed. There was a basin and a jug of water. It seemed to me I had been given the guest room because I conked out first. I stood on the little balcony and looked across to the identical little cottage, where the sound of voices ebbed and flowed. There was a smell of coffee. The sunflowers were like soldiers, standing on guard all night. As I made my way back across the little field, it struck me that it was so like one on Inisheer that I remembered when I shot the film for Jim Plunkett on J.M. Synge.

Mick Murray had taken the car into the village for a spin. He was stopped by the locals who were so amazed to see a car. This was 1968 but some of the villagers had never been in a car. Mick gave them their first ride, up and down the village street.

We said our goodbyes to the old couple who had made us all so welcome. I could see Mick was keen to get back to Bucharest. We had a film to make and we had lost time.

Back at the Athénée Palace, there was an invitation from Ceausescu waiting for us for the next day. We joined the long line of State cars in the driveway of the palace. Felicity turned many heads when she stepped out of the car, in a pink cocktail dress. Mick Murray was sent as the chauffeur to park the car a quarter of a mile away, because he happened to be driving. He was understandably in a bad mood when he caught up with us later. This was after Simon had caught his foot on the car mat, fell out of our vehicle and stretched full length onto the red carpet. The officials thought we were a very important delegation but, after this arrival, our importance seemed to diminish in their eyes.

Most of the diplomatic corps were at the function, held in an amazingly long and beautiful room. There was a lot of KGB people and local secret police. Some of the major delegations had a very heavy security presence. By chance, we were standing near a senior cardinal of the Roman Catholic Church who was in deep conversation with his secretary as we slowly moved along. He must have been in his seventies. When we finally reached the President, the little old cardinal extended his hand to Ceausescu who glared at him and turned his back, not giving him his hand. I looked at the cardinal's face. It seemed to have cracked up and collapsed. The old man was deeply hurt and embarrassed. He fumbled out of Ceausescu's presence. It was an insult to Rome, as much as to the little cardinal.

An official announced that we were next, introducing us as the delegation from the Irish television service. I was first and extended my hand to the President who smiled and shook my hand warmly. I moved on as quickly as possible. He met the other members of Mick's team but I have never forgotten the expression on the face of the cardinal. The President was very popular at the time but it gave us a glimpse of things to come.

After the visit to the palace, things settled down again. We started filming fairly intensively in the city. We asked many people what it was like to live in Romania in August 1968. It was high summer so the living was easy. People looked well. They were happy. There was a strong Turkish influence. There was the Romany gypsy element. There was an elegance that was quite striking. In the Athénée Palace, I looked for the English Bar that had been so popular in the 1930s but it was no more.

Our team was carrying two 16mm Éclair NPRs and a Bolex 16mm silent camera. Denis had a Nagra recorder, rifle mike and ancillary equipment. We had been away so long in Germany and now in Romania that it was necessary to check how good the shooting was and if the cameras were

Waiting to meet Ceausescu, Godfrey Graham, Simon Weafer and Denis O'Callaghan

operating correctly. We used to develop short pieces of film, about a foot long, in a small developing tank to check focus and exposure accuracy.

The test pieces of film were stuck on the tiled bathroom wall, but they began to disappear. If the secret police had been more subtle, they could have taken one frame. I would not have noticed. We had been warned that all phonecalls would be monitored. We were frequently approached by people selling currency but we were not sure if it was fake or not. It was all part of everyday life on a daily basis. There were people in the hotel from all over the world. They were definitely not tourists. Everybody was engaged in some scam or other. It was impossible to buy a gold ring of any kind, even for couples getting married; hence the mad search on the train and the counting of our gold rings. Everything was available in Bucharest and I mean everything!

We had decided by this stage that Karl was CIA. He asked us to have lunch with him. Mick made some excuse, we were too busy shooting. Karl persisted so we made a date for our next day off the following Saturday. He arrived at the Athénée Palace at 9 o'clock with a mini bus. We all piled in. When we were leaving the outskirts of the city, he told us that we were going to Mimea for lunch. Two hours later, we were on the Black Sea coast.

At the hotel, we had a drink and went into the dining room. A vast curved staircase led to the upper floors. Waiters arrived with silver salvers and presented lobster and crayfish. Some Romanian sparkling white wine arrived. There were all kinds of fruit. We enjoyed an excellent lunch.

The occasion was surreal. No other guests were in evidence in the hotel. It was like a scene from an old black and white movie. One of our team had mentioned to Karl some weeks earlier that he liked lobster. This lunch was the result. The more we learned about Karl the more intrigued we were by him. We got back to Bucharest that evening. Later, we found out that Karl owned the hotel and had interests in shipping. A big hitter in both Romania and the US, he was involved in every market, especially the black market.

Some days later, I bumped into Karl in the lift of the Athénée Palace. I had run out of money and asked him to lend me ten dollars until the next day. He asked if that was enough. When he opened his jacket, I could see blocks of notes in sterling, dollars, Romanian lai and German marks. He said I could have whatever I wanted but I told him that ten dollars would be fine. When we first met him, Karl had told us he was in exporting and importing … yes, currency!

We had been in Romania for six weeks. The heat was a big problem. Most of us had lost about a stone in weight, lifting and carrying equipment. In the city, people had a siesta but this wasn't possible for us because we were working. Most of all, we were homesick.

Bucharest's main concert hall was just around the corner from our hotel. I discovered there was a festival in progress, honouring Romania's most famous composer George Enescu. He had died recently. I managed to get a ticket for a concert the following evening that cost me the equivalent of about €1. All the theatre tickets were subsidised, which meant everybody could go to the ballet, opera or a concert. It was a most wonderful concert of marvellous music.

Mick Monaghan was interested in a hospital just outside Bucharest because Karl had told us that it was where people not sympathetic to the regime were being kept. It was a psychiatric hospital and Mick wanted to get some footage of this place. There was a lot of security and it was going to be difficult to get in. There was a park where members of the public would go. We saw children playing.

I suggested a picnic in the park, with the Bolex camera hidden in our picnic basket. A girl who had been helping us as a translator agreed to accompany me and we strolled through the gates and got into a good position 50 metres from the building.

We spread a rug on the grass and, for half an hour, we had some wine, cheese and bread, looking as relaxed as possible. The camera was under a napkin. I managed to hide my head and the camera behind the basket and get some good footage without the security guards seeing us. Many people were under detention in that hospital.

One evening, after a day's shooting in a museum, Babie invited Simon to join him for a drink in the officers' mess and took Simon to the HQ Army Officers' Club. Simon said it was like a plush nightclub. At about midnight, official cars started to arrive. Lots of high-ranking officers were running up the steps. Babie looked out the window and quickly left the room. It was not long before he was back, very upset and with tears in his eyes. 'The Ruskies, the Ruskies, they are in Prague', he told Simon. It was 21 August 1968.

Simon felt he had to get Babie back to our hotel. He took him to his room and phoned me to join them. This colonel in the secret police was very afraid. We had to find Mike Monaghan quickly. After ringing his room, we remembered he had gone to some tourist event in the city but we did not know where.

The magnitude of the information began to dawn on the three of us. 21 August 1968. Relations between the West and Soviet Russia were tense. If they invaded Prague, we were on the verge of a war that could include nuclear weapons. Simon Weafer from Ringsend was one of the first from the West to be aware of this ground-breaking news. How would Ceausescu react? At that stage, there was little we could do, so I went back to bed. Babie crashed out on Simon's spare bed, having drunk a number of Irish whiskeys. It was now 2 a.m.

I tried to reach Peter McNiff overnight without success. He joined me at breakfast. I told him what I knew. He did not believe me. I said that I was perfectly serious. Members of a team away for some time often kidded each other about this and that. Suddenly, there was an incredibly loud noise. Then tanks began to pass the window. Peter was a different man. He was on the phone to the RTÉ newsroom in 30 minutes. He gave a good, if sketchy, report into the 8 o'clock news at RTÉ, based on what he knew and continued to report on the on-going crisis for the next two weeks.

We had a unit meeting to discuss the implications for us. Mike Monaghan said there was a plane at mid-day and we could leave but we all

Nicolae Ceausescu

Bucharest the morning after the Russians entered Prague

opted to stay and cover the crisis. Our lives were going to be even more uncertain. We just did not know what was going to happen next, but whatever it was, we were going to be there. We had this important meeting outside so we could not be bugged ... on this occasion, in a car park.

Within a few hours, hundreds of thousands of people had assembled in that big square because Ceausescu was going to address them. Our team was fragmented slightly because of the situation. Mike was trying to get permissions to get into certain meetings. He asked Denis O'Callaghan and me to cover the big demonstration.

We managed to get through a huge crowd. We didn't understand the Romanian language but it was clear that Ceausescu was annoyed by the Russian move. We filmed the whole speech and, as the crowd dispersed, we made our way back to the Athénée Palace and linked up with Mike, Felicity, and Mick Murray. It was becoming clear that Ceausescu was out on a limb and that he had said things the Russians were extremely angry about. 'You have invaded our Slavic brothers,' he roared at the Russians.

Romania had been invaded ten times in its history. Was it going to happen again? The situation was serious for the Romanian people. There was immediate mobilisation of the army and the auxiliaries. Large numbers of tanks and armoured cars became a common sight. Later that evening in the hotel, Mike told me we had been given a special invitation from the President to go to the parliament building the next day and film his policy speech on the crisis. Apparently this was the first time that any TV unit from the West had received such an invitation. The speech was to be given at 10 o'clock the next morning. We assembled in plenty of time, not sure what to expect, and arrived at the parliament building with our passes and under escort. We wore suits and jackets.

We were given a very good position for our camera and sound. It was amazing to film this speech. The members of Parliament understood the gravity of the situation. Ceausescu had angered Russia and the West was on the verge of a response to the invasion of Prague.

Later that morning, we had another meeting and tried to determine what we should do in the coming days. Mike phoned RTÉ headquarters and told our people we were happy to stay and that we would require an extension of time and money to cover the crisis. Our own newsroom was extremely excited that they had a unit in Bucharest so close to Prague. They were happy for us to stay indefinitely. Our families had to be told that we were delayed further. We also made sure our footage of the Parliament speech was got out by plane that same day – there were no satellite links.

Earlier, we had planned to try to get a camera onto a train going by the Plousty oilfields, a no-go top security area, which we considered very impor-tant in the original film we were shooting. Mike asked Simon if he would shoot a sequence and take someone with him for company. Felicity agreed to go. Apparently, it was quite tricky. Soldiers and some officers were on the train but Felicity managed to distract them while Simon got the shots. They came back with a great sequence, tracking past the oil installations, which went into the film. Mike was shooting with me in Bucharest at the same time. This was the advantage of having an assistant cameraman and more than one camera on the unit.

23 August is Romania's National Day. Mike Monaghan had got clearance for us to cover a huge military parade in Bucharest. We got a good position for our camera and sound. It was in front of the main reviewing stand so when Felicity, Denis and I were setting up, Ceausescu and the government ministers were behind us. The place was crawling with secret police and KGB agents. We recognised one KGB man because Georgio and Babie had pointed him out in downtown Bucharest the previous week. He came over to us and asked for identification. We referred him to the local police who

had cleared us. He moved off. Just before the parade, he approached us again and wanted to look at our equipment. He was a menacing, big fellow. A bit frustrated because I was trying to shoot, I said that that they shouldn't have put on this big parade especially for my birthday. He spoke good English and was not amused at my remark. This Russian had no sense of humour. In fact, 23 August was my birthday.

I had never seen anything quite so big as this military show of force. At the head of the parade were thousands of men, women and children in national costume holding giant banners extolling the virtues of Communism and pointing out the links with the Soviet Union that were so strong. Then 30 or 40 tanks arrived, followed by huge trucks with guided missiles. You have to remember that, at this time, the Berlin Wall was a constant menace to freedom. A few years earlier, the world had come through the Cuban missile crisis had brought it very close to a nuclear war. Suddenly over the roar of the tanks and heavy armour, an even greater howling sound covered us like a blanket. When ten MIG jet fighters flew just above the trees and telegraph poles, nearly knocking Felicity, Denis and me off our feet.

The next day, I phoned my own boss at the studio in Dublin, and was careful about what I said because of the circumstances. I happened to be making the phonecall from Simon's room. I was talking in generalities but at the end of our conversation, he asked me about the current position. I said we had heard that there were 25 divisions of Russian troops surrounding Romania, based on the statement given by the President the day before. I was cut off immediately. Right at the end of the phone conversation, I had forgotten to be cautious about what I said. Simon was livid that I had made the call from his room. He was convinced he was going to be taken away. We got out of the room in double-quick time and went down the backstairs, spending the rest of the day downtown. Nothing happened. The police had other, bigger things on their mind.

It was now three days after the Russians entered Prague. Film units from all over the world began to arrive in Bucharest. BBC's *Panorama*, NBC, all the major networks, the Japanese, all arrived at the Athénée Palace Hotel, but were put under house arrest and not allowed to leave the hotel. We met some of these people and some we knew already. They were hopping mad that the Irish unit seemed to be able to go anywhere.

I was having a drink in the hotel bar late that evening. A man came in who looked as if he had been through the mill. He ordered a scotch and sat

Filming military show of force in Bucharest. Felicity Connolly and Godfrey Graham.
(Photograph: Denis O'Callaghan)

down beside me. I saw he had an exposure meter around his neck. We got talking.

He was a cameraman from German television. His name was Wolfgang. He had just come out of Prague. He said it was a nightmare but he had managed to get out with great footage. I asked him how he did it. He said that after shooting the Russian tanks entering Prague, he got back to his Mercedes in a side street, removed the roll from his camera, wrapped the can of film in a newspaper, removed the hubcap from one wheel, and stuffed the package against the tyre and replaced the hubcap. He reloaded his camera quickly, sat in the car and ran the film through the camera before throwing it in the back of the Merc. He got out of town as quickly as possible. Arriving at the border, he was stopped and searched. The Czech soldiers went through everything and snatched his camera, opened it and took out the film. They confiscated his camera but he got out with the hidden real footage.

I thought that was a clever ploy. Everyday, we were shooting footage and getting it out and our own newsroom in RTÉ was very happy with it, syndicating it all over the world.

An NBC director came up to Denis O'Callaghan to ask what network he worked with. Dennis replied, *The Skibbereen Eagle*. When the NBC man asked how we were doing this, we were nonchalant, saying 'that's the way we operate'. It was amusing to see that the other networks could not get out of the building. We had been in the country for almost two months. We were known to the authorities and to the secret police. The President knew who we were. We were on the inside track. For once! RTÉ were always the minnows on big occasions. We never had the resources. This was different.

The other networks also noticed we had a large crew. They queried how we could have seven or eight people there. This was how RTÉ operated in the 1960s and 1970s and how we made so many extremely fine documentaries. *Panorama* used crews matching ours when they were making similar documentaries, as did other networks. They still do on some documentaries, particularly drama.

We were invited to the American embassy. We thought under the changed circumstances this might be cancelled. It went ahead. The embassy was situated on the edge of one of the many parks near a lake. I remember being on the balcony with other guests and bumping into Karl and his fiancée. Surprise, surprise. An old upright radio was on a table. *Voice of America* was reporting on the crisis. Our party was introduced to the American Ambassador. He looked very grave. After initial pleasantries, I asked as tactfully as I could what he felt would be the outcome. 'We are on the brink of the Third World War,' he said. 'We shall know within 48 hours.' We all had a stiff drink. It was twilight; the trees beside the water shimmered in the last of that day's light and there were some canna lilies at the water's edge. I wondered what would become of us all if the worst happened.

Before we left sweltering Bucharest, the police informed us that we could not leave the country on the Orient Express until we had new passport photographs taken. Mike asked me to look after this. The difficulty was that our team had been 'stood down' two days before departure and I had to locate everybody, people that had gone all over Bucharest.

I had to go via Calea Victoriei and then the Boulevard Carol before I found a small photo studio. All our team was photographed there over the space of a few hours. The photographer was using an Exactor 35mm camera, which looked as if it had seen better days. Next day, I called to collect the pictures only to be told, in somewhat broken English, the sad story that the pictures had not come out. The photographer, in a typical Latin way, became very emotional and almost threw himself on one knee in an attempt to convince me that he was devastated by his failure. My problem was I had to get everybody back again, searching our favourite haunts in a city that was unbearably hot that particular day.

I went back the next day, the day before our departure, and the pictures were fine except that we were hardly recognisable. We had all lost over a stone in weight, having been away for nearly three months in the sort of heat you get in Eastern Europe. Our new photographs didn't match the shots in our passports in any way so we felt that this was going to cause us problems at the borders. To our great surprise, it didn't matter. They weren't interested once we were leaving Romania, Czechoslovakia and Hungary.

We were on board the train and ready to go, when we heard that Interpol wanted to arrest Karl urgently. I doubt they ever caught up with him, somehow. Karl had told me that, when he was staying in Dublin in the 1950s, he had asked the hall porter for some female company and was amazed to learn there was none in those innocent days.

We arrived at the station on the Czech border where we had all the problems those months before, travelling in the other direction. My passport was looked at and one official thought it was forged. He took the passport and left us. Suddenly, I had no papers. By now, we had been through so much I said we'd get over this latest problem, telling the team that, if they took me off, it would take Frank Aiken, our Minister for Foreign Affairs, ten days to get me out.

As we came to the Austrian border, an official from the West walked over to our compartment and gave me back my passport. We got back to Vienna and travelled on to Munich, where we had left the Mercedes bus, and returned the metal cases to the German television company. It felt like we were coming from another world and that we had been away for a year. We motored to a ferry and got back to Dublin.

Some 25 years after my visit to Romania, I was working on a programme, called *Check Up*. When I heard Ann McCabe, the director say we were going to Romania, my heart skipped a beat. It had changed a lot. Ceausescu was gone. The revolution had happened.

The assignment was to go back and find some of the lost children who had been forgotten, in the orphanages. It was an upsetting story to cover. It was also November, really cold, miserable and dark.

We got into our hotel, not the Athénée Palace this time, but into a

Bucharest that was very grim-looking. I paid a visit to the Athénée Palace, which had been shelled during the turmoil, and had a coffee with the night porter, chatting with him about the old days. When I asked if he knew Babie or Georgio, he looked at me blankly.

After a night's sleep, we were taken in a wreck of a car to visit these very poor orphanages. Inside, I saw some of the most upsetting scenes that I have ever photographed. We went to visit one of these hospitals each day. Most Irish people have seen the horror I speak about on television, my pictures were shown on the *Late Late Show,* and *Check Up* broadcast a complete programme. We filmed in an abortion clinic, where I saw sad women queuing to be dealt with. We met a doctor who was almost in tears when he explained that his equipment was primitive and that he had no staff. There were young Romany girls with their mothers. The sequence we shot was deeply disturbing. I know things must be better there now, I hope so. One orphanage was more horrific than the next.

Then there was some time to look around Bucharest. I tried to see if I could find the little apartment where Babie and our friends had lived. I found my way through the city at night, remembering the topography, and found the little apartment building and the small entrance to the flat where we had gone up the stairway all those years before and had such good times. I went up to the second floor with my little bag of presents in the hope that Babie or Georgio would still be there or some of their family. I don't know what I was thinking of 25 years later. I knocked on the apartment door. There was no answer. I tried again. Nothing

Sadly, I walked down the stairs, disappointed. Two travelling people came out of the wind and the rain into the porch to shelter. I approached them. They drew back, frightened, but did not move away. I tried again. I suppose they thought I was the police or selling black market goods. I reached out again. This time, they took the parcel containing tinned salmon, Bewleys chocolates and two Baby Powers. We parted.

The next day, we went to another orphanage. The children were tied up, like wild animals. We met some Irish people who were working there to help the children. The task was so huge. Today, I find it hard to pass a poor Romanian in a Dublin street without thinking of the old days in Bucharest, and giving them some help.

RYAN'S DAUGHTER
Summer 1969

W E KNEW THAT DAVID LEAN was about to shoot a film, *Ryan's Daughter,* in Dingle. RTÉ was making a documentary, which I was to shoot. The director was Adrian Cronin.

After the long journey from Dublin to Dingle, we booked into the famous Benners Hotel. We had dinner and I decided that an early night was a good idea. It was about 10 o'clock when I hit the sack. My bedroom had an enormous bed in beautiful rosewood, with a bunch of grapes and fig leaves carved in the centre panel. The windows were very old with coloured glass at the sides. There were more grapes and Grecian figures in the plasterwork on the ceiling.

As I drifted off to sleep, I wondered what the next fortnight would bring. David Lean, Freddie Young, Robert Mitchum, John Mills, Trevor Howard, Sarah Miles, Robert Bolt. Would I actually meet these people? As the last of the daylight faded and the night became darker, I became aware of a faint light travelling across the ceiling. A sea mist had drifted in off Dingle Bay. I could see it floating past the large windows. The light on the ceiling seemed to float and hover in a ghostly way, then suddenly increase in brightness as the coloured windowpanes threw shafts of light about my room. I wondered if David Lean could be doing some night shots. I got out of bed and crossed to the window.

At that time, Benners Hotel had a large back garden with many shrubs and trees, plus two herbaceous borders. It was covered in mist, creating a surreal scene. I could see a tall, spindly man carrying a light attached to the end of a long bamboo pole. He was wearing a Panama hat and baggy trousers like Charlie Chaplin. I could tell from his awkward gait that he was not young. The light consisted of a large bulb connected to a cable that ran through the hotel's kitchen window. The mist created a halo around the bulb. In his other hand, the man carried a large butterfly net on the end of a shorter bamboo cane. Moths and butterflies were attracted to his light and, for some time, I watched him moving to and fro, in a kind of slow dance, before returning to my bed for that early night.

Our team had a seven o'clock call the next morning and I was first down to breakfast. An elderly gentleman walked into the dining room, greeted warmly by the staff. They obviously knew him well. When I was finished, I paused at his table to wish him good morning and told him that I had watched his dancing light on my ceiling the night before. He introduced himself as Fatheringail from Norfolk and said he been coming to Dingle for years, because the area had more beautiful moths and butterflies than anywhere else in these islands. He asked me what I was doing in Kerry and I explained that we were making a film about David Lean's film, *Ryan's Daughter*.

That morning, we went to where Lean was shooting on the coastline, looking across at the Great Skellig. When we got there, the weather was quite fine and the main feature unit was some 50 metres away, doing a shot of an old army vehicle moving along a roadway and stopping opposite a standing stone. Our director Adrian Cronin suggested that we keep reasonably far back, about 20 metres, and we put up the 20-1 zoom lens. The feature unit comprised about 60 people, along with many vehicles. We watched them finishing off that particular shot. The unit began to de-rig and get ready for the next shot.

Fifteen minutes later, we noticed a figure move away from the unit and walk towards us. To our surprise, it was David Lean. He came over to us and said, 'Good morning, I presume you are the Irish television unit. My name is David Lean. Anything you want you can have, as far as I am concerned. This is Ireland, you are from the Irish television service, you get the priority.' Adrian Cronin thanked him and introduced everyone. David was very relaxed and he swung around to look at my camera, the French NPR, an excellent 16mm Relex camera with a 20-1 zoom lens.

He commented to me that he knew this camera and had shot some material with one. He asked if he could look through the viewfinder. David latched onto my camera, moving the zoom and panning the camera. A very nice instrument, he said. This was the man who had made *Brief Encounter,*

On the set of *Ryan's Daughter* in Dingle with David Lean. Colm O'Byrne, Joan Collins, Adrian Cronin, MGM publicity, Joe O'Brien, David Lean and Godfrey Graham

Great Expectations, Lawrence of Arabia and *Doctor Zhivago,* looking through the lens of my camera. It was a special moment.

David said he would arrange for some of the stars of the film to give us interviews, and people like John Mills and Robert Mitchum did so. We also interviewed Robert Bolt, who was writing the screenplay.

Robert Bolt was extremely interesting. He told us that he and David had originally planned to make an intimate, small-scale film in Ireland, a love story. However, that changed when they saw seen the magnificence of the locations in Kerry, locations that David wanted to shoot in 70mm Panavision. As a result, it was no longer a small film but one with a very broad canvas. The film began to grow out of all proportions.

In February 1969, Robert Mitchum flew to Stuttgart and purchased a Targa Porsche at the factory. He drove and ferried his way to Ireland and then on to Dingle. He was accommodated at the Milltown Hotel, the only guest with eleven rooms at his disposal, and a staff to look after him. He used to take phonecalls from prospective guests, discussing the merits of the hotel with them before adding that it was under new management.

As the spring blossomed, Mitchum began to become fed up with the fastidious way in which Lean approached the film. He became more frustrated, as he looked from his bedroom over the hotel's large, disused back garden. It seemed he had an idea. He got his hands on some marijuana plants. The mind boggles at how he managed it. The secret garden bore fruit. A very successful crop was achieved and made available to some of the crew later that summer.

Mitchum had agreed a fee of $870,000. In his wildest nightmares, he never thought he would be in Dingle for ten months. When we met him, he had moved from the Milltown Hotel to a large, rambling house near Dingle Bay. The white Porsche was parked outside. We had a drink and relaxed for a while and I remember that Joe O'Brien, our electrician, seemed to have a great rapport with him. They both had an amazing knowledge of horses and horse racing, all over the world.

The relationship between Lean and Mitchum never got off the ground. It was a shame that two men, who had given so much to cinema, could not get along. Perhaps there could have been better leadership from Lean, if he had tried to reach out to the actor. Their backgrounds were so different. Lean, a director of classic films, all painstakingly crafted, and Mitchum, who started his career as a knock-about actor. He had an instinct for performance in the hands of a director who saw and understood his basic instincts. *River of No Return*, for example, in 1954, *The Night of the Hunter* in 1955, *Cape Fear* in 1962, *The Sundowners* in 1960 and my own favourite, *Farewell My Lovely* in the 1970s, proved beyond any doubt that he was a superb screen actor. These two men loved movies, undoubtedly, but in a totally different way. Perhaps

Interviewing actor Robert Mitchum: Godfrey Graham, Robert Mitchum, Bob Finlay and Adrian Cronin. (Photograph: Colm O'Byrne)

it was to do with David Lean's sheer Englishness in contrast to the true American, Mitchum.

The first day the RTÉ film unit was filming in the village on the top of that high hill, near Dunquin. My camera was rolling on a medium shot of the street, with some of the feature film unit preparing the next shot. Suddenly I noticed Lean walking towards camera. Mitchum was about 20 paces away, walking in the opposite direction. I stepped away from the camera and looked in another direction. I don't think either man was aware that we were rolling on them at the time. They stopped, hesitated for a moment or two within a few feet of each other, but did not speak before they passed on. We weren't aware of the significance of this body language until long afterwards when we realised that the relationship between the two men was anything but good. The shot appears in Adrian's film and, on mature reflection, speaks volumes.

Mitchum used to bring friends to the screening of rushes without clearing it with Lean, which infuriated the director. Mitchum also used to fling parties at his large house near Dingle Harbour, with ladies flying over from London for these events. But no invitation was ever extended to Bolt or Lean.

Robert Mitchum had been a big star for so many years, we were curious to ask him how he was enjoying his stay in Ireland. I remember Adrian Cronin saying to him that he seemed to have been here for a very long time. Mitchum replied, 'Yes, I came in the February and then after winter came the spring, and now it's the summer. This is going on forever. David Lean is a perfectionist. Anytime he wants to do a two-shot, it's like Hannibal crossing the Alps! In Hollywood, you know, we make films in seven or eight weeks, and some of them turn out to be *Casablanca*, *On the Waterfront* or *Cape Fear*.' However, he added that Dingle was a nice place to watch change.

Mitchum said that Lean should have been given some canvas, brushes and lots of paint so he could paint his pictures all by himself, taking as much time as he liked. He remarked that it seemed to him Lean was using up the budget of ten million dollars on rehearsals. This kind of talk got back to the front offices of MGM and did not give a good impression. Critics hear rumours, too.

I was always interested in those films Mitchum made soon after the war. He was so natural on screen, always believable. He could out-perform most people off the screen and yet he was not taken seriously. I thought his performance in *Ryan's Daughter* was a most subtle effort but, in the hands of another director, he might have given an even more powerful performance; he was cast against type.

Every Irish actor seemed to be working on *Ryan's Daughter* or waiting around for David Lean to shoot their scene, as weeks went into months. Some lives were never the same after. It was great to meet the Irish stars like Marie Keane, Niall Toibín, Des Keogh, Philip O'Flynn, Eoín O'Sullivan and Arthur O'Súilleabháin. Des Keogh says he was hired for three weeks and kept for six months.

While shooting the documentary, we met Jack Gallagher, the wardrobe master, an amazing professional. He was looking after Mitchum's wardrobe as they shot a scene near the village on top of a high hill. Mitchum was doing a walking shot and his hat blew off several times. Jack pounced on it, brushed it off and it was ready again. An amusing sequence in the documentary, showed the frustrations of film-making and the dedication of the team.

Another person we met during our Dingle stay was Norman Savage, the film editor who had worked with David Lean on *Doctor Zhivago* and *Lawrence of Arabia*. We spent an amazing day with Norman in the cutting room as we watched him cut a sequence and build up the shots and the sound. It was a shot with some young girls teasing John Mills, who played Michael, bouncing a ball. It was absolutely fascinating. He talked to us about how he enjoyed working with Lean, who had originally been a film editor, so they had a lot in common. It also meant two editors in the same cutting room. That was another story.

Surprisingly, David Lean invited us to come and look at the 'rushes', the previous day's filming. Directors, the director of photography, designers and soundmen look at the material day after day and it is a very intimate and stressful process. It was therefore a very unusual concession for the RTÉ film crew to be invited to join his team. We went into what seemed a converted schoolhouse or church. Two 70mm Panavision projectors and a projectionist were flown over from Hollywood. We looked at some beautiful material that had been just recently shot.

Lean and his director of photography, Freddie Young, had decided that the most stunning place to locate the village would be on one of these high hills. So they built an entire village there.

Although it was a fantastic thrill to meet David Lean, it was even more fantastic for me to meet Freddie Young. I had studied and watched his work for many years. He was the director of photography who most excited me as a young cameraman. We spoke a lot and, when we shot the interview with David Lean in the bar and I needed more illumination, Freddie told me to ask his team for whatever additional lighting was needed.

Photographing David Lean was very important. We were doing this in one of the film sets, the pub in the village. Lean was there on time. He was wearing a dark polo neck sweater and slacks. Adrian's first question was why did he come to Ireland. Lean said it was the mountains and the seascapes that you could not get anywhere else in the world quite like them.

Lean said that he had settled into Dingle so quickly and happily, and found great support from the local people. Some of the garages in the town had assisted in the construction of vehicles and showed great skill in light engineering. After shooting had finished, Lean set up an editing room in the Great Southern Hotel in Killarney where he and Norman Savage and his staff worked for months.

Adrian asked him what his next film would be. David paused and said he was going to have a rest but thought he would then be going to India. There was something magical about the picture of Lean, his charisma leaped off the screen.

When I think back to that time, not forgetting that surreal scene of the old man with his light and butterfly net in the mist-filled back garden at Benners Hotel on my first night in Dingle, it strikes me that film making is not unlike collecting rare months. You need to be lucky. The image on the film can disappear, as can those rare winged creatures flying close to the hunter's lamp. After all that preparation, money, script, actors and director, you may fail to achieve your dream and have to start all over again, just like a hunter with a rifle or butterfly net, who experiences that sudden sense of loss as the intended prey escapes his grasp.

Lean was not the easiest man to have a rapport with. He refused to be interviewed by Alexander Walker, the distinguished critic from the *Evening Standard* in London. The then editor of the *American Cinematographer*, Herbi Lightman, was allowed to watch the filming of *Ryan's Daughter* but was not granted an interview. This created bad vibes back in Hollywood.

When the National Society of Film Critics saw *Ryan's Daughter* on a particular Sunday at the Ziegfeld Theatre in L.A., there was general disappointment in the film. The Society invited Lean to come and talk with them about the movie. It was organised by Nat Weissman, through the MGM publicity department. Weissman and his wife collected Lean from a transatlantic flight, under the impression that they would be meeting a group of critics to have some dinner and talk about the film. However, when Lean's party got to the hotel, they were met by Richard Schiekel, chairman of the American Film Critics Committee. They left Weissman and his wife outside the door of the boardroom and took Lean into a large room where they sat him at one end of the table. Then they proceeded, one by one, to attack David Lean on all the aspects of the film, telling him how they had found it flawed in so many different ways. David Lean was deeply shocked by this experience, which he was later to describe as one of the worst in his entire life.

One of the most severe critics on that occasion was Pauline Kael, who published one of the toughest critiques in America in *The New Yorker*. I quote, 'As a director, he is a super-technician, and probably he doesn't really have anything he wants to do in movies except to command the technology. He probably enjoys working his characteristic gentleman-technician's tastefully-colossal style. But tasteful and colossal are – in movies at least – basically antipathetic. Lean makes respectable epics, and that's a contradiction and self-defeating. Humourlessly meticulous, his pieces have no driving emotional energy, no passionate vision to conceal the heavy labour ... The only reasons for placing this story in 1916 were to legitimatise the fact that every idea in it is shopworn, and to build sets. For years, during the making of a Lean film, publicity people send out photographs of the handsome director standing in the cities he has built, and then the movies arrive and he never seems to have figured out what to do in those sets. They have a gleaming pictorial look, a prepared look – everything is posing for a photograph... [Bolt and Lean] don't have it in them to create Irish characters; there isn't a joke in all the three hours (three and a half, including intermission), except maybe the idea that an Irish girl needs a half-dead Englishman to arouse her'.

It was almost 15 years after *Ryan's Daughter* before Lean made another film. He was quite traumatised by the level of criticism directed towards *Ryan's Daughter* and wanted to get away from features. He and his wife started to go on tours, visiting many parts of the world. He bought an Éclair NPR 16mm camera with which he shot sequences on many of these trips. He still needed to be looking through a film camera, to see the flickering of the shutter. It was obviously a passion with him for so long that he couldn't stop. He did send his footage to Hollywood for processing where people in the laboratories were very complimentary about his camera operation and lighting. It's not surprising that a director who has created such wonderful cinema should have these abilities and sensitivities.

On that first day in Dingle, when Lean spent about an hour with Adrian Cronin and our unit, he did seem particularly interested in the camera I was using, the Éclair NPR. This is the type of camera he chose for those lonely wilderness years. He had set up a 16mm cutting room and projection facilities in his house in Rome so he never really stopped the hands-on connection that was to keep him going, in a sense, for those 15 years before he made his final film, *Passage to India*.

FRANCO'S SPAIN – 1969

AINDREAS Ó GALLCHÓIR and Patrick Gallagher were proposing a major documentary of Franco's Spain, a country that had not changed much politically since the Civil War in 1936. We went in our Mercedes film bus to Britain and then on to Bilbao. We proposed to be away for about a month.

It was the beginning of August when we arrived in Bilbao. We didn't have any hotel accommodation and, for the first few hours we tried, without success, to get a hotel. Aindreas thought if we slipped over the border into France, we might have a better chance. We looked at the map and decided to go to St. Tropez, about an hour's drive. We had heard, of course, of St. Tropez. We were not exactly in the jet set ourselves so we were not fully aware tha, in August, most of the jet-setters of Europe would be there. When we arrived, we quickly realised that we had gone from the frying pan into the fire. A couple of hours later, having searched for a hotel or B&B all afternoon, we began to realise that we were in some trouble. Eventually, we were given a phone number at a hotel by a woman who said her sister had a villa nearby, overlooking the town. We rang her. A woman's voice said, yes, to come and she would see what she could do for us. What a relief.

After a number of wrong turnings, we came up to a substantial building 'Villa Marina'. The owner must have been watching or an auto system must have been in place, because the gates began to open. Simon drove in. Aindreas had hired a car. Paddy and Carmel Deignan were with him just behind us. They were fine gardens. We got out. Suddenly three Alsatians appeared from nowhere, snarling and barking. It was quite alarming. Then a woman's voice gave what sounded like a command. The dogs stopped

Filming Aindreas Ó'Gallchóir's documentary on Franco's Spain. Godfrey Graham, Patrick Gallagher and members of ETA

dead and slunk away but never took their eyes off us. A woman stepped from the door. There was no smile. She was about 40, very good-looking with blonde hair in a sort of plait that went across the top of her head, rather like the style worn by many German women in the 1940s and 1950s. Aindreas shook hands and explained our predicament. She softened a bit and said that she had six rooms. We did not care what the rate was as she explained the details in perfect English.

We began to take our overnight cases out of the film bus. I could not see mine. It must have been put in first. The result was that, by the time I got my case and joined my friends in the beautiful wood-panelled hallway, all the rooms had been allocated. People were going upstairs and being shown their rooms. I was a bit disappointed. Then suddenly, the woman appeared at the top of the stairs and slowly walked towards me. I said that she had talked about six rooms, what was going to happen to me? She apologised. I sat down on my case, thinking that at least I would have a roof over my head and that I could hit the couch if necessary. She came back to me and said she would be away that night, perhaps her room would do.

I followed her up the hand-carved staircase. Just off the large landing, she pushed the bedroom door open. It was a delightful room with delicate pink wallpaper. She explained again, after showing me the en suite, she would be away and that her maid would look after us in the morning and give us breakfast and take our money. She picked up a small suitcase and a jacket and was gone. Most of our team were tired and got an early night. Having already met the dogs, we weren't that keen to explore the garden.

After an early breakfast, we were on our way back to Spain. We motored for about an hour or so into lush rural country, cornfields as far as the eye could see. We were impressed by the good roads. They were straight and extended over vast distances that would have traversed an entire county in Ireland. Simon, who was driving, had fine eyesight, developed when at sea with Irish Shipping. He drew our attention to some workers, about 1,000 metres away, standing in a circle, about a dozen of them, with a very large ox. We pulled over, then we realised they were threshing corn or wheat in the age-old manner. Aindreas suggested we get a sequence. We approached the man with the ox. Aindreas went into a sort of mime, illustrating that we wanted to take some pictures and sound. By then, Colm O'Byrne, Terry Wade and I had got close to where the people were standing, with our equipment. The old gentleman smiled. He thought we wanted to take stills so the whole operation stopped dead. Aindreas stepped forward and, like a conductor of a small ensemble, conducted the man and led him into action with the great ox, which was pulling a roller in a circle. Other workers were sweeping up the precious grain and others were taking the sheaves and storing them to one side. For us, it was a great stroke of luck. We realised these people were a unique community, with their own distinct dialect. They preferred to work in the old ways.

I got some great character studies of faces and hands and the method they were using. Like all rural people who work in remote areas, just as in our own country, they were weather-beaten and bent, shaped by the work they had done on the land for decades, and burned by the merciless sun. I thought of Kavanagh's *Great Hunger*, that universal masterpiece, as I looked through my viewfinder at these workers on the land where, season after season, they extracted the crop that would sustain them, just like the workers on the stony grey soil of Monaghan. We thanked them and left.

By now, we were beginning to realise how intense that sun was. It was not quite 11 o'clock. We did some shooting en route. We went to rendezvous with some Basque nationalists. Arrangements were already made. Seán, an Irish man, who knew Spain well, was doing research for us. He was waiting in the Basque region next day. We drove into a mountain area and into a small village. Seán was there with three Basque men in a house. We exchanged courtesies. Aindreas had warned us this was a secret meeting that the police did not know about. All were in ETA and on the run. We were on a veranda, shaded by a wooden frame, heavy with vines laden with jet-black grapes.

It was a relief to get out of our sweltering film bus. We set up a five-hander on a camera dolly. Paddy Gallagher, the three Basques and our interpreter. Two other men said nothing as they moved about quietly, looking over the first floor balcony into the small street where, occasionally, a car or a horse and cart would go by. We knew what their job was. The long discussion seemed to go well and the body language and attitude reminded us of people we had met making programmes in Ireland. We had some wine and local cheese, then we were on our way again to see the vast monument to the fallen of the Civil War. Its scale was massive as it rose out of a small hill.

Our aim was to get to Madrid that same night. It was a three-hour journey. Our film bus had been designed by Simon and Bob Finlay to their specifications – very solid, with tracking platform facilities front and aft. These were carried on the roof, were very heavy, and made of steel. Mercedes had not really put a big enough engine into this van so the problem was that the top speed was 55 m.p.h. It was nearly midnight when we found our way to our hotel in Madrid. There was a wet cloud of heavy, hot air hanging over the city. Our hotel was situated on a wide thoroughfare, which was very noisy. I am a light sleeper and asked the receptionist if there was a quiet room. She said there was but it had a small window. I took it but, when I got up to the room with my personal case and the 16mm camera which, of course, you never leave out of your sight, I was shocked. The room was so small they must have actually built the double bed in the room. It had a small window, about one square metre, but it was quiet.

When we got down to breakfast, the papers were full of what was happening in Northern Ireland. Derry and Belfast were in flames; Catholics had been burned out of their houses. I remember Colm O'Byrne saying he had to get back there immediately, he had to cover this. Colm had worked a lot in Northern Ireland but he had to stay with us, of course.

That day, we were to meet a Spanish nobleman of Irish descent, whose family had come to Portugal with the Flight of the Earls in 1607. His large apartment overlooked a magnificent square with fountains. He was wearing a double-breasted grey suit. He was very tall with grey hair, sporting a green tie that he said he wore specially for us. His apartment, air-conditioned of course, was full of beautiful paintings, classic and modern. I noticed a number of works by Picasso. He offered us chilled wine from his own vineyards. Aindreas and Paddy felt that you could not rush the interview with this individual. He was so appreciative that we had come to see him. The links with Ireland were still of great importance to him. He told us of his forebears. They had served with the princes in Portugal for about 20 years before coming to Spain, gradually leaving the army service. Having come from lands they possessed in Ireland, they turned again to the soil. With the monies they had been paid by the Portuguese and Spanish kings, they purchased land in Spain and went into wine and had been ever since. As we began to film, I thought of my history teacher telling me of the shattering experience for those who had to leave and, even worse, the people completely leaderless and on their knees for generations afterwards in Ireland. Living history in my viewfinder again. What an education. Although I was in the service for nine years by then, I never lost the excitement of the personal discoveries I was making.

Our next destination was Toledo. Next day, Simon was not feeling so well. Stifling heat, long straight roads, all morning we motored and, by about noon, there it was, Toledo, shimmering in the heat haze. We drove our van up to a high position where we could get a good look at that famous square castle the Alcázar, the four distinct towers. The building was a fortress and was once the imperial residence. Later, it became a military museum and a regional library. During the Spanish Civil War in 1936, the building was almost demolished. Toledo is known as the City of the Three Cultures, a reference to the Christian, Islamic and Hebrew traditions that coexisted happily there. The richness of its architecture is quite extraordinary as a result of these different cultural and religious backgrounds. El Greco, the painter, decided to settle in Toledo where he produced the bulk of his most amazing works.

We had chosen a great position to photograph the building from and I used a Red 5 filter to cut through the heat haze. That filter also increases contrasts and gives magnificent cloud effects. We were shooting in black and white, of course, as we had not moved into colour.

Next day, we discovered the bullfight was on so we got tickets. There was a feeling that if we had gone through the proper channels and asked permission that we might have been refused permission to shoot so I just took the faithful Bolex and Colm had his nagra recorder. I had read Ernest Hemingway's novel about Spain and bull fighting. I found the whole event unsettling. All the different acts were played out like a religious ritual, the procession looked like accolytes in a church, their costumes and the great horses were magnificent, of course, against the almost yellow sand.

There was tremendous excitement as the bullfight started with just the two, the man and the beast, staring into each other's eyes. I wondered was all this really necessary. There was no doubt in my mind, however, about the courage of both. The bull, from a noble breed, bred to fight. The matador with his consummate skills and courage. All this completely captivated the audience. Suddenly in my viewfinder, the whole scene seemed to light up. The shapes, the colours. I knew man's primitive needs were perfectly fulfilled by the excitement, the passion and the danger this provided. It was not too long since the gladiators in Rome and other parts of Italy and Spain had taken on wild animals and been torn limb from limb by these creatures in front of the noblemen and populace of Rome. It struck me that the bullfight was the nearest thing in contemporary society to the forum in Rome and that is why it is still fascinating people. We got a good sequence although, sadly, it was a kill.

As we left our seats high up in the stands, the setting sun was shooting fingers of amber light through a high tree in a gap in the bullring. There was a smell of jasmine in the air. I stopped and took a last look back and saw the long curved track in the sand, blood-stained, where the carcass of the young fighting bull had fallen and was dragged away.

We had left Simon in bed at our hotel in Madrid. He was still unwell. Aindreas called a doctor for the next morning. The prognosis was that he

The city of Toledo with the Alcázar

had a problem with his kidney area and should return home immediately. This was quite a shock. We were all concerned. Next day, Simon returned home. This meant we were one down so Simon's valuable work loading magazines, driving and focus-pulling now fell on my shoulders.

We had been trying to get an interview with Franco for a week without success. Andy had gone through all the proper channels but we weren't making any progress. We had contacted the Minister of Culture's private secretary who said he would speak with Franco's secretary and see if something could be done. A week went by without success and we were doing other work but it looked as if we weren't going to get that important interview. I always felt the interview we had done with the Basque Nationalists, in spite of being done in a very secretive way, had been known about or discovered by the Spanish police and that there was a block on us, as a result, when we made the approach for the Franco interview. We found, too, the police and army presence was very evident and that there was a distinct tough, cold, official Spain. Of course, Franco was still very much in control and his influence was very obvious. We noticed, too, a rigidity in the Church authorities as well.

CURRENT AFFAIRS

IN 1964, I had worked on 64, RTÉ's first current affairs television programme. We covered the British General Election. Most of our programming up to then had been in Ireland. Getting a chance to shoot in Britain was new. Gerry Murray directed and Terry Gough was the sound recordist. We based most of our shooting in Liverpool, a Labour stronghold. Our equipment was an Auracon 600 that had to be powered off-mains. When you were shooting away from a mains supply in the street, a 12-volt battery had to be used. This was highly inconvenient and showed how limited our equipment was in those days. The newsroom has portable power.

We filmed in the Cavern, missing the Beatles by one night! We did, however, have Cilla Black in full flight. It was one of the most cramped cellar nightclubs I had ever filmed in. If there was an emergency, it would have been a death trap. We met some of the leading Labour Party movers and shakers, including Michael Foot and Bessie Braddock. Gerry Murray won a Jacobs award for the programme.

It was good for RTÉ to be seen spreading its wings outside its own territory. At the time, I was on the shortlist to go to North Vietnam but Mr. Frank Aiken, our Minister for External Affairs, was not amused and we were effectively prevented from travelling. It was a very lively time. Programme makers were very vocal, laying the ground rules, having recently made them up for themselves. There were people like Lelia Doolin, Eoghan Harris, Bob Quinn and others. In a sense, it was like being on a university campus. In due course, it led to the book, *Sit Down and Be Counted*.

Seven Days, *Today Tonight*, *Prime Time*, what a pleasure to be part of that team working in Current Affairs programming with reporters of the calibre of Brendan O'Brien and Olivia O'Leary. Producers like Michael Heney, scrupulously careful but not afraid to take on vested interests or governments when necessary. I worked with Heney and Pat Cox in the US on the presidential run-up when Gary Harte looked as if he might pull off the presidency. One day in Boston, we arrived late and found Harte in the last sentence of his speech on the podium. We grabbed our equipment and ran to the steps at the back of the platform, where the Senator had already got into his limo, the engine running. I bent down to his window, my camera tucked under my arm. He opened his window. I told him that we were from Irish television. I have never seen anybody get out of a moving car more quickly. 'What can I do for you, chaps?' he said. Michael Heney asked could he spare the time for a quick interview. We did it where we stood.

We also met Senator Bolger, Governor of the Commonwealth of Massachusetts, who entertained us in his private rooms and brought us to see the Legislature in action. Our own Eddie Bolger, the electrician of our unit, asked the Governor about possible connections between their two families. I have to say the Governor looked like Eddie Bolger and was also short in stature.

In the mid-1980s, two producers joined the Current Affairs division – John Blackman, an Australian, and Paul Loughlin who was Irish but had spent a lot of time in Canada. One day, I was walking down the corridor of Montrose. Passing my supervisor's office, I got a call. It was Stuart Hetherington who asked if I could I be on a plane to London at four o'clock with my soundman, then on a flight for Oslo at about eight o'clock. This was not how Stuart usually operated in programmes. A foreign job always had some days' notice or even weeks. Obviously, Stuart got no notice of this assignment, or the cameraman involved had cried off at the last moment. Sheila was very used to me disappearing at short notice on assignments. There was really no recognition of the disruption to family life for staff like us.

John Blackman was directing this particular assignment. We arrived in London, then flew onto Oslo, getting there by about 10.30. We were wondering where we would be staying and what hotel. Then John apologised, announcing that we were off to an oilrig 600 miles out in the North Sea. As we raced across Oslo in taxis to the heliport, I wondered if we going to catch up with any sleep that day or night. There was a bright red Secorsci helicopter with its blades spinning when we arrived. We grabbed our camera and sound gear. The door shut behind us in the chopper and, when our eyes got used to the light, we realised about fifteen or twenty people were seated around us, all in bright orange survival suits. When Stuart gave us a suit each, I asked did I really have to wear it, adding that I understood we would be shooting en route and it would be very cumbersome moving around the cockpit and inside the aircraft. The laid-back Stuart replied, 'It's up to you guys, if we ditch, you will live for about ten minutes longer, with these on.' We put on our survival suits pretty damn quickly.

John O'Donoghue was the reporter and Tony Cunnane, the assistant cameraman for this particular assignment and we were heading not for a drilling rig but for a holding accommodation platform. In fact, it was a luxury hotel on stilts, with five-star cuisine, that catered for personnel on a rest period. A couple of hours went by. John and I shot extensively in the aircraft and now were shooting in the pilot's cockpit. We were in a position shooting on 16mm film behind the two pilots and could see nothing outside. The sea was absolutely jet-black. According to the navigator, we would see the rig at any moment. Suddenly, a tiny dot of faint light registered in my viewfinder. I continued to turn over. I was under-cranking to obtain maximum exposure. The light intensified and became brighter and brighter. I could now shoot at the normal 24 frames a second.

I have never been in space, not even in a high altitude aircraft that goes into orbit for a short time, but the scene as we approached the rig was the nearest thing to a space landing on a planet because the entire sea was black except for the brightly lit rig. The fact that we were in a steady helicopter approach made it feel as if we were in slow motion. A massive amount of light seemed to bounce off the rig as we jumped from the chopper. A tremendous force of wind hit us, nearly knocking us off our feet. We were ordered to hold hands and follow the leader in a sort of Conga, but I didn't hear any music. We were led to a door and I remember falling into the soft deep pile carpet. We were taken to a room where we unravelled ourselves from our Michelin suits. We were extremely hot, as there didn't seem to be any ventilation in the survival suits.

There was a marvellous smell of food. Our hosts took us to what we expected to be the canteen. We went through some sliding doors into what I have to describe as the dining room. It looked more like a Mayfair hotel with a piano tinkling softly. Five chefs were standing behind a long table, laden with roast beef, duck, turkey, lobster, anything you could imagine, with wonderful hot vegetables. By now, we would have eaten the leg off a chair. We had only had plastic food at airports since early afternoon and it was now 3.00 a.m.

After eating, our team was given accommodation in superb rooms with all facilities, including radio, television and tape stereo systems. Next morning after breakfast, we shot extensively on the rig and John O'Donoghue did a piece to camera before we were lifted off to the port of Stravana, where we were to be taken to see a rig being serviced in a dry dock. It was only when we saw this rig did we appreciate the vast scale of the platform we had been on the night before. Imagine a building about as high as Dublin's Liberty Hall, with another building of similar size on top, and then a tower crane on the top portion of that platform, and you will appreciate the height of this construction.

The producer, John Blackman, wanted me to get into a bucket on the end of this crane, which would lift me up to an extreme height. This took my breath away a bit. So I told him I would do it if he got in the bucket with me. We did this together. John is the kind of guy who leads a crew very well as if he is just one of us. There is never any doubt, however, as to who is in command. His experience in Australia, including using the electronic small hand-held cameras before they were introduced at RTÉ, was very valuable. He went on to be an executive producer in charge of special events, co-ordinating major happenings with regard to the EU and the Union, particularly when Ireland held the Presidency, on a number of occasions. John was in charge of that whole event, in television terms, and has also done presidential inaugurations for television, most recently that of President Mary McAleese.

I remember working with John Blackman and Emer O'Kelly on a programme in Rome. It was on May Day and we were near the Coliseum, filming a Communist Party parade, with dozens of red flags bearing the hammer and sickle. Nick Dolan, Eamon Hayes and I were moving in and out of the parade, at speed. After the sequence was finished, we got into our mini bus with our interpreter and the rest of the team and moved off, on our way to our next location. The radio was on. Suddenly, the interpreter and the driver began to listen more attentively to the radio. Apparently, a bomb had gone off in the Christian Democrats' headquarters. John asked them to take us to the area as quickly as they could. It was only about ten minutes away.

When we arrived, the building was smoking and there were several dozen people, along with two ambulances that seemed to be taking away the injured people. We were standing outside the building and I started to shoot. Eamon was recording. John Blackman asked if there was any chance we could get a higher position. There was no scope for this but cars were parked everywhere. So I told Nick to keep an eye on my back. I was wearing rubber-soled shoes so I stepped on the bumper, then the bonnet and then on to the roof of the nearest Fiat and started filming the building.

Two men, who were standing beside the car, exploded with rage. It was their car! I got the shots and we apologised profusely. Nick Dolan and John stepped in between the two men and me. It was a fairly dodgy situation. John told us to follow him. By this time, there was a heavy police and bomb-squad personnel presence at the location and a very heavily armed army unit. We tried to get into the building, showing our RTÉ passes. There was a lot of scrutiny. Eventually, a senior officer said, 'O.K. Radio Iran, you can go into the building.'

We filmed on every floor and in any room they would let us into. I think there were about six floors. There was dust everywhere. Eamon commented that it was just like being in Belfast. It was about 30 minutes since the explosion. John Blackman was in his element. Eamon had worked in Northern Ireland on many occasions in Derry and Belfast with the R.U.C. He was also well able to handle the situation. On our way back to the hotel, it was reported that another unexploded bomb had been found in the building. John just shrugged his shoulders.

Paul Loughlin was Irish and had spent some time working in television in Canada and the U.S. When he joined RTÉ, he started working in the Current Affairs area. He had a nose for a good story and worked with Brendan O'Brien on important material in Northern Ireland. I remember sitting in an R.U.C. Land Rover shooting as the police patrolled the area between the Catholic and Protestant communities, where steel barricades had been built to keep them apart. Not unlike the wall more recently built in Jerusalem. Paul was sitting behind me, calling the shots.

One of the most interesting programmes I shot with Paul was when a woman, who had vital information on a story he was working on, was in some danger or, as Paul would say, 'in some bother' from the bad guys. She was in London where the print media and others wanted to find her very quickly. I was going to have to produce pictures of the woman meeting Paul, without being seen. We needed a small crew so it was just Paul and I who went, and he organised a small plane, a two-engine turbo, to take us to London.

I had decided to use a 16mm Bell and Howell 50 feet magazine camera that I brought because it was small, about the size of two 20 cigarette packages put one beside the other. We were airborne within a couple of hours of Paul telling me of the assignment. At Heathrow, we were rushed through the private VIP arrival section – the only way to fly.

Paul was to meet our subject for dinner in a Mayfair hotel. My job was to establish that Paul talked to her. It was not certain then whether she was going to give us full co-operation so the situation was delicate, to say the least. My small camera, made in the 1950s, was mechanically driven and made noise when you were shooting with it. I had used it successfully in Israel on a number of occasions in very dangerous situations.

Paul and I split up and, after about 20 minutes, I entered the dining room. Someone was playing a piano in the corner. The woman of about 30 was sitting with Paul about three tables away from where I was. It was busy. I was lucky to get so close. I ordered an aperitif and looked at the menu. My hope was that I would get the shots and then withdraw, skipping dinner. Hotels of a certain quality always have beautifully starched white table napkins. So I wrapped mine tightly around the little camera. Then I reached over and took the other three napkins and did the same with them. I stuck the little package together with some camera tape, hoping this muffling of the camera would cut down the sound as much as possible. I was using a very fast film and a lens with fast light transmission speed. The lighting in the dining room was low so I was hoping for the best.

I got a sequence. In those days, working with film, you could not simply run the picture back to look at it as we do with video today. I told the head-waiter I had had a change of plan. He treated me very coolly. It struck me that he must have thought me very odd, a guy with an Irish accent who ordered a drink, sat at a table for four, then abandoned the table at short notice, leaving four clean and impeccably-starched table napkins in a rumpled heap with a piece of camera tape sticking to one of them. Very strange!

I waited for Paul in the foyer of the hotel for about 40 minutes. He arrived with the woman. There seemed to be a good atmosphere. Paul introduced me and I tried to read the body language. She was very tired looking and a little frightened. Paul announced that we would all be flying back to Dublin straight away and asked me to get the hall porter to order a taxi. It emerged later that Paul had convinced the subject to come back to Dublin for her own safety.

Paul's experience in Canada turned out to be very useful in the Current Affairs division at RTÉ. He went on to work on other major stories for the station but he was certainly one of the most interesting people to work with in that particular sphere.

Joe Mulholland was editor of *Today Tonight* for some years and transformed television Current Affairs at RTÉ. I had earlier worked on the first current affairs programme in 1964, which was called *64*. I then moved to *Seven Days* and nearly went to North Vietnam except Frank Aiken had other views about that. Then I moved on to *Today Tonight* and, ultimately, *Prime Time*. I always liked the opportunity of contributing to good current affairs programmes. There was a great sense of adventure and immediacy about it.

Brian Farrell was to go to Israel to conduct a major interview with the President of Israel, Chaim Herzog. Joe Mulholland was to direct this programme himself. Pauline Kelly was his production assistant – a lovely personality, one of the best P.A.s RTÉ ever had. My father had known Chaim's father in the 1920s and 1930s in Dublin. He was the Chief Rabbi and a most respected gentleman with a long flowing beard, according to my father. Chaim Herzog was born in Belfast but had grown up in Dublin. In those days, there was a thriving Jewish community of some 5,500 in Dublin. Gentile cleaners or maids would go into Jewish houses to clean out the fire and reset it on Saturday, the Jewish Sabbath, along with other housework.

As our El Al 747 reached Tel-Aviv, there was a tremendous cheer from all the people on board when the wheels of the aircraft touched down. We had had a rigorous security check in London before leaving and there was another detailed check of everything we had with us on our arrival. The next day, we were expected at the President's private residence at 10 o'clock. I had never experienced a tougher security check. Every member of our team was scanned personally and then every piece of equipment was gone through in the presence of three security officers. We expected this, of course, but what we didn't bargain for was that they would take my camera, an ACL 16mm camera, and remove the lens and the 400-feet magazine from the body of the camera to check if there had been any modification to the camera. They were looking at the camera gate to see whether a single-shot

Joe Mulholland with the then President of Israel, Chaim Herzog

weapon had been specially engineered with a snub nose barrel.

We finally met the President and his charming wife. They were a warm couple and always loved to welcome people from Ireland, particularly Belfast or Dublin. The President told us he had only happy memories of Ireland where he had grown up. Brian Farrell, Joe, Pauline and the rest of our party settled down as if we were among friends. Ireland was the common bond that we shared. After lunch, we set up a shot in the living room, where Brian and the President settled into a long discussion. Brian touched on his links with Ireland, his education here, his involvement in the 1939-45 War and how he had been in the British Army and was in the first wave of troops who burst into Auschwitz and saw where the Jews had suffered such indignities and death in the Holocaust.

At one stage, we were strolling in the President's garden and he mentioned that he was within SAM rocket's range of some of the Palestinian factions and it was only when the Israeli army pushed them back a few miles that he and a lot of the other residents in that quarter in Tel-Aviv were out of range. He said that a SAM could make a huge mess of your fruit trees if you were not careful. It was obvious that his time in Dublin had meant a lot to him. He said that it had shaped his character to a large degree.

When the interview was finished, we seemed to relax and took some more coffee together and enjoyed further chats about his memories of Dublin. I was mentioning that my father knew his father and that there was a nice ambience in Dublin in those days. I took some still pictures of Joe and the President. I mentioned to him that I had played cricket in Dublin with and against some of the Jewish community. They had their own club, called Carlisle. I met and became friends with people like Rodney Bernstein, Willie Samuels and Alf Solomon, which seemed to interest him greatly.

Our production team also spent some time in the Palestinian areas. We visited refugee camps, where Arabs had been moved to temporary camps in 1944. There is a picture of a very dignified gentleman living in appalling conditions who made wooden farm instruments and had a philosophical approach to being in the camp but hoped that one day he would have his home and his land back.

The fact that Jerusalem has a strong Arab quarter and that all the great religions are represented there with some important shrines, seems to point to the fact that, ultimately, it must be a capital city that represents all the great religious traditions and not just the city for one dominant tradition. This would seem to me the only fair way forward. Just as the Jewish people longed for a homeland, they should be the first to see the need Palestinians have for a homeland, too.

PORTRANE PSYCHIATRIC HOSPITAL

Lelia Doolin and Sheamus Smith were producing *Seven Days,* which went on to achieve great distinction as a current affairs series. We had heard conditions were bad in Portrane Psychiatric Hospital and I was sent there with the instruction to get internal and external footage. It was unusual for a cameraman to be sent out on a job on his own. Thousands of patients were in mental institutions all over the country.

It was January. We had been given permission by the hospital authorities to film. I did a sequence of the exterior. Then the official accompanying me allowed me to enter one of the buildings. The first thing that struck me was the smell of stale cabbage water and urine that pervaded the corridors.

Patients were shuffling around slowly. It was cold and the sight of the unfortunate people, some of whom were still in bed in the afternoon, touched me deeply. I photographed extensive detail of all this and my escort took me then to an older building, which had a wrought-iron roof. He led me to the doorway and ushered me in and, in a moment, I realised he had left me there on my own. I cautiously entered a long corridor, and I have to say the sights I saw there were even more saddening than those I had experienced earlier. I was conscious that this house seemed to be occupied just by men, some in long overcoats, many were unable to make any eye contact.

It was one of those moments that all cameramen experience, when you have doubts as to whether you should record what you see in front of the lens. Ultimately, you have to fall back on the professional reason for your presence. You have a job to do. So I spent another 30 minutes or so shooting another 200 ft. of 16 mm black and white footage. It is sad to think that many of these people were committed to Portrane, not because they were psychiatric patients, but because of circumstances in their family, which had nothing to do with the state of their mental faculties.

I know there has been much progress in the treatment of psychiatric patients and some major break-throughs in drug therapy. The policy of closing down these institutions was enlightened but only if the patients are given aftercare and continuous monitoring, so they can continue to benefit from their new situation. It was experiences like Portrane that enlightened me about the different strata in Irish society and of the glaring injustices. The idea of housing patients in a small family-type set-up, which is now widely used, is so much better, but more resources are still needed urgently for the treatment of the mentally handicapped.

CHARLES J. HAUGHEY

I had worked with Rory O'Farrell at the beginning of Telefís Éireann in the film editing rooms. Later Rory became a master film editor and, later still, set up as an independent editing house. After some years, he became Charles J. Haughey's media adviser.

We met again when I was shooting with *Seven Days* and they wanted an interview with Haughey who, at that time, was Leader of Fianna Fáil in opposition. We met in the Leader's Rooms at Leinster House. Rory welcomed us like old colleagues. Some time later, Mr. Haughey arrived. We were lit and our sound recordist wanted to mike C.J. Mr. Haughey looked around, as if somebody was missing that he had expected and said to the producer, 'Where is the make-up artist?' We had not brought one. C.J. turned to Rory, rather abruptly and said, 'Get a make-up artist down here quick.' A phonecall was made by our production assistant to Montrose. We were asked if we would like some coffee, it was arranged. We were a bit on edge as a result of what had happened. Rory was also disappointed. It was certainly not entirely his fault. We don't always have a make-up artist with us. We were ready to go in about an hour after our arrival. Mr. Haughey was properly prepared for camera and lights.

There is a lot of nonsense in the media about make-up. Anybody who goes on camera regularly needs make-up. Some people have rather red flesh tones that must be covered with a more flattering foundation. All news-readers on television wear make-up. Guests on the *Late Late Show* and other shows are made up. What is wrong with politicians wanting the same basic professional service?

The next time I bumped into C.J. Haughey, it was the night he won the confidence vote from the Fianna Fáil parliamentary party at Leinster House in that smoke-filled room. He won it by a few votes – I think just five. In the corridor on our way to set up, we passed Geraldine Kennedy and Bruce Arnold. They looked like two bloodhounds that had smelled the blood of their quarry at last. I can't blame them; their phones had been tapped by that administration.

A sound colleague and I were set up in an adjoining room. We were lit and had a small dais where a mike was in position. It was most unusual not to have a producer with us. *Seven Days* had got clearance but we were all alone.

For some days, there had been great speculation as to the future of C.J. The heave against him had had great bitterness in some quarters. Haughey must have been going through terrible pressure. Suddenly the solid wooden doors burst open. It was Charles J. Haughey, immaculately dressed in a dark blue suit, smart shirt and tie. Although not tall, his carriage was superb, he was bolt upright. He strolled into the room, quite alone, however, no aides of any kind, no friends or foes. He walked straight up to me and said, 'Who are you?' in a kind of tone that frightened me. It was menacing. I noticed he was perspiring. At that moment, I did not know if he had survived the vote. He asked again, 'Who are you?' He was well within head-butting range. I replied, 'I am a member of the Radio Telefís Éireann staff.' I was so fright-ened. I was not prepared to give him my name. C.J. glared at me and said

Charles J. Haughey
pondering his future

Haughey at a press conference after he won a vote of confidence.
Bertie Ahern looks on intently. (Photographs: Derek Speirs)

nothing more. After a few moments, I said, 'When you are ready, Mr. Haughey, could you please go over to the dais?' He spun on his heels and moved across to the lit position where he settled himself and seemed much more relaxed. Then followed the famous statement when he said how happy he was to have been given the vote of confidence required.

In my entire career, only one other person frightened me quite like that before from very close range. It was in Bucharest and his name was Nicolae Ceausescu.

SOME IRISH DIRECTORS AND PRODUCERS

JAMES PLUNKETT

WORKING WITH JIM PLUNKETT in the Wicklow Hills, you could see how much the area meant to him. He loved the isolation of the walks high up on Djouce Mountain, the remoteness of the Feather Bed, the mystery of Glendalough. Long before he moved to Coolakeagh House in County Wicklow, he and Valerie spent many holidays in small cottages there when the children were younger. John Beckett, the musician and composer, sometimes stayed nearby. They were great friends.

Shooting the feature on J.M. Synge, Jim included the rivers and hidden valleys that Synge had adored. My son Ian, just eight years old at the time, came on location for a few days with us. Many years later, Ian was to produce and direct the tribute programme to James Plunkett that RTÉ made after his death. Jim's empathy with Synge was considerable. He was a socialist, but one with the imagination and vision to look beyond constraints of any kind, not one of the narrow, dogmatic variety.

Jim and I called on a house where Synge's family used to live in Annamoe. The present owner, John Boorman, received us warmly. We did some shots around the rambling old period house. Plunkett's series, *The Wicklow Way*, with J.B. Malone, was very popular in the 1960s. Malone had a regular column in an evening newspaper. I shot some of these films. Jim would work with J.B.Malone again, and Aengus McAnally, when RTÉ had moved to colour, making a major film on the Wicklow Way which was, of course, the forerunner of official walks all over the country.

In his film about St. John Gogarty, Jim cast Ulick O'Connor as Gogarty. Ulick had written the biography of the writer that was part of the Irish lit-

James Plunkett in the Wicklow Hills he loved so much

erary revival series. Our film was shot in Dublin and the west of Ireland, particularly Connemara. Gogarty had acquired Renvyle House, a wonderful solid house with walls said to be six feet thick, which sadly, was burned down by some of our so-called patriots. Now a hotel, it was located at the water's edge. We filmed in and around the house, which had a marvellous atmosphere.

Jim had not been well on the journey from Dublin. Later that night, I called to the cottage where he and Valerie were staying and was shocked to find him as weak as a kitten. Valerie was very worried. She told me a local doctor had seen him and was not unduly concerned. On my return to Renvyle House, I told Ulick of my concern. Ulick was adamant that we should get another opinion and, fortunately, there was a doctor on hand who Ulick persuaded to see Jim. Driving a red Morgan car, he followed us to Jim's cottage where, within ten minutes, he had administered an injection, telling Valerie if Jim was not much better in the morning that he would send them both to Galway by ambulance. I think it may have been salmonella poisoning. The next day, the doctor sent them to Galway Regional Hospital by ambulance.

In the throes of his illness the previous night, Jim asked what would happen to the shoot. I reassured him that we would all carry on. In the morning, the company had a meeting and decided to keep to the schedule. It was odd without Jim, but we had the script and the shooting plan. That morning, we were to visit another house that Gogarty had acquired on Tully Lake. We filmed Ulick, in his role as Gogarty, sitting in the back of a rowing boat, as the gilly rowed him to the house on the island. It was a sweltering June day. The house was situated in the centre of the small island, surrounded by trees and some exotic plants. There was a small meadow of high grass, full of butterflies. The colonial-style house had an outside staircase to the top floor.

Seán Keville had brought a portable generator, run on petrol. There was no power in the house or anywhere on the island. We lit and shot Ulick playing a scene as Gogarty in his study. In the dialogue, he talked about people in both political and cultural circles whom he did not think much of, which was understandable as some of them had burned down his house. We did a sequence in the little meadow. It was like a secret garden from long ago that had reverted to its natural state, the kind of place so full of nostalgia and memory that you could feel it. Jim used these visuals for a sequence in the film to illustrate, with great effect, some of Gogarty's lyric poetry.

Having spent three days in Galway Regional Hospital, Jim was taken to Dublin by ambulance. Apparently, he had a narrow escape and if Ulick and I had not discovered his plight, the story might have been very different. Another director, Laurence Byrne was sent down to take over for the remainder of that shooting week.

I met Jim Plunkett right at the beginning of the television service in 1961, when I shot some of my first transmitted footage for him. Our friendship continued for the rest of his life. You did not have to know Jim for long to realize he was a committed trade unionist. He had worked with Big Jim Larkin in the hungry days of the 1920s and 1930s, when he was a clerk in the gas company. He had also worked closely with Big Jim Larkin's son, young Jim, for many years in the Workers Union of Ireland, before they amalgamated with the Irish Transport and General Workers Union, now SIPTU. Jim Plunkett had strong feelings about the amalgamation, not entirely sure it was a good thing.

John Irvine, a senior manager in RTÉ in those days before he became the Assistant Director General, told me Jim was tough but honest in all negotiations. Jim was equally complimentary about John Irvine, telling me you could do business with him, knowing that, when a deal was struck, it would be honoured. Jim Plunkett's example was responsible for a commitment to the trade union movement in me and many other young people working in broadcasting in those days.

I knew Jim had been a radio producer, scriptwriter and editor for a number of years with Radio Éireann and it was great to be able to draw on all that experience. He was one of the first two radio producers trained by the BBC as a television producer/director. Imagine what it was like for me and others to work with somebody who had written *The Risen People, The Gems She Wore, When Do You Die, Friend?, About 1798, Farewell Companions, Strumpet City* and *Circus Animals*. It was an honour to be James Plunkett's lighting cameraman on the Synge and Gogarty films, the tribute to the violinist Hugh Maguire, the production about the National Youth Symphony Orchestra, the little film about the fiddlemaker, Willy Hoffman, which Jim loved very much, and, of course, the tribute to Cyril Cusack.

It was such an amazing privilege just to be around when he was doing

Cyril Cusack

that type of work. The marvellous thing was that Jim was a director who had the soul of a writer. He was involved intimately with the visual but, for him, it was the story he was telling and the performance of the actors that were paramount. The clever camera work was never his priority, nor using the camera like an aerosol spray, which is so fashionable today. This gave me a wonderful freedom as a cinematographer. It allowed me to just take off, knowing he trusted me. We collaborated for so many years. A trust developed, something unspoken. I listened and watched him carefully, beginning to sense what would please him on the screen. We both felt that the camera should not bring attention to itself. Instead, the camera is an instrument that should draw the audience into the fantasy of the story. It should be subtle, the viewer hardly realises it is there at all and the lighting mood was so important.

I spent happy times with Valerie and Jim. They met at the Royal Irish Academy of Music as children. Valerie went on to play the cello, Jim was introduced to the viola. They were childhood sweethearts. Coolakeagh, their house in the Wicklow Hills, was a haven, looking straight at the big Sugarloaf Mountain. I spent many a windy winter's night with them in front of a roaring turf fire where Jim's hound dog stretched out and always fell asleep in the grate. The dog seemed to enjoy the music, Mozart and Beethoven, that Jim played on his record player almost as much as the rest of us.

Valerie's death was felt so deeply by Jim and the rest of the family. Jim remained in the house for some years. It meant so much to him because Valerie and he had been so happy there. He must have felt that he could not leave it because of the memories interwoven in his heart. He battled on, only to lose his only daughter, little Valerie, in her forties. Jim did his best to write and I used to see him but his health had not been good for some years. It is not easy being alone, no matter how good your family is. Some loved ones are simply irreplaceable and their loss slowly destroys the one left behind.

In the last year or so of Jim's life, I met him quite frequently. We would go down to the seafront in Bray for lunch, sometimes to Finnegan's in Dalkey. Jim was on a stick by then. We also went to the John Field Room at the National Concert Hall and heard the superb RTÉ Vanburgh String Quartet. I would try to get Jim as close as possible to the players so he could smell the resin on their bows, almost within arm's reach. He listened and watched with rapt attention. These sessions gave him great satisfaction and, afterwards, we would cross the road and go around the corner to Hourican's Pub, in Leeson Street.

Sitting there after the concert, Jim started to reminisce about our work together, I suppose we had just listened to the Vanburgh for a couple of hours, music was in our heads. Jim knew Hugh Maguire for a long time and admired the Allegri String Quartet, one of the best in the world in the 1950s and 1960s, led by Hugh Maguire, who had also been leader of the Bournemouth Symphony Orchestra and, when we were working with him, on that film about his life in music, he was leader of the orchestra at the Royal Opera House, Covent Garden, where we filmed him. We talked about our time working on the film *The Jealous Mistress*, the title being a reference to the fiddle and how unpredictable the instrument was in the wrong hands, I suppose like dealing with a mistress in another context.

Willy Hoffman was a fiddlemaker who had a shop in Lincoln Place. Hugh Maguire told us how he got his first fiddle there from the original Mr. Wilhelm Hoffman who had come from Germany and opened his business in 1919. This shop was opposite the old Turkish baths and part of it was still there when we made this film. Joyce mentioned this particular building in one of his works. Jim's memories of this film were very vivid. I think it was one of the loveliest things he ever did. Jim was fascinated by the skills of Willy Hoffman because of his feeling for the music and instrument, so, when we went into the shop, it was like going into some sort of a dream. Hanging above our heads in the dim light were cellos, fiddles, violas of all shapes and sizes, reflecting beautiful rich reds and browns in the dim light. Joe Mulholland had done an earlier film on this same magic music shop and when Jim and I found ourselves back there again for Jim's film about the fiddle maker, we were able to use some of the original footage which I shot for Mulholland. It enhanced the film greatly.

Jim Plunkett had always played in string quartets and also, of course, with Valerie when she played her cello at home, and in the Radio Éireann Symphony Orchestra in the 1950s as a temporary player, from time to time.

I visited Jim in Loughlinstown Hospital with David Kelly, who played Rashers in *Strumpet City*. He was frail but so happy that Cathal Goan at RTÉ has decided to retransmit *Strumpet City* after so many years. As we sat either side of his hospital bed, Jim told us that the news had cheered him up a lot. Tony Barry directed *Strumpet City* and Ken Murphy photographed it. All the actors and technical crew had done a superb job and it is still RTÉ drama's finest hour. It is good to see it is now available on DVD.

David Kelly and I were so shocked to hear of Jim's death. When we visited him in Loughlinstown Hospital, we had not felt things were quite that serious. David was away working on a feature and I was also out of touch for some weeks. Before we knew it, Jim had passed away. I don't think anybody else I have ever worked with was so stimulating on so many different levels. Jim was a real friend.

GOLA ISLAND DIRECTED BY ODRAN WALSH

I seem to be drawn to Donegal a lot. I worked on a film about Gola Island. We landed on the island after a rough crossing. We had made provision for two women tocome from the mainland to cook and look after the team during our two-week stay. I remember we brought a gas-driven fridge and a seven-inch black and white television set, for which Tony O'Connor organ-

The tiny harbour on Gola Island

ised an aerial on the roof and got a perfect picture because the Olympic games were going to be on during our stay. There were very few people still on the island. The postmistress was there and two or three others who were going to leave within a few days. The McGinleys, the O'Donnells and the McGees, all fine people with a great heritage on Gola.

We settled into the house, which was warm and cosy. It was October and we began to film our surroundings, the little harbour, fishing boats and great oyster boats and, within about 48 hours, we were settling in well. Suddenly, we were hit by the most almighty storm. It struck at dawn and, as the little house began to rattle, dark clouds rolled in from the Atlantic.

We had seen some porpoises the day before coming in very close to the beach. One of the fishermen told us it was a bad sign and the weather was going to worsen. We managed to get a sequence on film of these porpoises. We found ourselves completely stormbound. We lost the radiotelephone at the post office so there was no way we could contact the mainland. After a day of this, Odran Walsh suggested we get out and shoot the storm. We got ourselves up to some cliffs where we could get some very dramatic seascapes and waves pounding against the cliffs, with massive spray covering us.

We had no transport on the island so we laid our hands on a big wheelbarrow, mounted all the equipment on it, covered it with tarpaulin and pushed it around. After some hours of being drenched, there was a clearance and wonderful clouds started to roll in. Light re-appeared. We got a magnificent sequence of the ending of the storm. I used some flashguns to simulate lightning in the interiors and under the wooden-structured roofs of some of the remaining old houses, now in ruins. There were one or two old photographs on the walls of families and the people who dwelt in the house long ago.

The next day was marvellous, with bright sunshine from dawn. The school was across the island. Odran decided that we must go there to see if we could see the details of the school and maybe get inside if it was open. The little school was intact, its door open and the classrooms almost as they had been when the last children were there some eight or nine years before. We filmed a nostalgic sequence in the room. We were so happy when we found the key in the door of the big old cupboard in the corner and opened it, to discover the students' exercise books. Little art books with drawings of seabirds, donkeys and rabbits, which we handled with great care and ten-

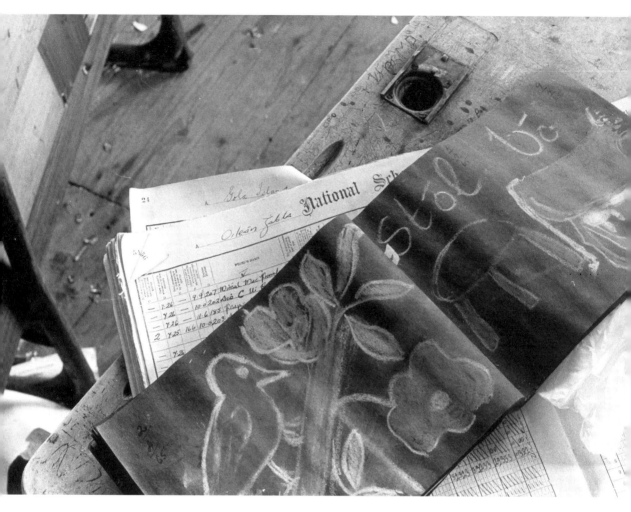

The remnants of records, Gola schoolhouse. (Photograph: Peter Dorney)

derness. We could sense the personalities of each child still in the classroom. Odran found the register of names. It was one of the most moving sequences that I ever photographed.

We spent quite a lot of time in boats on the water further out on the Atlantic, looking back at the island and then moving around the island with the camera very low and close to the water. The sea was quite menacing and there was a very heavy swell. We did extensive shooting of many seals. Odran selected the music of Mahler's *Third Symphony* to illustrate the profound power and beauty of the sea, which was very effective. It was going to be another couple of days before we returned. We did a sequence with the postmistress speaking on the radiotelephone to the mainland at night about somebody who had become ill and needed a boat. We were to go back to the mainland the next day. Two or three islanders, who had been working with us and were now leaving their homes for good, were walking around as if in a dream. They did not want to go.

We filmed them as they left. I was shooting from a separate boat. As they crossed to the mainland, I saw they had a dog with them, which we had played with on the island. I noticed a man tied a rope and stone around the dog's neck. He flung the animal into the sea. I managed to get a shot of the dog struggling before he disappeared. We could not believe it and were very upset. Odran shouted out to ask why he had done that. The man said the dog would never settle on the mainland. Then we saw they were about to get rid of another animal. We couldn't believe what we were seeing.

In due course, Odran and his editor put the film together and the event of the dog became the pivotal sequence in the entire film. The Head of Features was very concerned about this sequence and said we could not show it. The argument went on for six months. Odran would not allow them to touch the film. Eventually, the film was transmitted to great critical acclaim and a controversy that lasted for about six months in the print media.

SEÁN O'FAOLÁIN AND NIALL MCCARTHY

One of the most influential directors I had the privilege of working with was the late Niall McCarthy. I photographed a film about an unmarried mother for him, still a sensitive issue in Ireland in the mid-1960s. It was shot in a documentary style and Fidelma Cullen played the unmarried girl, with Niall Buggy. We were influenced by the film *Cathy Come Home*. Other programmes included a film about the town of Ennis, another on the Wall Street Crash of 1929, written by Tom McGurk, and a film about Padraig Pearse, scripted by Ruth Dudley Edwards.

Niall had also made a film about Emmet Dalton and his memories of his time with Michael Collins. We listened to Emmet tell how he had been sitting in the armoured car beside Michael when Collins was hit, and how the body was brought to Dublin by sea because the roads were not secure. The shock of the event still moved Emmet.

Then a major series came along, called *We The Irish*, based on Seán O'Faoláin's book. I was lucky enough to shoot most of that series. It was

Seán O'Faoláin

great to work with Seán who was 72 but, mentally, one of the youngest people I have ever worked with. His grasp of Ireland of our day and his ability to assess the progress that we had made since independence was quite brilliant. He had great clarity of mind. Nothing clouded his vision, unlike some others, who spent their time whingeing about the old enemy.

Seán had a lot of experience working in radio and Niall McCarthy had managed to get him involved in television, although he was not attracted to the new medium. Niall had to persuade him to make television documentaries. He phoned him one day and said, ' We need you.' Seán invited him to talk with him in Killiney. They clicked in an amazing way. If this chemistry had not occurred, we would have been deprived of a whole series of quality documentaries with Seán's wonderful wit and scripts. We don't make them like this anymore. I have a hunch that a significant number of the Irish TV audience would view quality programmes like this, if given the opportunity.

One of the programmes, *Saints and Soldiers,* was based on his book about St. Columbanus who walked from Bangor in Northern Ireland to Rome. Seán was with us and he was marvellous company in St. Gallen in Switzerland and Bobbio, Northern Italy.

For myself, I felt a special sense of following in the footsteps of St. Columbanus as Seán told the story of this monk's great faith and iron deter-

Crew of *We The Irish*: Margaret Cassidy (nee Kelly), Godfrey Graham, Niall McCarthy, Simon Weafer, Seán O'Faoláin and Denis O'Callaghan

mination, walking to Rome with his party of eight or nine monks. What an achievement. And Seán, then in his seventies, standing over the tomb of the Great O'Neill in Rome, thereby linking our noblemen who travelled for different reasons to the same resting place. It took my breath away then and, after nearly 30 years, still gives me a tingle.

At this time, Seán talked to me about knowing the poet Patrick Kavanagh and how Paddy, having written a poem the week before, was wondering when, if ever, he could produce another. Observing him in a pub looking into his pint of Guinness moaning, 'Oh, dear God, oh dear God', Seán felt compassion for his plight. The short story writer, Seán stressed, could always try his hand at journalism in the meantime, if he suffered from writer's block.

I have always felt that the time spent with Seán O'Faoláin was very special. You could ask his opinion about anything and know that, on balance, he was right most of the time. He was always in search of the source of the creative impulse. The Irish are an island people. We have been cut off for generations. Seán was like a beacon, proud of our unique history but determined to look outward and to change our vision and, in so doing, create a new modern nation because our people deserved better.

One night, Seán took us to a restaurant in Rome he loved where nuns waited at table, wearing the full long habit. They were from a famous order that was expert in all the best wines and ran this restaurant to help support

We had to hide the camera and equipment. One photograph shows the gear, in the other, we have hidden them on our persons. Niall McCarthy, Phil Eustace, Godfrey Graham and Roy Bedell

the convent. It was quite a bizarre situation. I remember a couple of days later, after we had been busy shooting and had experienced an amazing Roman thunderstorm which went on for hours, Seán and I were having coffee in one of those stand-up coffee shops on a corner, so typical of Rome. He told me that *Playboy* magazine was publishing his stories and had already carried three of them. It pleased him that he could reach contemporary young people through the magazine. There was talk we might come back to Rome to shoot another film, this time in colour, about the Vatican.

On another day in Rome, we managed to get permission to film in the Papal gardens, an incredible oasis of peace. We looked out for El Papa but he wasn't walking in his garden that afternoon.

On the Vatican film, the unit had been filming in Rome for about four days and Seán was going to arrive in the morning. I went with Niall to the airport to collect him. We saw him in the distance coming through the arrivals wearing an immaculate grey suit, carrying an old briefcase and a smart Panama hat. He greeted us, adding 'good to see you, boys. I know just the place where we are going to dine tonight'. He was like a young guy just out of college, ready for adventure.

At one stage in the shooting of the Vatican film in 1974, Niall was very keen that we would get up on the very top of St. Peter's. There is an observation balcony, circular in shape, right at the top and you can go up by lift.

Page 1:

KNOCKADERRY
KILLINEY
CO. DUBLIN
Tel. 85.1939

To All Whom it may Concern,

Which includes Niall, Godfrey, Simon, Denis,Maire de P.,
Margaret and our invaluable friend who slits the thin
spun life (to its great improvement)

It was a most happy and rewarding experience, and
when I think of all the detailed minutiae involved
I am full of admiration for your patience and
persistence, and wondered last night as I looked at
the result , in the opening piece (at) how smoothly it
all jelled into a unity of intent and mood. If anybody
ever did a Time and Motion study of the making of such
a piece I wonder how many separate movements would be
seen to have gone into the making of even two minutes
of film. And all this you had to perform with
accuracy in the face of wind and weather, geography and
the uncertainties of man (and woman) for every foot
of the film and of the road. My sole regret is that

Page 2:

it could not have been done in colour, because
thanks, I suppose, chiefly to Niall and Godfrey,
the eye-food was so good. It has been for this
writer fascinating to see words and thoughts
bedding so happily with image, over and over again,
so beautifully that I honestly kept on wishing that
the speaker could have been kept clean out of
the box, and let the images be enjoyed without his
presence.

Not for any priggish passion for total honesty
but (a) to make a point and (b) to show that I am
not being a flatterer I will tell you my only two
slight moments of visual hunger: the pictures of
Grianan Aileach, and of the close-up approach to
New Grange. How well I remember the day we had to
do Grianan Aileach having travelled so far and
so bloody coldly, there was fog.∎ I don't know how
Godfrey got even the dark images he did

Page 3:

get. The New Grange close-up is a matter of
opinion. But the point I am making is that
even if we had to go to Grianan Aileach three times
specially, to get the sun, and so to get the views
from the parapets, we should have done it, and Niall
would, I am sure, have wished to do it if (Hold
your breath, RTE!) it was not evident that the whole
programme was being done on a shoe-string. Oh, I
know - a very expensive shoe-string! But you cannot
do a film like that on whatever one-tenth of whatever
the total sum allowed apparently was.

Anyway, those two small moments apart, I feel
most happy about it. ▓ I enjoyed every moment of
the experience, greatly admire the amount of tact
displayed by all concerned, and am pleased to be
associated with the work of you all.

Cheers,

Seán

So we enquired. But we were refused. No professional cameras were
allowed. I took apart the camera and spread parts out amongst the crew. It
was a large 16mm camera, and proved difficult to hide in our shoulder bags.
We got to the top of the dome only to find a security guard on duty so we
rotated continuously, putting the camera back together, grabbing a
sequence before moving again to shoot some more.

After the first programme of the *We The Irish* series was transmitted,
Seán O'Faoláin wrote a letter to Niall McCarthy and the film team. Loreto
McCarthy has kindly given me her permission to use it here.

TRIP TO TURIN

In April 2000, Universita Deglistudi de Torrino celebrated the centenary of
the birth of Seán O'Faolain. Marie Arndt and others, together with the Irish
Culture Relations committee of the Department of Foreign Affairs
arranged the event. The Irish Ambassador to Italy, Mr. H.E. Joseph Small,
attended the event, hosted by Rector Magnificus of Turin University,
Professor Rinaldo Bertolino.

Seán O'Faolain's daughter, Julia, gave a wonderful paper, as did Maurice
Harmon, Terence Brown, and the pioneer of O'Faoláin's work in Italy,
Giuseppe Serpillo. I was asked to contribute and gave a talk on my memories

of working as a cameraman and a friend with Seán. I took with me Niall McCarthy's film, *Saints and Soldiers*, which I had shot. The large audience was captivated. They had, of course, listened to distinguished visitors talk about O'Faoláin for two days; then, suddenly, there he was talking to us about his beloved Italy.

Niall McCarthy's film starts at Clonmacnoise on the mighty River Shannon, then moves to St. Gallen in Switzerland and onto to Bobbio in Northern Italy and, finally, to Rome, tracing the journey Saint Columbanus made with his eight or nine monks from Bangor, County Down in the Middle Ages. At the end of the screening, I noticed Julia O'Faoláin was in tears to see her father suddenly again, on the big screen. She knew I was attending but was not aware that I had Seán's film with me and that it would be screened. Just to be part of such an occasion was so evocative and brought back so many of the memories I had of those films with Seán O'Faoláin and the times we spent together.

ERIC CROSS — *THE TAILOR AND ANSTY* FILM, DIRECTED BY LAURENCE BYRNE

The *Tailor and Ansty* have passed on to their just reward. I was lucky to shoot a film about the remarkable couple who were the subject of Eric Cross's famous book. I had met Nancy McCarthy in the context of the Cork Film Festival. Nancy told stories of knowing Ansty and the Tailor, recounting how, as a schoolgirl, she cycled down to Gougane Barra to spend time with them in their little cottage beside the road. The Tailor, a small crippled man, spent time in his small field, keeping an eye on his cow. On long summer days, he would keep watch on the road to see all the comings and goings, chatting to all manner of people, young and old alike.

Nancy told me she would be tired after the 40-mile cycle ride from Cork. Ansty would sit her down before the turf fire that burned summer and winter and offer her buttermilk and freshly baked bread. The Tailor had beautiful Irish which visitors and students found of great value. In our film, we spoke to local people who had been close friends, and we visited the cottage.

After Eric Cross's book was banned, the old couple was subjected to abuse, and some of their close friends expressed the anxiety that they were in physical danger. They had a good friend Guard Hoare, who lived in Ballingeary. He cycled out to them once a week to make sure they were safe, and to warn off a certain element.

The worst thing Nancy told us about was the day that Holy Mother Church struck. Three priests arrived at the little house, determined to see the Tailor. They forced the old crippled Tailor onto his knees at the fireside and made him burn his only copy of Cross's book. As Nancy told us of this gross abuse of the old man, tears welled in her eyes.

As you pass the cottage on your left, the road stretches on to Gougane Barra. I believe it is one of the most beautiful and haunting places I have ever seen. Hills surround the lake. Not a sound, especially in the twilight, a small church. I have travelled widely in Europe, Africa, North America and New Zealand but nowhere have I found such a place that seems to project you back to pre-Christian Ireland. The elements of water, light, sky, the hills and mountains seem to make a collective statement.

Ansty and the Tailor are at peace now. They lie together beneath a tombstone fashioned by their loyal friend, Seamus Murphy. In the late evenings as the last shafts of light fade, and a wild bird skims over the lake, I like to think

Eric Cross, author of *The Tailor and Ansty*

Bill Skinner filming *The Oxford Elegy* (Photograph: Noel Green)

the souls of that unique couple fly on the back of that creature to a place of peace where prejudice and meanness do not exist.

To meet Eric Cross and to listen to his stories of the fight in Dáil Éireann about his book defies belief.

BILL SKINNER AND THE FILM THAT NEVER WAS

Bill Skinner grew up in Britain and had an Irish mother. He fell in love with Ireland and, later, discovered the Táin Bó Chuailgne. He was captivated.

Because no one knows how Queen Maeve, Cúchulainn or Ailill looked, Bill and his production designer, Lorna Moran, decided to design a series of masks for the main characters. Lorna created a stunning collection, drawing from the Japanese Noh theatre. We shot in west Wicklow in the Glen of Imaal for four weeks in the early 1970s. It was exciting from a cinematography standpoint. We were in natural forest and mountain country. Can you imagine the Battle at the Ford? Both actors over six feet tall, up to the waist in a fast flowing river. Cúchulainn and Ferdia, fighting to the death, using swords and spears and the secret weapon thrown at the opponent on the surface of the water, which entered his body – what a macabre concept. Man has not changed much!

We shot Queen Maeve in her chariot racing through a forest, on her way to an assembly with her chieftains. Then another sequence in Studio 1. Maeve in her tent near the battlefield as she played an ancient board game resembling chess. Lorna created strange figures from out of two different coloured soaps. I was using Eastman colour and shooting in 16mm. Brian Cleeve was script consultant, Pat Hughes the production assistant and researcher.

We had finished shooting. The lab in London reported we had an excellent negative. Then disaster struck. There was a major objection about the treatment we were using. I don't propose to go into the pros and cons of the issue. Suffice to say the Irish people owned the Táin. There were objections from other interests, saying we were using their version. Talks took place but to no avail. The thousands of feet of Eastman colour negative remained in the London lab for years. What a waste. The project faded into the mists of time from which it had come. It was the creative imagination of Bill Skinner and others that created programmes of significance, most of which made transmission.

I always felt this film would have helped viewers appreciate our unique heritage but it was not to be. This riveting story from the dawn of Irish mythology has everything. Love, hate, jealousy and heroism. It stands as an example of our uniqueness. In Radio Telefís Éireann, in those days of actual public service broadcasting, this project was attempted with gusto and dedication.

I did, however, shoot Bill Skinner's film on *E.J. Moeran*, the composer, and *The Oxford Elegy*, the music by Vaughan Williams. These films were finished. Both were made in England and Ireland. The Moeran film was the first colour production transmitted by RTÉ. Moeran, had been influenced by Vaughan Williams and Bax, was an example of the type of English person who falls in love with Ireland and the Irish. It is, I believe, a kind of love affair that lingers for a lifetime. Bill Skinner also loved Ireland. He had the best eye for composition of any director I worked with; it was impossible to improve on his composition.

On the Moeran film, we shot in Norfolk on the Broads and on the coast. The English countryside is quite different from Ireland. You can see and sense the care of centuries. It helps when you have not been invaded since the Romans. The Irish locations were Kerry and Kenmare, where E.J.

Moeran lived for some years. He was haunted by the beauty of the mountains and bays of Kerry, and spent time on the rivers and lost coves near Kenmare.

Moeran's violin concerto is captivating. For the second movement, we shot a fair day, described in music, from which Bill and I shot a fine impressionistic sequence, like a Jack B. Yeats image. Moeran's two string quartets are perhaps my favourites. I have come to string quartets late in life. The RTÉ Vanburgh has recorded a number of them beautifully. E J. Moeran met his death in his beloved Kenmare, at the harbour, falling in off the end of the pier. He was laid to rest in the little graveyard just outside the town.

Getting back to Bill. His film, *The Oxford Elegy,* was based on the Matthew Arnold poem, *The Scholar Gypsy,* with music by Vaughan Williams. Skinner conducted the RTÉ Symphony Orchestra, as it was then. The score required singers; Hans Valdemar Rosen led the RTÉ Choral Group.

Bill Skinner was a producer/director who could lead the creative team in musical terms, then direct the film on location in Oxford over three shooting sessions in different seasons, as required by the narrative. This was some trick. What a talent. Bill conducted the RTÉ Symphony Orchestra, recording the score for the film. He decided that the music was of such importance he would shoot the entire film to musical playback so the pictures were shot to the exact section of the score required. This meant the timing of the action with actors had to be exact. This was marvellous for me, operating the camera. Soundman Denis O'Callaghan was playing the Vaughan Williams music so the tempo floated over the scenes of the rivers and the little bridges in Oxford, the fields, the roadside inns, and the gleaming spires. Then, at night, the scholar gypsy passing over a bridge in the snow against a night sky, all with the marvellous score. I felt I was dancing with my lens, sucked into that amazing story.

The people in Norfolk and Oxford were surprised to find a film crew from Irish television making a film in Oxford about a story written by Matthew Arnold. I never understood why programme-makers in RTÉ looked to Britain only in political terms, obsessed with the turbulent history of the two islands. We never looked further afield, to the possibility of superb programme ideas in Britain. *The Oxford Elegy* and *E. J. Moeran* were two exceptions.

FROM MUSIC AND DRAMA TO POKER

ONE EVENING AFTER A PERFORMANCE of the Cork Ballet, I went back with Billy Hunt to meet her mother, a most charming and delightful person. John Cunningham was also there. We were talking about this and that over a few drinks. We got around to jazz because Billy loved jazz. She started to play records of Stan Kenton and Woody Herman and some of the great singers that we loved so much, like Frank Sinatra, Peggy Lee, Eydie Gormé and Ella Fitzgerald. Billy asked had I heard of Cork's own jazzman, Bobby Lamb. I said that I hadn't. She told me he had gone to the US and he was with Woody Herman and played with Sinatra, Sammy Davis and, later, Ella Fitzgerald.

She took out an LP called *The Children of Lir*. Composed by Bobby Lamb, it was a jazz composition based on the Irish legend. She played it and we were very impressed. I thought it was an amazing piece; pre-Christian Ireland had always interested me. I contacted Bobby some months later and we met for lunch when I was in London. Over the next 15 years when ever I was in London shooting, we would always meet and he, and his wife Rita and I would go to lunch and discuss music and films. I got to some concerts with the Trinity Big Band.

I wanted to work with Bobby some time in the future. Bobby lent me a recording of his music entitled, *The Dublin Suite*. It was a musical description of a day from dawn to dusk in Dublin. Each of the musical movements had different characterisations. When I put my idea for a film based on this suite to Muiris McConghail, the programme controller, he backed my suggestion and was most helpful.

It was fun to incorporate the many different characters of my city. The big man shopping in Moore Street, the children enjoying street games, the lonely old lady making her way home late at night. Most of all, the river, the

Children playing instruments from John Lynch's film of *The Life of Bobby Lamb*

Bobby Lamb

main arch of the body that is Dublin. Reflections of buses passing to and fro in the river like ghosts, looking for lost souls on their way home. It was a departure for a lighting cameraman to direct in those days. Things were never more rigid. Permission was granted by the producer/director body.

As part of the plot, I wanted one of our characters, a young Dublin boy of twelve, on his bike to deliver a very important letter to the Shelbourne Hotel. On his way, he would meet some pals driving a horse and cart. He would chat with them and be delayed.

A chap from the Liberties agreed to supply the horse and cart. John Cooke, Phil Eustace, Jim Coghlan, Joe McKeever and I were all waiting at the top of Grafton Street at 11 a.m. There was no sign of my horseman and cart. After 20 minutes, I was getting worried so I took the crew into the pizza restaurant at the top of Grafton Street for a cup of coffee. Our young actor, the boy on the bike, was standing by, but we could do nothing. I would have to call off the sequence. We were all sitting by the window and Phil jumped to her feet, pointed and said, 'There they are.' A man driving a horse and cart was coming down St. Stephen's Green just by the College of Surgeons about a hundred metres away with a helper, all right, but it was not the team I had hired!

I shot out of the restaurant and ran across to speak to the horseman. All the traffic had stopped at the lights. I asked him was he by any chance a

Shooting *The Dublin Suite*. (Photograph: Mary Bracken)

replacement. No, he said, he knew nothing about my arrangements and was on his way to a job. The lights changed to green, he was off again. I ran beside him, and people in a double-decker bus must have thought I was out of my mind! I asked him if I could have an hour of his time for £50. I was amazed how quickly he pulled over to the pavement, just in front of the Stephen's Green Club. The two guys were typical Dublin characters. 'OK,' they said, 'What do you want?' The sequence worked even better than I thought – it had a spontaneity as a result of the haphazard way it came about.

There are few words in the film; it is a total music and picture experience, with no dialogue or commentary. John Kinsella, Head of Music at the time, assisted me in every way with the RTÉ Concert Orchestra. Alan Smale led the orchestra, which was conducted by Bobby, and Johnny Devlin produced the music score with the orchestra.

Twelve years elapsed. By now, Bobby Lamb and I were good friends and it struck me what an amazing film could be made of his life from his beginnings in Cork to when he said to Rita he was going to have to go to the US.

The story of Bobby's life is quite amazing. He went to New York in the 1950s and managed to break into one of the major big bands of all time, the Woody Herman Big Band. He was there for several years, working latterly with Sinatra, Ella Fitzgerald, before he decided to come back and use London as his base. Mike McCarthy, the head of features at RTÉ, gave us his support for the project. Bobby's life story made a marvellous subject for the RTÉ film, which John Lynch directed. We drew on Bobby's jazz experience and filmed at the Henley Regatta, where Bobby and the Trinity Band had the residency for sometime. We shot in Austria, Cork and London. Filming in Cork was the most interesting. We shot flashbacks of Bobby's early life. John Cunningham played Bobby's father. It was great to have him with us. It brought back memories of the Cork Ballet.

One of the nicest things that ever happened to me was that Bobby dedicated the new symphony, *The Children of Lir* to me for my encouragement over 25 years. There is a CD on the Naxos label, featuring the National Symphony Orchestra of Ireland, conducted by Bobby Lamb and narrated by Fiona Shaw.

The Dublin Suite was premiered at the Cork Film Festival, sold abroad and shown on RTÉ and Channel Four.

CHARLES LYNCH, CONCERT PIANIST

My father admired the concert pianist Charles Lynch during the mid-1940s, 1950s and right into the swinging 1960s. Lynch was our leading piano performer on the international concert stage. During those years, there was just no one else at that level from Ireland. Dad followed his career, attending concerts when he played in Dublin. I was at performances he gave in the 1950s and 1960s. It was fascinating to see him and listen to him play.

I had the good fortune to shoot the tribute programme that Bill Skinner made about the life and music of Charles Lynch. It was the mid-1980s when we met and made the programme and Charles was still giving recitals, although the demand for his performances had lessened. The new generation of pianists had made their impact. Michael O'Rourke, Hugh Tinney, Veronica McSweeney and John O'Conor.

I thought Charles was a somewhat sad figure when we met him in his digs in Cork city, an elegant house near Montenotte overlooking the River Lee, where he had access to a piano. His life as a journeyman pianist had taken him to Britain and all over Europe and, after the war, when access became easier, to Paris, Budapest, Madrid, Brussels and Berlin. He was away for long periods.

Charles travelled down memory lane with us. He talked about the concerts he had given in some of the great concert halls in the world's capitals and strange experiences in odd corners of the world, when he thought he was actually in some physical danger, and trying to get his fee from shadowy impresario figures. We took Charles to Blarney. He had some family connections in that lovely area. The trees and the countryside are so lush in May in that area of County Cork. We did some sequences of him walking under some fine chestnut trees in blossom, heralding in the summer that was to come.

Charles was over six foot tall and still had good carriage, a fine looking man of about 70. It was time for afternoon tea. The hotel was comfortable. Bill Skinner and Pat Hughes ordered the standard afternoon tea. Charles, who was so courteous and reserved, suddenly sprang to his feet and asked, 'Could we have cream buns, please?' Bill said that, of course, we could have cream buns, then all went quiet. As I looked at Charles, I thought of what he must have seen in his long career and the amazing people he would have met. Bill asked him of all the music he had played, what had meant the most to him. 'An impossible question to answer,' he replied. Then there was a pause. 'Rachmaninoff, I met him, did I tell you that, Bill?' Bill said no. 'Yes,' Charles said, 'I met him three times. We discussed particularly his piano concerto Numbers 2 and 3 which I had played many times.' It struck me that I was sitting beside a man who had known Rachmaninoff. What a moment. All my life I had listened to my father play the whole Rachmaninoff repertoire.

Suddenly, the tea arrived on a large silver tray, followed by the sandwiches and cakes, and then a special tiered salver with about six cream buns in a little tower. As we got through the sandwiches and so on, I saw that Charles had short-circuited that course and was now into the cream buns. He became like a character in a Billy Bunter story, pals all around on an outing of some kind. Charles confided in us that he actually knew this hotel served freshly baked cream buns every day and that was why he had suggested we have our afternoon tea here.

I felt Charles was truly a lonely, isolated person. A solo artist travels alone most of the time. It is difficult to make strong friendships. You have to follow the work. Living out of a suitcase for a long time. He had no piano of his own. When I see a plate of beautiful cream buns in a shop window or on a tray in a hotel today, my thoughts always go back to Charles Lynch, that wonderful pianist, that lonely figure who was our greatest concert performer for three decades.

EARLY VISITS TO THE THEATRE

I was eight years old when my parents started to take me to the Abbey. First the pantomime. I was fascinated by the mystery of it all. Then I saw my first Seán O'Casey play, *The Plough and the Stars,* followed by *Juno and the Paycock.*

Mary Lavin in Bective, Co. Meath by the River Boyne close to her home

I remember when they started to fry the real sausages, Hafners, what a marvellous moment. At that time, M. J. Dolan, Cyril Cusack, May Craig, Harry Brogan, Eileen Crowe, Sheila Richards and F. J. McCormack were performing. This was the old Abbey Theatre that was to be lost in a fire. The Gate was a great favourite with my parents. Longford Productions, then Hilton and MacLiammoir. They wanted to get a look at European theatre. The Abbey, good as it was, tended to spend too much time staring at our own collective national navel. Of all the plays my parents saw in the 1940s and 1950s, Shaws's *St. Joan* was the most thrilling. My mother raved about Siobhan McKenna's portrayal of the French heroine. I missed it and have always regretted not seeing that unique production.

Mary Lavin's short story, *The Cuckoo Spit* was to be filmed by Deirdre Friel. She cast Siobhán McKenna and Brian McGrath. I shot the film. My mother would have been overjoyed but, sadly, she had gone to her reward by then. When I photographed the film, I felt she was near me. I have always liked photographing women. Shooting them and, above all, lighting them so they look their best have always been a priority.

Scripts with a more dramatic storyline are lit accordingly, in a more dramatic style. I was using a new Kodak Eastman colour film, which was an improved emulsion with smaller grain that Tony Iles, the Kodak motion picture expert suggested I try. Tony gave me encouragement when Kodak sponsored an exhibition of my still pictures at the National Theatre.

When I met Siobhán and Brian with Mary Lavin we hit it off straight away. It was marvellous to have Mary Lavin with us. We shot at Mary's house, Bective, in County Meath, set in rolling meadows where the River Boyne lazily flowed through her land. I went back after the film and Mary let me take the photographs that appear here. Nearby was a forest whose trees and pathways provided an opportunity for delightful sequences of Siobhán and Brian strolling together, as their relationship developed. The story had been partly set in Mary's house. I had by this time worked with some of our leading actors, including Cyril Cusack, Donal McCann, John Kavanagh, Aideen O'Kelly, Jack MacGowran and David Kelly. Siobhán was quite exceptional. So strongly Irish and steeped in the background of Galway and the traditions of the Taibhearc Theatre, yet an actress of international stature. She could hold her own in any company, and did. She was given the classic roles in Synge, O'Casey, Chekhov and Ibsen.

The interesting thing about the Lavin story was that the central character

Siobhán McKenna and Brian McGrath

Filming Mary Lavin's *The Cuckoo Spit* in Stephen's Green: Godfrey Graham, David Fitzgerald, Michael Walsh, Tony McHugh, John McColgan (assistant director) and Deirdre Friel

was a sophisticated contemporary Irish woman in her late 40s, who was attracted to a younger man. In a sense, Siobhán McKenna could play herself at last. She embraced the character with gusto. To photograph her was a treat. Her natural elegance, the way she moved. I took great care about how I lit her.

We filmed in St. Stephen's Green where Brian and Siobhán had decided to meet. We were very lucky with light. A magical summer sunlight shone through a large tree, catching Siobhán as she kept her rendezvous with her exciting young man. There is a Henry Moore sculpture of Yeats nearby. The two circled the bronze, attracted to one another, yet separated by the symbolism of the great figure.

I shot night exteriors in Mary Lavin's garden at Bective, using a big lighting rig with four high lighting towers, with Dermot O'Grady and his crew. I remember there were eleven takes on a long tracking shot. Artists' fluffs, sound mistakes and camera error meant we were caught out by the dawn and had to re-shoot. But, as the daylight transformed the scene, I realised that a dawn mist was beginning to form so we shot wild flowers and a spider's web in the meadow, with the dew glistening. Our time was not wasted; these shots were used in the film. Siobhán remained a good friend, and we worked together again when she played in Tom Murphy's *Bailegangaire* at the Druid in Galway. That performance was breathtaking but an immense physical and mental challenge at that time in her career. What a loss Siobhán was to her family and the Irish public, she left us far too soon.

Brian McGrath has gone on to establish himself as a fine actor on stage and screen. We still meet and reminisce about our time with Mary Lavin and the crew who worked with such enjoyment on the film – some films leave special memories that remain forever.

A JAR WITH BRENDAN BEHAN

Birgitta Pierre was a production assistant, later a journalist with *The Irish Times*. She wanted to make a documentary about Brendan Behan and asked me if I would shoot it. I explained that, as a staff lighting cameraman, I would have to do it in my own time and employ a freelance crew, otherwise I could not be involved. Birgitta agreed. She was Swedish and had fallen in love with Ireland. She was full of ideas and loved Behan's work. I invited Joe McCarthy from Cork to operate the camera with his soundman Tony Perit. I was the director of photography.

I phoned Niall Toibín, the world's best interpreter of Brendan Behan. Birgitta, Niall and I put up a third of the budget each and are the owners of the property. Beatrice Behan gave us permission to use Behan's material. That was a great vote of confidence. We shot the film in late November 1970. Strangely, it was not eligible to be screened at the Cork Film Festival because it was in 16mm. But the festival's director, Dermot Breen screened it at a special viewing for critics.

We did a sequence on the banks of the Canal near Baggot Street Bridge in Dublin. Niall recounted the story told by Brendan Behan of his turbulent relationship with Kavanagh and how he had offered to decorate his flat when Kavanagh was going home for a few days to Inniskeen, County Monaghan. Behan was known to say he always had a problem with people who were not from the city. In fact, he had a pathological horror of country people. When Paddy returned to Dublin, he found that his flat had been decorated, but black all over.

Niall played a scene in Kilmainham Gaol that was very powerful, cooped up in his cell like a caged animal. He did not say a word. The scene was riveting. We went to Hollywood for the sound interiors, because we wanted no street or city noise on our small budget. That's right, Hollywood in County Wicklow. We found a little pub that was as quiet as a grave, at ten o'clock in the morning.

Niall Toibín as Brendan Behan

Another day, our film team was assembled on Sandymount Strand, waiting for Niall who was filming in Ardmore in the morning. We wanted to start shooting at 3 p.m. There was no sign of the great man. Birgitta was walking up and down, her footprints cutting out a trench in the sand, becoming more and more frustrated. This was her first film. The main actor was late. At 4.15 p.m., as the light was fading and turning a beautiful pink, Niall's car arrived at the sea wall. We could see the burly figure of Niall get out and open the boot. Even from a hundred yards away, I could see our star was in a bad mood. Niall took off his jacket, flung it into the boot, took out a pair of boots and begin to walk down the steps, straight towards us. Birgitta had not noticed the body language. Joe, Tony and I were in no doubt what was going to happen.

Our director said, 'At last, what on earth kept you?' Niall exploded. 'You think you've got problems? I have been working with one of the most incompetent directors. Take after take and I am in no mood to be admonished by a director on her first film. Please do me a favour!'

After a while, they both calmed down. Birgitta wanted a sequence of him walking, thinking of an imagined meeting he'd had with Joyce. Or perhaps he'd just observed James in Paris. There were a number of wide shots, followed by close shots of Behan's boots on the sand. Behan passes and looks at camera, his memory drifting back to Paris. Niall Toibín was suddenly right on target and in character, despite the earlier argument. The true pro was delivering. I watched him in my viewfinder as the shutter flickered, and marvelled at his power. By now, the sun was slanting low and had turned even redder. People who saw the film complimented me on the mood and look of that scene. Little did they know that the whole thing had been such a grab.

This is the poem that Behan wrote about an imagined encounter with Joyce in Paris. It was used in voiceover for those shots on Sandymount Strand.

THANKS TO JAMES JOYCE
by BRENDAN BEHAN

Here in the Rue St. André des Arts
In an Arab tavern pissed
For a studious French I construe you
Ex G.I.s and a Russian pissed.
All of those things you penned I praise
While in France, I swill Pernod in return
Proud of you as a writer we are
And grateful for the Calvados we owe you.
If you were me and I were you
Leaving Les Halles
Holding all this Cognac
On a full belly bawling
You'd write a verse or two in my praise.

The Troubles in Northern Ireland exploded in 1969. In Birgitta's film, she dealt with Behan's involvement with the IRA in the 1950s, he had carried dispatches to London and that he had come from a strong Republican background. This was essential in order to understand Behan's life. The film also dealt with how Behan 'fell out with the IRA', as he put it. 'They sentenced me to death in my absence. They can also shoot me in my absence,' he said. Behan spent time in Borstal and the 'Joy for his activities.

In 1971, the BBC complimented the film but they would not transmit it. RTÉ liked it and thought Niall Tóibín's performance superb, but they decided not to screen it, because of Section 31. It was shown in America and Sweden and at film festivals. It has never been screened on any Irish or British television network.

GAMBLING

The director, Michael O'Connell, who had been the film editor on Odran Walshe's film about Francis Ledwidge that I shot, got in touch with me. He and Pat Kenny were working on an idea about gambling. They wanted to do something with a number of high rollers. After some enquiries, Michael told us he was trying to get in touch with Terry Rogers and some friends. There was an inner circle met on one night a week in different premises on different nights. Yes, it was poker! On a dirty, wet, wind-swept night in February, we met in an upstairs room in a house on Talbot Street, near the railway station and almost under the bridge at Connolly. Every time a train went by, not just the room but the whole house shook.

Rogers was well known. He had no problems appearing on camera but the other three gentlemen did not want to be identified. Pat Kenny sat in on one of the first hands and one of them explained that it was just a warm-up hand. Our job was to light and shoot the game and to establish the players. I lit the action with our electrician in as moody a way as possible, just using some cross light so we could identify the cards people were dealt.

Kenny became engrossed in the action and was startled when he noticed large numbers of very high domination notes in little piles beside each player. One of our team whispered to me, asking whether this was for real or was it just funny money. After about an hour, Michael got some additional shots of the players and the atmosphere in the room. There was a break but we were not quite sure if that was it. There was a cocktail cabinet full of whisky and brandy and other strong stuff but none of the players wanted any of that. They were more interested in a big pot of tea.

It was about 10.30 p.m. by now. We began to realise the players were only getting started. Then suddenly, there was a huge noise, a train that sounded as if it were coming down the landing and out through the big window onto Talbot Street. But play continued. These guys meant business. Our camera watched their faces and their hands. I tried to shoot what the players were holding. There were some objections to this. Poker players do not like a third party looking over their shoulder, especially when there is a couple of grand on the table.

As the night wore on, Kenny broke into the conversation on camera, pointing out to Rogers that there was more money on this table than the average person earned in two years. Rogers agreed, adding that was what happened in some card games. A little bit later, Kenny commented that he could not believe there was as much money on the table as would buy the average semi-detached house. 'Yeah, and one of the players around this table is going to walk out onto Talbot Street with that money tonight,' Rogers replied. Most of us had never seen this kind of money exchanged quite like that before.

Pat Kenny and I had worked in Current Affairs. We had made some programmes in Paris and also some science-oriented programmes in some of the universities. I found that he had a great grasp of the sciences and was very comfortable in that area. Of course, he was a chemical engineer. I missed not working with Pat in Current Affairs when he moved across to other programming, I thought his work had been first-class. He was eventually to follow in the footsteps of Gay Byrne, and has done extremely well. I am not sure whether Gay Byrne could have made the switch from hosting a chat show to Current Affairs as successfully as Pat has done in the other direction.

Pat Kenny.
(Photograph: Frank Miller)

POLES APART

JOHN BETJEMAN

JOHN BETJEMAN WAS IN IRELAND from 1941 to 1943 as Press Attaché in the British Embassy. He said somewhere, 'I was a spy, I think.' At the time, he tried to learn some Gaelic. Some of his works were autographed Seán O Betjeman. He was an IRA assassination target, apparently. The gunman happened to read some of the poet's work and Betjeman was promptly crossed off the hit list.

During his stay in Dublin, he was invited to play in a cricket match at St. Columba's College in Rathfarnham, at the foot of the Dublin Mountains. Betjeman had played a bit of cricket at Marlborough but was not much good. In the early 1940s, the British Ambassador in Ireland had an occasional cricket team and invited Betjeman to play. The poet was terrorised when he realised that he might have to bat against St. Columba's demon fast bowler. The story goes that he hid behind the little pavilion, hoping he would not have to go in when the fast bowler was in action. He is not the first batsman to be frightened at the thought of facing the fast bowler on a sticky wicket.

I spent a fascinating day with the poet laureate in Chelsea in his dinky little house there, along with Nuala O'Faoláin and Tom McGurk. It must have been the mid-1980s. He welcomed us very warmly and seemed to have lots of memories of Ireland, which were very vivid to him as if he had been there in recent times. In 1941, during the War and our Emergency, things had not changed much in Ireland in the previous 30 years. John visited Mullingar and Belvedere House and had written some stories about the family and eccentric people who lived there in the years before. John soaked up the echoes of the earlier Anglo Irish generation in other towns and villages,

John Betjeman

those who enjoyed a privileged existence. For many of those people, it was a way of life that was shattered by the changes in 1921 and the new Republic that was to emerge.

Betjeman was like blotting paper; keenly aware of the traumatic experience his kinsfolk had during the transition. His poetry reflects this. In Dublin, the Georgian squares delighted him. He was captivated by Parnell Square and North Great George's Street although, in those days, when I lived there in the early 1940s, some of the properties on North Great George's Street had fallen into very bad repair. Despite this, the old elegant street had its beauty, which still remained. If only Betjeman could see it today and what has been done.

The Rotunda Hospital was another one of his discoveries, particularly the church in the heart of the original building. John told us how he found this church quite by accident on a dull January day, when he pushed open the door only to discover the Aladdin's Cave of the shadowy mystery and timelessness the place seemed to have still, with its deep silence. The plasterwork is of the very highest order and was quite captivating, he told us. He described how he just sat there, alone in a strange city in a country full of memory, with a different history, of course, to his own. Yet there were so many familiar symbols of Britain and the Empire now all passing away around him. Nelson's Pillar was just a stone's throw away.

John Betjeman had the ability to observe a place and be inspired by his memories of his childhood at Highgate and, later, in Cornwall, small vil-

Alex Haley with Godfrey Graham and Niall MacCarthy. (Photograph: Michael Lee)

lages, hidden-away beaches and little harbours. Cornwall was the inspiration of much that is in *Summoned by Bells*. Betjeman's days at school were both happy and unhappy. The Ulster poet, Louis MacNiece was at school at Marlborough at the same time. Betjeman's infatuation with women is well known. His powers of observation, his boyish instincts for a girl, even when he was well past youthful manhood himself. Always the eternal optimist. Even if he could not have the girl he desired, he could possess her in a poem.

ALEX HALEY AND HOLLYWOOD

It's every cameraman's nightmare. Until somebody at the film lab views the footage, you don't know if the work of everybody on the film is 'safe'. This is particularly so when shooting on film. The lighting cameraman has the ultimate responsibility. An error by him, a camera fault, a film magazine leaking light, a film stock fault (rare but occasional) can all mean disaster.

I was shooting in Hollywood with Niall McCarthy and Tom McGurk on a film about the 1929 Wall Street Crash, based on a book by Gordon Thomas and Max Morgan Witts. We had been filming for a week and were in discussions with Paramount Studios. They were considering a mini-series based on the book, to be produced by David Walpole who had just finished the *Roots* series.

One evening at my hotel, there was a message asking me to phone Stuart Hetherington at RTÉ. The lab in London had bad news. The last programme I had shot was faulty. The camera, the same I was using in the US, had a defect and the result on film showed a serious lack of image steadiness. What a bombshell! A cameraman has to take great care with the whole process, as does his assistant who loads and unloads the film magazines. I was working with Michael Lee, who was always scrupulous in these matters. He went on to become senior cameraman in the RTÉ news division.

The first thing I had to do was to tell Niall that all the footage we had shot in Hollywood was in danger. I suggested that we process 800 feet of Eastman Colour in a local laboratory. This would be done overnight and we could view our pictures in the morning. Niall was realistic about the situation, not angry, but obviously very concerned.

We were at the laboratory at 7 a.m. and were ushered into a rather plush screening theatre. We sank into the leather seats and the lights dimmed, as we feared the worst. A superb image hit the big screen, well exposed, rock steady, pin-sharp. There were sequences of downtown Hollywood and footage of the Los Angeles Book Fair. Niall and I left with our hearts high and compliments from the projectionist ringing in our ears, although it struck me afterwards that he probably said this to all his clients. I later found out that the London lab had had a fault in their printer!

We sought an interview with David Walpole who said we could come over to his Beverley Hills home. He was charming and very hospitable. After the shooting, we talked more about the possible mini-series on the 1928 Crash and Tom McGurk enquired how Alex Haley was. David said that he had been speaking with him on the phone the day before in New York. Quick as a flash, Tom asked for Haley's phone number with a view to talking to him about his book, *Roots*. Tom arranged an interview in New York a few days later.

Alex Haley lived in an apartment building in a rather average end of town. We arrived at there 8.30 in the evening. He was quite friendly and put us at our ease. We settled into the interview, which went well. It is sometimes after the actual interview has finished that the subject really relaxes, and you get even more interesting anecdotes. There was loads of coffee on hand and Niall complimented our host on the quality. Alex started to tell us a story of how, a couple of weeks earlier, he had been working late and felt he needed a strong coffee. Having discovered that he was 'fresh out', he decided to go to the all-night corner shop, five minutes from his building. It was after two and a dry night but, as he left his apartment building, it started to rain. He picked up a jar of coffee at the shop and was walking back. He turned a corner and was confronted by three black youths, two tall guys and a short fellow. Alex got a shock, greeted them and attempted to walk on. The biggest guy pushed Alex back and he fell on the pavement, smashing the jar of coffee, which went all over the ground. Two of the youths lunged at him, one with a knife in his hand. Haley told us that he had never been more afraid than at that moment. He broke out in a sweat. His pores seemed to open. One of his assailants said, 'We want your money, man, and all your cards.' Alex told him to take everything. The biggest guy reached and grabbed Alex's jacket and pulled him closer with one hand, holding the knife close to Alex's throat, staring into his face. Then he said, 'Jesus Christ, man, it's Alex! Gee man, it's Mr. Alex Haley. Give the man air!'

They moved back a couple of paces. One of the youths tried to save some of the coffee on the roadside which, by now, was wet and floating away into the gutter. Alex thought it might have been his blood a few moments earlier. The four ended up sitting at the edge of the sidewalk in what Alex said looked like a group playing a crap game. The youth who had recognised their victim as Alex Haley, the man who had changed their lives by writing *Roots*, apologised again and tried to express what the book had done for them and a whole generation of black Americans. This was before the term African American was in common usage. They told Alex that, before *Roots,* poor black Americans had no heritage he could be proud of and, with little education, their backgrounds were confused and lost. Educated black Americans were aware of the links with the countrys their parents and grandparents had come from. Consequently, they could connect in a more logical way with their 'placement', as it were, in American society today. The four wet figures sat on the edge of the pavement for what seemed a long time. Alex never got his coffee that night but, as he told us, he got much more.

INTO THE EIGHTIES

DESECRATION 1980

IT WAS 1980. The Arts Council had commissioned Neville Presho to direct the drama documentary, *Desecration*. He co-wrote the story, which is set on a fictional island. It was decided that Inishbofin, off the Galway coast, would be the location. Neville asked me to photograph the movie.

The plot centred on an amateur archaeologist, beautifully played by Eamon Keane, and a ten-year-old island boy who shows an interest in old crosses and ancient plaques set in the walls of the old monastery, not unlike those seen at Clonmacnoise. The monastery lies on a peninsula across the harbour at Inishbofin where the ferry from Cleggan docks.

In the story, tungsten, used in the manufacture of light bulbs, is discovered under the monastery. A local group, determined to support the mining, is led by a gombeen man of property with political connections who owns almost everything on the island. Tom Hickey played this role. Another group is formed to resist the desecration of the monastery.

I love islands and island people. They are surely a race apart. The visual potential is always dramatic and hauntingly beautiful. Inishbofin is no exception. Our 15-strong unit set off in October on the ferry. A wooden trawler about 60 feet long, it had no wheelhouse. The skipper was Paddy O'Halloran, now retired, a giant of a man, not too young, but still at the height of his powers. He stood holding the arm of a great tiller, looking like an ancient mariner or the captain of an Egyptian felucca drifting up the Nile.

The Atlantic, however, is a different kettle of fish in October, when the equinoctial gales tend to rage. All our camera and sound gear, along with Gerry Birmingham's lights, were stored below, under the battened-down

Tom Hickey and
Godfrey Graham

hatches so our complete company was sitting on deck. That day, there was a gale force five, with a heavy swell and rain driven in by the wind. At Cleggan Harbour, we felt the swell but, as we moved out into the bay, the open sea hit our little craft. The situation worsened quickly. The problem was there was absolutely no protection. We were all covered with great heavy tarpaulins, which the skipper had on hand for just these conditions.

I was sitting beside Eamon Keane. We were reminiscing about Jim Plunkett's *When Do You Die, Friend?*, a drama about 1798, on which I had worked as a second unit cameraman to Stuart Hetherington. Eamon said to me, 'I don't feel like dying today either, Godders.' As soon as we hit the open water, Eamon blessed himself and said he didn't like the sea and hated rough water. We were hit seconds later by a very heavy wave. I have shot a lot of film at sea in lifeboats in very rough weather over the years, and was able to continue filming because the potential to get marvellous shots tends to concentrate the mind of a cameraman.

I began to realise that Eamon was really frightened. He put his arm around me for support to steady himself. We were now out of the shelter of the shore. I tried to get Eamon to focus on the next two weeks' shooting but it was no good, he was petrified. For some years, he had been fighting alcoholism with great courage. This storm was keenly focusing his mind. He whispered into my ear, under the increasing noise of the sea, that he would give up the booze for the duration of the shoot if we survived. I said that was a bit drastic but he explained that he meant just himself, and not me, too.

Paddy O'Halloran was rooted to the tiller, like an Arctic explorer, completely exposed if a heavy wave took him overboard. He had one crewmember, a young man about 30 with a gold earring in one ear, who looked pretty strong. Should the worst happen and the ancient mariner disappear, only his first mate would be left. There were rough seas and no wheelhouse! We were in the Atlantic with no protection for the vital steerage man. If we lost rudder control, the ship could founder in what by then were relatively dangerous waters.

First mate Paddy Joe O'Halloran on the way to Inishbofin

I paid more attention to Eamon, as another wave hit us. I began to appreciate why they had insisted all the gear be stored below. There were a couple of calves down there, too, and we could hear them wailing from time to time over the noise of the wind. Sitting on heavy boxes and a couple of life rafts, some of us were better off. At least we weren't sitting on the deck with wet bottoms. Nobody was wearing lifejackets. That was the way it was then. Eamon was green at this stage. Paddy Birmingham was fine, toughened by years of working on locations in all weathers. Pat Hayes took the whole storm as a piece of light entertainment. Conditions improved once we were in the lee of the island, and we finally docked safely.

Neville and I had a quick meeting as we got our equipment out onto the quay. We decided, bearing in mind the rough trip, that we would just let the company settle in at the Doonmore Hotel and have a good night's rest. We knew we would be losing a half day's filming but reckoned that we would get better performances from the actors and better film quality all round if we were rested.

For some six weeks, our designer had been constructing some beautiful stone heads and plaques, to be used in the monastery for the very important sequence of the desecration. As the days wore on, we caught up and were actually ahead of schedule. It's a great feeling on a unit when people know things are going well. There is a sort of spring in the step that's infectious. The October light on Inishbofin was so beautiful and you get clearer visibility and more slanting sunshine. The colours are shifting, too, creating more delicate hues than in summer.

Eamon Keane stayed off the drink, keeping his promise, known only to him and me. He went on early morning walks, enjoyed his food and looked so young again. He was a classical actor, with a timeless quality and superb voice, who could be cast in plays by Synge, O'Casey and many others. I saw him in an Abbey production of *The Dandy Dolly* by George Fitzmaurice. He was breathtaking and the production was more like a ballet than a play. Eamon could have performed with any theatrical company in the world and distinguished himself. He performed with the Radio Éireann rep company for many years.

On Inishbofin there is an area with a number of lakes. Beautiful wild lilies were growing there, along with other fauna and flora, and it was quite lush, unlike the ruggedness of the rest of the island. Eamon Keane's character, the amateur archaeologist, lived in a little cottage full of things that would interest a ten-year-old island boy. Among these, was a telescope on a tripod, a pair of old World War I field glasses made by Zeiss, a barometer, charts, and ships in bottles. We shot a very nice sequence there in twilight. There was a huge, high-back winged chair which Keane's archaeologist character called his submariner's magic chair, telling the little boy how important it was to remember things from the past. He explained to him that, if we learned about those things, we would discover what our grandfather and great grandfather were like, what it must have been like living in those days. The little boy was responding to all this.

That night, the island was hit by another severe storm, so bad I was sure it would blow itself out by morning. We had a busy day planned. A helicopter had been booked, at great expense, for a rescue after an action scene on a cliff but, at breakfast, the wind was as bad as ever. The Met Office said there would be no let up for at least six hours. Nothing could be done. We called a meeting and decided to do interiors planned for the next day. The actors were prepared quickly in make-up and wardrobe. Gerry and I began to light the room as quickly as we could. I was looking at Pat Hayes, who was not his usual bouncy self. Without asking him, I knew what was wrong. The storm was as noisy as ever. It was clearly audible and would cover all the scenes we were planning to do.

Pat took Neville aside and gave him the cans. Holding the headphones, it was quite obvious that we had a major problem. Neville began to shake his head. It was mid-morning. When in doubt, call a coffee break. Neville, Pat and I went into an adjoining room, where Pat told us that, while we could do it and play about with it in the dubbing suite afterwards, the storm sound would never be fully lost. It would have been quite different if we were filming in a city or in a supermarket, where the audience would expect background sounds.

On this occasion, the alternative would be to record it with the existing sound of the storm and then take the actors into a dubbing suite later to re-record a clean track with them. It would be different, acoustically, but the sounds of a ticking clock and a fire crackling in the corner, people coming and going in a room, the teapot pouring tea, the tinkle of cups on a tray, all these could be added to create a satisfactory, believable atmosphere. The problem, Neville explained, that the budget there was not a big enough to pay for these post-production facilities, so we would just have to wait until the storm died down.

By late afternoon, the storm had abated so we got our sequence and had it finished by about 8 o'clock.

Some days later, we were to shoot the final part of film, the desecration of the monastery. In the script, the faction on the island who wanted the mining was by then incensed by the other group, who frustrated their plans and prevented them from progressing. Actor John Murphy, in his role as the leader of the pro-mining group, was going to attack the beautiful structures and ancient plaques under cover of night, aided by a dozen men.

For Gerry Birmingham and myself, it was our biggest lighting rig of the film. We always knew that it would but hadn't bargained for the problems we would face in pulling it off. The monastery was on a spit of land, stretching out into the sea at the other side of the harbour. We planned, with the help of the ESB, to hook into the power pole nearest where we would be shooting. We had checked the pole some weeks earlier and knew it was functioning. We had six 5kw lamps, two 2kw lamps and four or five smaller 500w lamps. Gerry had brought two coils of heavy duty cabling with him on metal spools.

Our problems started when we checked out the pole again the morning of that evening shoot. It was dead. As a result, we had to hook into a pole some 60 metres further away. This meant our cabling would not reach to where we would be placing our lamps. We were in big trouble. It was going to take all day to get our lamps and other equipment, camera and sound, into position to light the vital scenes of the desecration of the monastery at night.

Neville and I wracked our brains as to how we could get over this problem. Urgent enquiries on Inishbofin showed there wasn't a generator big enough to power Gerry Birmingham's lamps. Neville contacted Belfast. Being an engineer, he had dealt with companies there and was able to procure the right size generator but we would not have it until lunchtime the next day. We stood down the cast and crew. Gerry covered his lights and cables, and battened them down in case there was a storm overnight. Neville, Pat, our assistant cameraman, Alan Butler, and I decided to spend the afternoon shooting scenic and other material which we would later cut into various elements of the film.

At 12 o'clock the next day, the generator arrived by ferry and was dropped onto the ground. There was also extra heavy cable, as requested by Gerry. Neville and I breathed a sigh of relief. Suddenly, I realised that there were no wheels under the generator. It was built on a steel base. It must have weighed a ton. Neville asked how we were going to get near enough to where we wanted it. Not too near, Pat Hayes pointed out, because generators make a lot of noise. In fact, the terrain was so uneven on the peninsula and there was a deep culvert, so we couldn't have got it past that point, even with wheels on.

Somebody once said that, what he loved about making films, was the physical work required – carpenters, electricians, construction – all necessary before the cinematographer, the creative director or sound recordist could do a damn thing; nothing could be done without all these others skilled people. How right he was!

We scanned the monastery across the water, some 1,000 metres away. Suddenly, Neville shouted, 'I've got it. A raft, we'll build a raft from oil drums and wood, we can use some of the flats we brought for tracking.' We discovered there were a small carpentry workshop and boathouse nearby. We spent the afternoon, under Neville's guidance, constructing the raft. It was completed, with the generator on top of it, by 5 p.m.

We hired a boat with an inboard motor and our company moved. We got to the rocky beach where we laid the tracking boards and manhandled the generator as far as we could up above the high water mark, tucking it under the culvert so that it would muffle the sound as much as possible and not give Pat too much trouble. The extra heavy cable, which had been brought from Belfast, could now reach the spot where our lamps would be, just 200 metres away. Pat Hayes said that, if he did hear the generator noise, he could lay the sound of wind over the desecration scene to create more atmosphere, even if there was no wind on that particular night.

A night sequence like this can have terrific impact. We used cross and back lighting to create silhouettes. Some of the men going to desecrate the old monastery would carry pickaxes, sledgehammers and flaming torches. My job was to create a very dramatic effect so that some of the beautiful stone plaques could be seen splitting into a thousand pieces. Some twelve men were going to destroy the old monastery. The archaeologist, played by Eamon Keane, and the young boy would try, in vain, to stop the attack, ultimately falling on the ground amid the beautiful stones and shapes, which were being hammered by the mob.

The plaques had been built for the film, but with artificial materials, not stone. We had to be careful that this could not been seen when they were cut open and broken. We recorded additional sounds of stone breaking, separately, to lay over the action. We did get a very good sequence but it was a huge amount of work, bearing in mind the preparation and the difficulties. Time was forgotten. In fact, everything was forgotten in the desire to create the images on film that the script demanded. It was 3 a.m. by now and the first hint of dawn was approaching.

As I lay in bed that night, I went through every shot, wondering how things would cut together and how the lighting would look. It was one of the most demanding films on which I had ever worked but one that I will remember with great happiness. The camaraderie of the team was marvellous and I think we ended up with a good movie.

PAINFUL CASE

I HAD WORKED ON DOCUMENTARIES a number of times with John Lynch. John, along with Michael Voysey, had adapted Joyce's short story, *A Painful Case*. John asked me to be the lighting cameraman on the production. John did extensive recces all over the city. Sadly, my father died in the run-up to the shooting. I felt he was very close to me during the production and I remember all my colleagues gave me close support.

Joyce's story is set in Dublin in 1908. For me to get the chance to light and photograph such an intimate story, set in my own city in the very streetscapes where I grew up, was an absolute joy. We were shooting in December, which has that lovely warm light of winter, which is fleeting and can cause its problems, as the days are very short. I tried to create on screen that atmosphere Joyce invokes in that marvellous story when Mr. Duffy meets Mrs. Sinico.

A small theatre was required for one of the sequences. I remembered going to school with the Loreto nuns in the kindergarten a few doors from where I lived in 35 North Great George's Street. It had a beautiful little concert hall. The art director, Michael Grogan, John and I checked it out and it seemed to suit perfectly. It had not changed since 1900. It set my mind racing to go back to my first school to shoot a sequence in a film based on a Joyce story.

The main characters in *A Painful Case* were Mrs. Sinico, played by Sian Phillips, Mr. Duffy, played by Michael Lally, and Mr. Sinico, the sea captain, played by Ray McAnally. Working with these artists was a tremendous experience. John created a lovely rapport, which made the task, though challenging, a great pleasure. Des Perry and Olwen Foueré, who played Mrs. Sinico's daughter, also contributed a great deal to the success of the film.

For another scene, we needed a restaurant with the authentic atmosphere and décor of the early 1900s. I suggested the back salon of Bewleys on

Westmoreland Street, one of my favourite rooms in all Dublin, with the flickering coal fires and red velvet snugs, resembling a Dublin pub, dominated by marvellous chandeliers, which are either Russian or Turkish in origin.

John had cast over a dozen Dublin characters, mostly men, to populate the restaurant. Great care had been given to the selection and costuming. We managed to create a superb sequence, where Mr. Duffy, a dry old stick, dined alone most evenings before returning to his lonely single room in Chapelizod. The film was very successful, produced in association with Channel 4, and went all over the world. It was part of the series, *Irish Love Stories*, devised by Muiris MacConghail and Jeremy Isaacs of Channel 4.

John Lynch was invited to show the film at the Jerusalem Film Festival. He was met by a limo at the airport. Whilst travelling into the city, he was given the programme for the festival. Flipping through the contents, he noticed that his film *A Painful Case,* and two Wim Wenders productions, had been circled with a red pen. John was a little unsettled by this discovery and enquired of his escort whether there was any difficulty with these productions, and why they were they marked this way. His companion said, 'Oh no, Mr. Lynch, these are the films that have been completely sold out!'

Royal Television Society's (Republic of Ireland Centre) visit to the James Joyce Centre. (Photograph: Denis O'Grady)

Sian Phillips in James Joyce's *A Painful Case*. (Photograph: John Curtis)

Apparently, they had to hire an additional small art cinema for three extra screenings of the Joyce short story.

All six films in the *Irish Love Stories* series were very successful. I always wondered why the Drama Department could not have extended the series by reaching into the rich treasure trove of Irish short stories that are only waiting to be brought to the screen.

LAUREN BACALL

I arrived with a sound colleague and electrician at Dublin's Shelbourne Hotel, two hours before the appointed time for the interview with Lauren Bacall. I wanted plenty of time to rig and choose a location in the suite that was appropriately elegant. We had brought some lamps with Fresnal lenses that have a quality of light output similar to the Hollywood look. After 35 minutes we were ready. I ordered some coffee that, in true Shelbourne-style, arrived on a silver tray. We had a relaxed break. It was now one hour before Miss Bacall's arrival. The director was Joe Mulholland and interviewer, Paddy Gallagher. With five minutes to go, I was on tenterhooks. We appreciated what a temper this star was reputed to have.

On the stroke of 4 p.m., she entered the large room wearing a warm smile, dressed in a smart brown and white pinstripe suit, still very slim. I stepped forward and welcomed her to Dublin and introduced our team. I invited her to sit on an elegant chair beside a little lamp. There was a long pause. Lauren looked straight at me. She could see my Brockway exposure meter on a strap around my neck. 'Where is the director?' she asked

Lauren Bacall. (Photographs: Janet Wynne)

accusingly, jumping to her feet. It was now 4.15 p.m. and there was still no sign of the others. It was not easy to sweet-talk her. Somebody who mixed it with Bogart was in a league above me.

I always packed a still camera with me. I asked her if I could take a few photographs. This seemed to surprise her. She agreed and sat by a small table. Dermot O'Grady swung his 2K on Bacall. I asked him to soften it more with some diffusion. Lauren gave me a few looks, right and left. I got six frames but she was so tense. There was no way I was going to get a good picture. I thanked her and she got up, walked to a sofa and sat down. She crossed her legs and lit a Dunhill. There was the moment that I missed. The shot Bacall would never let me have.

Suddenly, the elegant doors of the suite were flung open. Joe Mulholland, followed by Paddy Gallagher, entered the room. To say they were nonchalant would be an understatement. Bacall swung around and stared at them. 'You are 35 minutes late, boys. I am not used to being kept waiting.' The three of them eyed each other. Apologies were extended. She circled around them, like a tigress stalking her prey. I wondered what was going to happen next. The crew shuffled in a corner of the suite, hiding behind a large potted plant. We must have looked like three hyenas on the edge of a kill, hoping for some scraps after the tigress had finished.

Lauren started to walk towards the window. You could see that she had started to unwind. She did not say anything. I knew the fight was over. Near the window was an easy chair. She sat and crossed her legs, lit a Dunhill and said, 'Let's talk about my book, boys.' I swung my lens on her. I was determined to light her as delicately as I could. She seemed to melt into my lens. The years seemed to drop away from her face. *To Have and Have Not, The Big Sleep, Key Largo,* I was back in the 1940 and 1950s, just watching her.

I don't remember what Paddy Gallagher asked her about at all but I will never forget those couple of hours I spent with Bacall in the Shelbourne Hotel.

ARTISTS AT WORK

LOUIS LE BROCQUY

I KNEW OF THE WORK of Louis Le Brocquy, of course. His creation for the images of the Tain, in response to Thomas Kinsella's working of that great saga is, in my view, one of the great artistic creations of the last 50 years in Ireland.

It was great to photograph the film documentary made by RTÉ on this great artist's work. Shooting paintings is a tricky business. You want to be faithful to the original work of art, at all costs. Louis uses so much white in his work. We did some shooting at the opening of an exhibition of his pictures in the Taylor Gallery, in Dawson Street in those days. Lighting and exposing white are a challenge. Le Brocquy layers white on white in a very subtle way but, once Louis saw what I was doing, he was happy, and so was I.

There were some magnificent canvases depicting the confirmation of young girls in their white dresses, on Bachelor's Walk. Louis had been sent a press cutting picture. Many years later, he produced a series of wonderful paintings based on this. It was a response to a real event. There was also a marvellous work of some beautiful doves. My favourite pictures of his are *The Family,* and another entitled *Tinker Woman.*

Soon after, we travelled to the south of France where Louis had returned, and we filmed with him in Carros near Nice, in his dramatic studio overlooking his olive grove. The studio had been designed by the Dublin architect Ronnie Tallon, whom I knew in the Blackrock beach days.

One afternoon, Louis's wife, Anne Madden, a painter in her own right, prepared a beautiful lunch for us close to the studio, served on the patio overlooking the pool where we later swam. As we lunched, we watched goldfish swimming in a small pool nearby, ducking in and out of the leaves and lilies, with other flowers floating in the water. I suppose that they had to

Louis Le Brocquy with Godfrey Graham. (Photograph: Jim Butler)

The artist at work in his studio in the south of France. (Photograph: Janet Wynne)

be careful of the heron. Suddenly, they would spring into life, all the colours of the rainbow. Louis painted a beautiful series of pictures of goldfish.

As I sat there that afternoon, it struck me what extraordinary places all over the world I had found myself in through my work, in the company of amazing people. Louis had two beautiful, big dogs that checked us out when we arrived but soon accepted us. We felt that we were all part of Louis's extended family for a few weeks.

We saw Louis at work, surrounded by some of the marvellous heads of Joyce, Beckett, Lorca and Picasso. Louis is one of the gentlest of the creative artists I have ever worked with. Unassuming and thoughtful but determined and focused. He revealed that there was no certainty, when he started work on a canvas, as to how it would turn out and that his original thoughts might not be fulfilled on the finished canvas. It was a revelation to me that an artist of his eminence should continue to have uncertainties.

We shot a major sequence in the Picasso museum and gallery in the small town of Antibes. It was fabulous to film some of Le Brocquy's canvasses of Picasso, Shakespeare and Lorca in this gallery overhanging the sea.

One day, we had lunch in Antibes. At the next table was Graham Greene. I was tempted to use my still camera but decided that the intrusion would have been in bad taste. Louis and I talked of cricket. He was at school at St. Gerard's in Bray. I had played against them when I was at Willow Park, and had been ticked off by the headmaster of St. Gerard's for shouting, 'run like the devil', when Johnny Wood hit the winning run! Father Stanley was spoken to by the headmaster. 'Stano' had a word with me, too, but he wasn't too bothered.

In the film, we shot an extensive sequence on the imagery that Louis had produced of the figures of the armies massing in the Tain. The images, combined with the music of Seán Ó Riada, were then moved about with fast cutting. We also looked at some of the ancient heads from pre-Christian Ireland that had inspired Louis.

Louis was about to illustrate Joyce's *Dubliners* for a new edition when he heard that I had shot *A Painful Case* on film. He was happy when I sent him a VHS of the film version.

The day before we flew back to Ireland, we took Louis and Anne to dinner. We were down at the seafront in Nice. He gave all the team a lithograph of Yeats, with a personal message to each of us. We presented him with the clapperboard that we had used in the film.

Michael Garvey and the unit filmed in County Cork, where Anne and Louis have a house. We shot a sequence near a massive rock that had a large hole through which the sea rushed in. The resulting sound and visual effects had moved the painter in powerful ways. An important sequence was created here and I got some still photograph, also.

MAINIE JELLETT

Bruce Arnold's Roundtable Productions and RTÉ decided to make a film about Mainie Jellett. In the course of telling the story, we met Hélène St. Pierre, a Parisienne woman who was in her early seventies. She was from an aristocratic French background. Hélène told us on camera that on 15 June 1940 she was walking up Kildare Street in Dublin and turned left in front of the Shelbourne Hotel, where she was astonished to see a poster held up by a paperboy announcing that the German army had just arrived in Paris. As she bought and began to read the paper, she was aware of someone looking at her, a tall angular young woman who said to her, 'Are you all right? You look a bit distressed.' Hélène replied, 'You would be distressed, the Germans

Hélène St Pierre and Godfrey Graham in her apartment during the Mainie Jellett film shot in Paris

have just invaded my home, Paris.' Mainie Jellett replied in French, 'Come to my studio in Fitzwilliam Square and we will have some coffee.' The two young women, one tall and gangly, the other, Hélène, bird-like and petite, seemed to have an immediate rapport. Over coffee, Hélène told Mainie that she also painted. Jellett immediately offered her 'atelier' to Hélène any time she wanted and said her brushes and paints were at Hélène's disposal. This was the kind of good-natured act that Mainie Jellett showed to people right through her life.

Our film was shot in Dublin, Donegal and Paris and in some rural areas of France. We spent some time in Hélène's large apartment, near the Opera House, overlooking some of the most prestigious residences. The back garden of the American Embassy, with its high trees, was near by. This exclusive property had been in Hélène's family since her grandfather's days. It had large proportions, especially the main salon with the magnificent tapestries that were over 300 years old. She had some magnificent classic and modern paintings, some striking pieces of sculpture. I remember a beautiful head of a young girl on the grand piano. There was some 18th-and 19th-century furniture, not surprising, I suppose, in a family that had a château in Normandy. That family had produced her distinguished father who served in the Great War and Hélène's brother, an eminent French novelist.

Our team was staying at a hotel nearby. However, I was given a studio room just off Hélène's large salon where there was a small divan and some interesting pictures with access to a balcony. Before our friends returned, Hélène talked of her time in the apartment when she was a young girl – the parties, her first love affairs, the nights she went to the Paris Opera House, only ten minutes away. She saw the Ballet Russe there, Diaghilev's company, with scores provided by Stravinsky but, when she told me that Stravinsky had occupied the apartment directly above her, I nearly fell off the chaise longue. 'Yes', she said, 'he played his piano there day and night.' When he played complete or parts of works, it was very interesting to listen to him but it was a very different matter when he was working on composition, going over the same passages of music again and again. That was more difficult to take. Then he would get up and walk up and down above her head for long periods. She met him several times in the rickety typical Parisian lift, with its wrought iron framework.

One of the interesting things about this fascinating woman was that she reminded me of my godmother, Madame Toto Cogley. They were both Parisian, bird-like in appearance, and loved the arts. When I was ten or eleven, Toto Cogley was still around but meeting Hélène fascinated me because it gave me a sense of what it would have been like to spend more time with my godmother in adult life.

Hélène has stories of Dublin in the 1940s. She was at dinner parties with Hilton Edwards and Micheál MacLiammóir. People like Austin Clarke, Seán O'Faoláin and Flann O'Brien. Roger and Pat McHugh, Charles Lynch, the pianist. She said that the conversation was marvellous, flowing from English to French to Irish, occasionally to German and back again, seamlessly. She told me that the Catholic Church came under sharp criticism at the time. Of course it was deep in the censorship period. All the leading Irish authors had been banned. Hélène was a neighbour of Archbishop John Charles McQuaid in Killiney. They met some times, she said, at suitable cultural events, which the Archbishop attended. She found him a fascinating character, who was extremely widely read and familiar with her brother's novels. He had a mind as quick as lightning and was not without humour. One day, he told her that he was fascinated by the stars and the universe and that he had a large telescope positioned in a tower-like structure in his residence in Killiney.

One winter afternoon in her home in Monkstown, she reminisced about dining in Jammet's Restaurant with another young French woman who could not get back to Paris because of the war. It was 1940. There was a party of six at a round table in the centre of the dining room. It was a few days after Hélène had bumped into and been befriended by Mainie Jellett, a day or two after the Germans occupied Paris. Hélène overheard a couple at the next table saying, 'Is that Lord and Lady Brookborough there with that party at the centre table?' Hélène and her friend would not have recognised them, of course. Brookborough was Minister of Agriculture in Northern Ireland and would become Prime Minister (of Northern Ireland) later that year. Together with his aides and a couple of security people, they were having their aperitifs and looking at the menu. Louis Jammet and his wife, Yvonne, approached the centre table to get details of their order. As they did so, one of the party said in a very loud voice, 'That's Paris gone anyway, we can't trust the froggies, they have no backbone.' The rest of his party concurred.

Hélène told me what a shock it was, and that Monsieur and Madame Jammet were quite stunned when they heard this. They ran the most famous French restaurant in Ireland, not just in Dublin. She described what happened next. The Brookboroughs' orders were taken – starters, main courses and wine. In those days, people came to Dublin from as far away as the UK and Northern Ireland for a decent meal. Other guests were being looked after at their tables. Twenty minutes elapsed, with some obvious impatience from the centre table, the shifting of chairs and looks towards the kitchen. The first course came and was placed in front of the VIP party. There were immediate objections, not one of the first courses was correct. There was flicking of fingers and grumbles. The waiter took away all the first courses, then came back again and meticulously took further notes about the first courses . He went back to the kitchen. Hélène and her friend were given their main course by a French waiter who knew Hélène and said in French, 'There are many ways to return an insult with interest.' Wine arrived and was poured from carafes. One of the aides jumped up and said, 'This is not what we ordered, it is not the burgundy we asked for, take it all away.'

After another ten minutes, the correct first courses arrived. By this time, Hélène and her friend had finished their main course, a delicious sole bonne femme. The next crisis was timed beautifully. Monsieur Jammet came forward and, with meticulous good manners, said to Lord Brookborough's party, 'No French wine is being served tonight because of shortages caused by the war and by the British embargo on trade across the Irish Sea which, of course, is neutral as is the Republic of Ireland.' There was another outburst from one of the aides. They accepted the earlier white wine, which had arrived but, as far as Hélène had observed, seemed to be lukewarm.

Soon after the wrong main courses arrived. The entire Brookborough party stood up, threw a few pound notes on the table and demanded their overcoats. Somebody said, 'Not only is Dublin a backwater, this whole country is a backwater.' With impeccable timing, Monsieur Jammet appeared and said, 'This is a French restaurant, good night.' When the Brookborough party left, the best burgundy wines were offered on the house to the entire clientele, which, by then, had increased substantially. Hélène and her young French friend made their way back to their apartment in the early hours of the morning.

Yvonne Jammet had a reputation in Dublin as a painter. She was a member of the White Stag Group. Louis Jammet was educated in Belvedere College. He joined the French Army in 1913, soldiered in the Great War and was wounded in his right arm, which he was fortunate not to lose. Louis knew what war was.

The young Mainie Jellett, played by Roslyn Renwick in the film directed by Godfrey Graham

Left to right: A waiter, Padraic Colum, Lady Longford and Michael MacLiammoir at Jammet's.
(Photograph: John Hedgecoe)

UGANDA

As SCHOOLBOYS, we collected pennies for the black babies. My school was run by the Holy Ghost Fathers. I got the chance to work on a programme in Uganda about the AIDS epidemic in the mid-1990s. It was profoundly sad in the villages to see whole generations of parents had died because of this horrible disease. We were taken to see their children, entering a number of houses. We discovered that 30 or 40 children, from four up to teenage, were being reared by their grandmothers. It was a pathetic situation.

We moved on to a Mother Mary Martin clinic and community close to Lake Victoria, where we were warmly welcomed. This community was operating a hospital. The first morning, we saw patients arriving for treatment. An old two-seater van arrived. The driver got out and dropped the back of the carrying area. I saw a young boy of about 15, lying on some leaves, looking very ill. Beside him was a large bunch of twigs and some small wooden logs. There were also two large bunches of bananas, one fully ripe and the other still green. The surgeon, Sister Maura Lynch, supervised his arrival and arranged for a stretcher. She told us it was the tradition for the family of the patient to look after their loved one whilst in hospital. So the firewood was for cooking food and the bananas for him to eat.

Sister Maura told us that the boy had some abdominal blockage and would need an operation right away. She would perform the procedure. This group of sisters had transformed the lives of these people. I thought again about how we had collected pennies for the black babies at Willow Park and Blackrock College. At last, I saw the imporance of the support from home. Sister Maura rejoined us for lunch. The operation was a success and the boy would be back in his village in ten days. When I see a bunch of bananas in a big Dublin supermarket, I can't help thinking of those other bananas in Uganda.

The next day, we travelled up country with the same nun. She wanted to have a look at a woman on whom she had operated some weeks earlier. That part of the country was so lush and our Land Rover made its way on the dirt roads, sometimes on no roads at all. We met the woman sitting on the mud floor of her little house. Obviously, she was expecting the visit. There was great warmth between the two women, and the body language was positive. Things had gone well, the consultation was over. Sister reached into her bag and withdrew a small silver box. Then she made the sign of the cross and gave the woman the Blessed Sacrament.

The extreme heat was beginning to take its toll on the team. The next day, Sister Ursula Sharpe said she wanted to take us up country to a village where things were said to be very bad. We didn't know in what sense. The settlement was near a small forest so at least there would be some shade. There were eight or nine straw shacks and some small stone buildings, with few people in evidence when we arrived. Two elders came forward and greeted the sister and our party. We were immediately brought to meet an old woman who seemed to be suffering from some kind of fever. Our team stayed back a little and we photographed the sequence as the sister began to treat her, both speaking the local tribal language. I thought the reason for so few people was that they were in the fields, or perhaps working in a small banana plantation near the village. After the woman had been settled down and seemed more comfortable, the two elders, standing nearby, approached our party and moved out of the house. Sister Ursula beckoned us to follow them. We walked to the far end of the village where there was a clearing with one house apart from the others.

The door was shut. I put my camera on the ground to rest my arm and squatted down. More talk followed. I looked at the Sister for some indication of what was to happen next. Our director, Stephanie nodded in the direction of my camera. John Rodgers had his mixer and rifle mike in his hands so I switched on the camera. The door began to open slowly. Inside seemed to be pitch black. I looked through my viewfinder, and saw that the house was full of small children, between the ages of four and ten. Their eyes gazed out at us with the most soulful expressions I have ever seen. The whites of their eyes shone as bright as snow.

In the centre, there was an old woman, who must have been 80, with her arms stretched out cradling as many of the little ones as she could. Some were her grandchildren. Their fathers and mothers were all dead. There was no sound save the whirring of my camera. None of us could say a word. There was some whispering between the nun and Stephanie to the effect that their mothers and fathers were all close by in the little graveyard near the forest. As we walked over to the burial ground, we were told that AIDS had decimated the entire village, leaving just the very old and the very young. Many of the children had HIV and would develop AIDS later. To see a noble tribe totally unequipped to defend itself from such a menace, despite all the efforts of the Sisters, was deeply saddening and made me feel very frustrated.

As we made our way through the trees to the graves, just simple mounds of clay, some with names, we were told that, every few days, there would be a procession from the remaining community, including the children, who came to pay their respects to their dead parents. Some of the little ones would play close to the mounds of earth under which their parents lay, not yet knowing the magnitude of their own tragedy. I think Stephanie must have known what we would see but had decided not to let us know in advance so the impact would be all the more powerful. Nothing has ever affected me quite like this. I felt so helpless and could only hope that our film may have made some small contribution to the global fight against AIDS.

Today, 15 million children worldwide have lost one or both parents to AIDS, 12 million in sub-Saharan Africa. By 2010, there will be an estimated 50 million orphan children in sub-Saharan Africa, 18 million of those parents having died from AIDS. Since it was identified in the 1980s, 20 million people have died from this virus and 38 million are affected.

We wanted a sunrise sequence, looking from the hospital complex, which was on the shores of Lake Victoria. I suggested to Stephanie that I would stay overnight at the hospital to be on site at 5 a.m. Stephanie agreed and gave me her ideas as to what she required. Then she and the rest of the team returned to the town six miles away. We would link up in the morning. The sisters looked after me well. A bottle of wine was produced as a special treat. These marvellous women told me why they wanted to serve God and these wonderful people, and that their founder Mother Mary Martin so wanted to bring them modern medicine, which would transform their lives. Despite wars and revolutions in Uganda, they continued to do this, despite the best efforts of Idi Amin, who was gone by then.

How good to see these happy children cared for by Sisters of Mother Mary Martin, with such love

I was given a room in a narrow, one-storey, cottage-like building, which had a thatched roof and six or seven bedrooms. I had my film camera, two magazines and a tripod. I looked at the door. It just had a wooden latch. That was all the security. All it would need was a hard push to open the door. On location as a cameraman, one is always conscious of the danger of being assaulted or of having one's equipment stolen, even in the most unlikely places.

I had been asleep for some time, I don't know for how long, when I was suddenly awakened and the door was moving. I had wedged my heavy tripod at the foot of the door. It moved again. I was on my feet and had the heavy metal magazine box in my hand as some form of defence. Then I heard footsteps moving away, a very light sound. The person was not wearing shoes. By now, I was wide awake. I got back on my little metal bed, a typical hostel or dormitory bed. I wondered could it have come all the way from Ireland, from some forgotten institution in the West, perhaps.

I thought of my family back home and wondered how Sheila, Lisa, Ian and Rachel were. What a strange life I lived, far away from all the people who

Sr. Margaret Quinn meeting some of the villagers on the occasion of the sinking of a new well near Lake Victoria

meant everything to me. There were more sounds outside my door and I was on my feet again. This time, more than one person was moving about; then they moved off. By now, it was almost time to get up. It could not be long before first light. My watch said 5.30 a.m. I gave my face a rinse with the water from a jug and basin, which had definitely come from the old sod.

I took my ACL camera and tripod and one extra mag from the box and opened the door. Looking around, I made sure there was no one in sight. A bird started singing, or, more correctly, croaking. It must have been a parrot or a cockatoo. It was still pitch black. There were some dense bush and some high trees running down towards the lake, about 300 yards. As I walked with the tripod on my shoulder, the camera in my right hand, and spare mag under my armpit, I thought how stupid I had been to suggest a sunrise sequence on Lake Victoria! I was extremely vulnerable on my own, and wondered whether my every move was being watched by those I had heard earlier. Were the eyes of some big, wild animal watching me?

I set up close to the water. Suddenly, I was aware of a noise and some very loud movement in the bushes about 20 paces from where I stood. I swung my lens in that direction. What was I expected to do if a large animal suddenly came at me? Shoot him with my 16mm film camera? From what I knew, it was

likely to be an elephant, a lion, a baby hippo, or maybe an even large wilde-
beest. Whatever it was, it bashed about in the bushes for a few more minutes,
then, to my great relief, left in the opposite direction, displacing a large
amount of scrub and bushes as it went.

By now, there was a faint sense of light in the sky over the lake. I reposi-
tioned and focussed with water filling three-quarters of the frame in my
viewfinder and the top quarter left to be occupied by the sun as it began to
appear. I undercranked so that the sun rose more quickly in film time. It certainly was worth the wait and what a superb sunrise that was!

Next day, our team walked a long distance in the bush with some of the
sisters. One of the community, Margaret Quinn, spotted my movement and
said, 'What's wrong, Godfrey, you are carrying your right leg.' I explained that
I had a hip problem and had been in a fair amount of pain for about a year or
so. I wondered how long I could keep going in my job. She told me that, when
we got back to the hospital, she would give me something that would help. It
was my first anti-inflammatory treatment, which was of enormous help then
and for the months ahead.

Some days later, we took our leave of these remarkable women who were
and are wonderful ambassadors for our country. As I got into the van, one of
the sisters said, 'I hope our people did not disturb you the other night.' When
I asked what people, she replied, 'Our guards, of course. We have night people who patrol our complex against robbers who come from up-country.' I did
not tell her what I had been through. It would have been great to have known,
however, that those night prowlers were on my side all the time.

A POTPOURRI OF PROJECTS

ROBERT GRAVES

ROBERT GRAVES' PLANE LANDED on time at Cork Airport. Tony Barry and our team were on the tarmac. Seán Lucey, Garech de Brún and 20 special Corkonians and the Press were very excited to welcome him to Ireland. I was standing at the foot of the stairs as Robert disembarked. From the moment I got the first shot of him, I was aware of his happiness to be on Irish soil at 80 years of age.

He moved down the steps as if he were about 50. As he passed me, he acknowledged my camera, which is not always what you want. In the terminal, there was a brief press conference. Robert's warmth was a delight. His old-fashioned good manners were charming.

His party was on its way to Seán Lucy's house, situated near the centre in a pleasant part of the city, a wonderful, large, rambling garden, and lots of trees. Tony Barry was keen to film a sequence as Graves wandered through the lush greenery so I observed Robert walking as if in a dream, moving under the branches of a weeping willow, appearing, then suddenly vanishing, then suddenly re-appearing from another pathway. He broke off some branches and carried these, like some Greek hero from mythology. I hand-tracked in front and behind him, for what seemed a long time. Graves had an infectious charm. Everybody was treated in the same courteous way. There was an Irish glint in his eye, which made you feel he was up to devilment, and was ready for anything!

The next evening, our team location was at University College, Cork, where our poet was to give a reading from some of his work. Nancy McCarthy, a very dear friend of Frank O'Connor, Billy Hunt, Mary

Robert Graves and Garech de Brún arriving at Cork Airport. (Photograph: *The Irish Examiner*)

Manning, Theo Dorgan and many others were in the large audience and everyone was captivated by this great poet who, at 80, presented his work with the gaiety and enjoyment of an undergraduate presenting his first offerings in a smoke-filled coffee house. The whole event was just captivating.

We then went to the residence of the Knight of Glin, Desmond FitzGerald. There was some family connection as far as I can remember. Graves seemed to be quite at home in the elegant rooms of this fascinating house. He threw himself on a chaise longue and was offered warmed malt whiskey, which seemed to go down very well. Garech de Brún added to the warmth of the company. Robert began to tell us stories of his time in the Army in the First World War, and how he commanded Irish troops, some of whom were rabid (his word) Sinn Féin members, and how they expressed to him in no uncertain terms, their attitude to the old Empire. Robert hypnotised them with stories of his Irish ancestry, which seemed to quell their irritable attitude. He asked why they were in the trenches fighting for England. It was to support small nations, they replied.

Robert also told us how appalling trench warfare was and that he tried to write some poetry to stop himself from going mad. He sang some wonderful Irish ditties, which he said kept his spirits up. I often wonder what would have happened if Graves had met Francis Ledwidge. I have a feeling they would have got on very well. Oddly enough, Ledwidge never wrote any poetry about his time in the trenches. It was all escapist material, a protective mechanism against madness, I suppose, so that he could think of his family and his beloved Slane and County Meath,

Next day, we were on the move again, to Limerick City where Robert had connections. One of his forebears had been a Church of Ireland Bishop of Limerick. I remember photographing him with a low-angle shot as he signed the visitors' book, with a great stained-glass window towering above him.

After filming, Robert said he was dying for a pint of Guinness. Our expert electrician, Dermot O'Grady, suggested a particular pub on the corner of O'Connell Street. It was a little bit scruffy but served the best pint, not only in Limerick, but in all of Ireland. After an hour of so, when we had all settled in nicely, Robert began to relate more memories from his eventful life in public school and university, and then his emergence as an important writer and poet. I asked if had he played rugby, and he said he had. I broached the matter of the other noble game, cricket. Robert glared at me and said he hated it and that only the English could invent such a stupid game. I had to admit to him that I had a fondness for it.

Robert was sitting on a very low stool. I was on a high stool next to him. The rest of our team was scattered about the place. He enquired how long I had been seduced by this cricket thing. I said for most of my life, but that I had recently given it up because of family and work commitments. I recounted to him how I was sitting in my breakfast-room, reading the paper one morning, and had suddenly exploded with a giant sneeze. My teeth flew out of my mouth and, with my eyes shut, I managed to catch them with my left hand, my wrong hand and, when I got my breath back, shouted to my darling wife, 'Eureka! I haven't lost it. My reflexes are wholly intact.' Shortly after, I returned to the sport and played for the next 20 years with her blessing. As far as she was concerned, if you were mad enough to be obsessed by something such as cricket, there was not much hope for you.

I looked at Robert. He seemed to have gone a very peculiar green, and his folded-up 6'2" frame was beginning to vibrate as he clung to his tiny stool. An alarming thought struck me. Was I going to be remembered as the man who killed Robert Graves? Suddenly, he sprang to his full height, his face now red, but bearing a sort of mad smile. He finally got his breath back, and I said I hoped he was all right. I looked at Tony Barry, who seemed very concerned. Robert put his hand on my shoulder and said, 'Dear boy, in all my time at public school, university and the army, I have never heard a better story.'

ABOVE THE ARCTIC CIRCLE

I photographed a film about the Norwegians with Odran Walsh. The highlight for me was that we went to Tromso, above the Arctic Circle, in the far north of the country, the last port of call for the great explorers. I had always been fascinated with Polar exploration so, to be in the very place where these men had departed from, was quite a thrill.

Twenty years later, I was to return to Tromso. This time not using a film camera but a Sony 300 SP, shooting on tape. Our team was led by Dermot Horan and Cathal O'Shannon was the reporter.

We were to make a voyage in a small steamer from Tromso in the black night, out into the Norwegian Sea, calling into a little coastal village. The plan seemed straightforward but you cannot predict what the ocean is going to do. We found ourselves in a sea Force 4 and it was intensely cold. Having had something to eat, we prepared to disembark at midnight to shoot a

Cathal O'Shannon – he was not using his bike in the Arctic!

sequence as the boat docked. We did not notice while at sea that it had been snowing, the docks were covered in snow.

We shot Cathal walking the deserted streets. There wasn't a sound. We found the inn we had been told was typical of that remote area of Norway. It was just after midnight when we entered. There were eight or nine people there, all locals. You could sense they were not too pleased to see us. It struck us that maybe they didn't like crews poking their lenses or mike in their faces, when they were having a quiet drink. Who could blame them? Dermot gave the soundman Cormac Duffy and me the nod, and we began shooting as sensitively as we could.

The bar was underlit but I don't remember adding extra light because that would have been more intrusive. I got shots of the barman and some of the customers. I felt a chill as I looked down my lens at some of those faces. I do not speak Norwegian. I did not have to. I knew what they were saying and thinking. We ordered some drinks. We thought this might break the ice, it didn't. We knew the steamer was sailing at 1.30 a.m. and were glad we would be on it. We split up around the little bar. Cathal ordered a pint of something. There was a bearded gent, probably the most unfriendly and unsavoury individual in the company, standing near Cathal who had his drink on a little shelf. The rest of our team was feeling a little more relaxed. The bearded man went to the men's room. In a few minutes, he rejoined the company and stood close to Cathal. He looked him in the eye, then proceeded to stick his finger in Cathal's pint, up to his wrist. It was quite a shock. Cathal did not know what to do, whether to punch him or not. You could have heard a pin drop. They outnumbered us. At this point, we had a boat to catch. We shot some more footage and finished our drinks.

Cathal is without doubt the best company on a shoot, full of fun, with some of the best stories I have ever heard, many against himself about his times with the RAF, later working with the BBC. He is a real pro. I looked at Dermot. It was time to go. We were happy to be back on board the little steamer. It was beautifully built, with lovely wood panelling. One felt you were on a ship from another era, perhaps the 1930s.

The next morning, we were up on deck early. The steamer was battling against a Force 6 gale on one of the angriest oceans, the Norwegian Sea, above the Arctic Circle. I don't think I was ever more cold on a shoot. It was difficult to hold my feet when shooting. At one point, the little ship lurched badly to starboard. It flung me across the deck, up against the bulkhead, smashing the front of my camera, shearing off the microphone bracket and mike. No major damage, luckily. The courage of those explorers leaves one so full of admiration, when you look at bleak icy wastes they struggled in, not forgetting two of our own, the great Kerryman Tom Crean, and Ernest Shackleton who explored Antarctica and other territories.

SEÁN Ó RIADA

I was photographing the film about the sculptor, Seamus Murphy, with Seán Ó Mordha and we were in Cork for some weeks. One evening after shooting, Seán said he thought Seán Ó Riada would be having his evening drink after lectures and he knew the pub he frequented, not far from UCC. We went in and, sure enough, there was Ó Riada, sitting up on a high stool at the bar. He greeted us and ordered drinks. I knew him slightly but O Mordha knew him very well, having made a number of studio-based programmes with him. We spent an interesting hour or so with him. He looked frail.

Some time after his premature death at the age of 40 in 1971, RTÉ decided to make a major documentary about him, directed by Seán Ó Mordha. It was a joy to try to visualise his music and life in an imaginative way.

I had met Paddy Maloney in the early 1960s when he was playing with Seán Potts, many years before the Chieftains were founded. I met him again in the context of this film because Seán Ó Mordha re-staged the inaugural concert of Ceoltóirí Chualann, in the Constitution Room in the Shelbourne Hotel.

Paddy Maloney and, by then, the Chieftains came together to honour Seán Ó Riada's memory. The film explored his contribution to Irish traditional music, the expansion and use of the harpsichord, uilleann pipes and tin whistle in new ways. Eamonn de Buitlear was part of the group in those days, a fine accordion player. His work now in wildlife film has reached the pinnacle of that genre.

I remember our time in Kerry where we tried to visualise the Nomas 1 and 2, classic compositions by Seán. There was a day on the beach at Dun Chaoin spent shooting skyscapes, mountainous seas. Some of the jagged rocks on the coast. Strange shapes. In Dun Chaoin, we went back along memory lane to where Seán had enjoyed some wonderful holidays, met some of the local musicians and found his cultural identity and inspiration.

Thomas Kinsella was on holidays with him in those days. They met the **seán**ós singer, Seán de Hóra and tried to understand his music and its roots.

Another day, we were moving the camera car from one position to another, some miles up the road, and I was stretched out on the floor of the camera car, resting my back with a cushion under my head. The car was moving along at about 40 mph. We needed a piece of film to illustrate very fast musical notations. We left Dingle town along that winding road with high trees, near the convent school. As I looked up, the sun was piercing through these trees and, suddenly, I realised the tempo of the images was ideal with that piece of music. I told Seán what I had seen and we went back to look at it together. We set our camera up in a low angle position with the sun bursting dramatically through the trees at the same speed, of course. It worked very well in the film, and seemed to catch the tempo of Seán's music.

We shot a sequence in Paris at night that I particularly liked, as we re-captured the period when Ó Riada spent some difficult times there, with no money and little food, living on bananas and red wine. Ó Riada was reaching out to other cultures. He played jazz in Paris cafés, but was essentially searching for some unique link from our ancient musical tradition that he could interpret for a new generation.

We spent some time in Seán's house at Cúil Aodha in County Cork where the composer's study was fascinating. There were books on Greek mythology and French novels. Arnold Schoenberg's *Preliminary Exercises in Counterpoint* was there. He had been inspired by the days of Greek leadership in philosophy. He tried his hand at film making. There was a 16mm Bolex camera, cans of film. In a corner was an Irish harp. Earlier, he played jazz in tennis clubs in Cork, on one occasion with Bobby Lamb. Seán made a decision to look to the Celtic tradition in all its elements, steeping all his family in the language and living in Cúil Aodha. He was a jazzman in one compartment of his mind and a classical composer at a more fundamental level. Ó Riada's film score for Synge's *Playboy*, played by Ceoltóirí Chualann ,and his work with that group were simply breathtaking.

Filming in Germany some years later, I brought the LP of the soundtrack of *Mise Eire*. Some friends there were most impressed. They had never heard Irish music like that, full of power and emotion.

DARKNESS VISIBLE / MANIC DEPRESSION

Eoghan Harris wanted to make a film about manic depression for a long time. He had the sense that, in a strange way, people suffering from that condition drew strength from the very things that haunted them. Spike Milligan, John Ogden, Johnny McEvoy and Stuart Sutherland were to be the subjects. We spent a week with each of these fascinating people. Mairead de Buitlear researched the film and did the interviews.

Spike and his wife, Denise lived in an old hops house in the country in Kent. We listened to Spike telling stories of his time in the army, the brutality and how they thought he was a suitable case for treatment. The electric shock treatment, to be precise. His memories of the Goons, with Harry Secombe, Peter Sellers and Michael Bentine. One man with so many talents.

I tried to light and shoot to make the room appear as unsettled as possible. It added to the strange feeling as Spike talked about his life full of periods of depression and then explosions of creative output. Spike played the piano for us and sang something he had written. When I asked if I could take some stills he agreed but could not relax. He seemed to want to keep performing.

Johnny McEvoy is a fine ballad and folk singer, performing all over the country and abroad, constantly on the road. When we were in his house, we were taken aback at some of his revelations about the difficulties he had because of his manic depression. He spoke of a nightmare performance in a Manchester venue when everything seemed to be okay but, as the concert progressed, he began to lose control. Johnny had to fight with all the strength he could muster because he was having an attack.

At Eoghan's suggestion, Johnny agreed to re-enact the performance so we could observe the pressures. We built a rostrum seven metres high in Studio 1 at Montrose. I lit Johnny with two follow spots. We used a moviola camera dolly so we had complete freedom of movement, circling Johnny as he sang. The studio was completely black except for those two lonely spots that helped to convey the utter loneliness of the performer.

Johnny told us how he had coped through the love and support of his wife and family. He talked of how he discovered the poetry of Dylan Thomas and how much it had both stimulated and consoled him during these bad periods. At one point, he put an LP on his turntable and we heard the amazing voice of the poet. It was easy to see how the soothing insight of Thomas had a healing effect on Johnny McEvoy.

John Ogden

Meeting John Ogden and his wife was fascinating. They lived in the same house in London but each had their own quarters, separated by a steel door. John's attacks happened without warning. We were all welcomed and Eoghan talked to John's wife first. She was also a distinguished pianist and used to accompany John on tours. John Ogden joined us. He was very welcoming and told us he had fond memories of visits to Dublin, where the audience was always very warm.

Eoghan asked John to play for us. He was a big bear of a man. The moment his fingers stroked the keys, it was electric. His command was breathtaking. I shot with the lens on the level of the keyboard as John played Rachmaninoff's *Third Piano Concerto*. His performance seemed to suck my camera in. From that position, I could tilt to a close-up of his head and then explore his eyes. We all seemed to be drained when he stopped. After we had finished shooting in the music room, I asked John if I could photograph him with my still camera. He agreed.

Author, playwright and university lecturer, Stuart Sutherland, lived in Brighton, a few doors from where Parnell had visited Kitty O'Shea. He was your typical, cool Englishman. His house was comfortable. Books everywhere. A well-stocked wine cabinet. He reminisced about how one evening, having returned home from delivering a lecture, he put on an LP. The music was the theme for the television series, *Van der Valk*. As he listened, the melody seemed to take him over. He moved towards the wine rack and began to juggle two very expensive bottles. He was experiencing an attack. He was out of control. On another occasion, in a London art gallery, he began to bid for paintings costing between £20,000 and £40,000, money he did not have.

We met Anthony Clare outside Britain's National Gallery in Travalgar Square at 6.30 a.m. Special permission had been granted for us to take Clare with us into the Gallery before it was open to the public. Tony wanted to show us some unfinished Michelangelo paintings to illustrate that here was another artist who had struggled. It was a strange feeling, surrounded by such marvellous works, all at our disposal. Tony brought his own particular insight to the film that was most revealing.

Observing artists as we did in the *Darkness Visible* series with Eoghan Harris was an amazing, enriching privilege. In fact, Harris is one of the five or six directors I worked with who really made things happen on the screen. He didn't always get it right but then who does? But I felt lucky to be part of his team and to see what he could create when he followed his instincts.

The year after working with John Ogden in London, he came to Dublin to play Rachmaninoff's *Third Piano Concerto* at the National Concert Hall. Sheila and I were there. The first movement went well, John had lost none of his powers. The second movement was also absorbing. My mind went back to the time we met him in London with Harris during the shooting of the film, when he played for us.

Sitting in the National Concert Hall, I listened to him playing the third movement, which I was familiar with. Suddenly, as the Rachmaninoff music took off into an exquisite run of notes, something snapped and my eyes filled with tears. I tried to control them but couldn't. My shoulders began to shake. Sitting beside me in the middle of the parterre, Sheila gripped my hand and put her other hand on my knee. I was totally overcome with the emotion and the music Ogden's performance had produced. It lasted for three or four minutes. Nothing like this ever happened to me before. It was a feeling of joy, an appreciation of Rachmaninoff's music and an awareness that, as one of Eoghan Harris's team, I had spent time with one of the world's great pianists.

ON THE MOVE AGAIN

RUSSIA

IT WAS EARLY MORNING in Connemara. A young woman had risen early, dressed, grabbed a cup of coffee and a piece of toast. She checked the strings of her fiddle, wrapped the instrument in a soft duster, gave the bow a wipe and was gone. Mary was on her way to Moscow. Some of her friends had got together and were giving a session in a small music hall in the Russian capital and at the Writers' Centre in Leningrad.

Eoghan Harris was the editor of *Cursaí* at the time and wanted to shoot a programme in Russia. Our film team was led by Michael P. O'Conghaile, a Connemara man.

Our Aeroflot plane arrived late at night in Moscow. A small battered bus took us to the outskirts of the city and stopped. The driver got out and lifted the engine flap at the back of the vehicle. He tinkered for about 20 minutes as we all froze. Two of us got out with a large torch and offered assistance. The driver shrugged and gave a grunt. At least, he could now see the engine. Ten minutes went by. He tried again. It started. By the time we reached the hotel, we were famished. I have never enjoyed a hot bath more than I did that night.

The first concert went well the next evening. The audience was intrigued with the uilleann pipes. All our musicians played well. Most had never been to Russia. The performance ended at 10.30 p.m. We had to be on the midnight train for Leningrad. A tall order, it was the fastest de-rig I ever saw.

We got to the station where Ed Lynch and I grabbed a porter and I jammed a twenty-dollar bill into his hand and said, 'Leningrad.' We threw the equipment onto his trolley and, like a Cossack commander, he charged down the middle of the platform shouting an order that seemed to have the desired effect. People threw themselves out of his way. In due course, we got to the Leningrad train. Most things do not work on time in Russia but the Moscow to Leningrad Express goes on the stroke of midnight. You can imagine how we felt as we fell into our sleepers, four to a compartment – Mike P., myself and two Russians. One was knocked out on his bunk, having drunk a bottle of vodka, and the other, a gentleman of Mongolian origin, was also asleep a half bottle of vodka clutched to his chest.

By then the train was getting up to speed. Mike put his head over the bunk and said that he was starving. There was no dining car at that time of night. He began to rustle in a brown paper bag and came out with some brown scones from Lydons of Galway. Sheila had given me an apple and a tin of sardines. We had nothing to drink and eyed the vodka, then thought better of it. It was one of the best snacks I ever had. The train hurtled through the Russian night. We were a long way from Connemara.

I got up early, before dawn. Mike thought a dawn sequence as we neared Leningrad would be effective. The first light began to chink through the window blinds at 5.30 a.m. I have never been able to sleep properly on a plane,

The fight to save Leningrad

train or boat. I had stored the camera in the bunk with me to keep it warm. I got out as quietly as I could, so as not to wake my companions.

I was so lucky. The snow was covered with a blue light, slowly changing to pink and then to red. I went to the end of the carriage and out through the dividing doors so I could get to a window I could open. I was hit by a blast of cold air that I will never forget. I looked through my viewfinder and the trees stretched as far as I could see. There was an occasional smallholding.

My camera was like a looking glass, I felt, showing me the outskirts of Leningrad but also opening up a vast tapestry of Russian heritage as the images rushed past my lens. I could almost hear the voices of the siege of Leningrad. Suddenly into my mind came the memory of seeing Dmitri Shostakovich striding into St. Patrick's Cathedral in Dublin in 1972 to hear his Chamber Symphony Inc played by the RTÉ Concert Orchestra. Of course, his seventh symphony is a stunning record of that struggle. It has always greatly moved me. Now I was actually here. My lens began to fog up. I let it run. It gave me a gradual fog effect and eventually the image disappeared.

I shot for as long as I could before the cold forced me to stop. The next day in Leningrad, I was walking down a street with a friend who pointed out a sign on a building opposite which said, 'Don't walk on this side of the street, the shells of the enemy will hit you. Stay on the other pavement.' This sign was left there to remind the current generation of that great sacrifice.

I got to Leningrad's wonderful Mariinsky Theatre for a performance of the Kirov Borodin's *Prince Igor*. To think of the music that has been performed here, the great ballets staged in this theatre. Tchaikovsky's *Swan Lake* and *The Sleeping Beauty*. Igor Stravinsky's *The Firebird* and *Petrushka*. Dancers like Nijinsky, Lydia Lopokova, Léonide Massine and Galina Ulanova. What names!

I walked up a magnificent staircase that curved like a swan's neck, into a beautiful room on one of the theatre's many levels. The rosewood panelling was breathtaking. A marvellous ceiling floated above us. There was a circular space beside a beautiful curved bar. As people got their drinks, they began to walk anti-clockwise around this space, in twos and threes. It was not long before 50 to 60 people were promenading, elegant couples, individuals, not in formal dress but well-dressed, smart. Older people who had obviously been coming to the Kirov all their lives. The prices were subsidised, one of the few good things in the communist system.

I joined the snake-like procession. All the people had a drink in their hand as they walked; I had my glass of red wine. I felt like a dancer in a ballet, promenading with such an assortment of different characters out of a Russian plot. I could almost hear the music, as everyone was forced to walk at the same tempo. It was if, at any moment, the Ballet Master would appear and take over the class.

As I walked, I could hear my ballet mistress Evelyn Birchall in her lovely St. Stephen's Green studio from 50 years earlier, screaming at me, 'Godfrey, don't hunch your shoulders like that, relax your head deportment.' I was ten. In those days, the great ballet companies came to the Gaiety Theatre. Sadler's Wells, the Ballet Rambert, the Antonio Spanish Company. I would queue for tickets in the 'gods' where the cheapest seats were located. From about mid-day, I would sit on the pavement outside the ticket office, armed with a flask and sandwiches. The doors of the ticket office opened at 7.30 p.m., by which time there were some 150 people in the 'gods' queue. You had to be at the head of the queue so that, when the doors opened, you could run up the ten flights to get a seat in the first or second row.

I saw *Swan Lake* there, *Petrushka, The Firebird, Giselle, Prince Igor.* My imagination took off. It may have been the Hungry Fifties but seeing those ballets and, most of all, hearing that music gave me a lifelong love for music and dance. Not as an elitist thing, just to live and breathe such beauty. And now to be actually in the Kirov Theatre in Leningrad.

Then the bell rang and the corps de ballet that I was part of snaked off to watch the real thing. My fantasy was over.

The Writers' Museum in Leningrad was also a very interesting building, housing a small theatre with great character and some beautiful plaster-work. The audience loved our traditional music and showed great interest in the group.

After the concert, we found ourselves in a beautiful little restaurant, full of tobacco smoke. Many of the audience were there and told us how much they had enjoyed the performance. Our host invited us to join them the next day at the Memorial to the Fallen. The scale of this statue is hard to describe. Imagine a vast figure, half the size of Dublin's Liberty Hall, and you get some idea of the magnitude. It depicts a woman in her 40s, Mother Russia.

It was the most moving large statue I have ever seen. We were all seized by the power of this marvellous work. Suddenly, there was a sound of a click. Our uileann pipe player was opening the box containing his pipes. He began to play the most haunting melody. It was wonderful to hear the Irish music rising up in this most Russian of surroundings. Snow began to fall.

Our piper's playing moved us all. Our Russian hosts were in tears.

The next day we had some free time. Dmitri, a young man from the writers' centre, invited me to have tea with him in a restaurant frequented by some of the contemporary Russian writers. As I walked along the canals, I was so impressed by the symmetry and colour of the buildings. There were some magnificent bronze statues of some of the heroes and artists. Their reflections danced in the water, as if they were still alive.

We took tea together from a handsome samovar, and the conversation came round to Dublin. He was so knowledgeable about Dublin's literary giants – Joyce, Wilde, O'Casey, Beckett and Yeats. He could not believe that I had worked with Patrick Kavanagh, Austin Clarke, John Banville, Mary Lavin, Edna O'Brien and James Plunkett, or that my grandparents' house, where I lived for the first seven years of my life, was now the James Joyce Centre and that I was a director of that institution. He was also interested when I told him that we run the James Joyce Film Festival at the house.

He took a small book out of his bag, saying it was for me. It was a book of Irish short stories by Frank O'Connor, Mary Lavin, John Banville and James Plunkett in Russian. I treasured the book for many years. Later, when the Society of Irish Writers was honouring James Plunkett for his 80th birthday, I had the great pleasure of giving Jim the little book from Leningrad. The presentation took place in the James Joyce Centre.

THE GATE THEATRE IN JERUSALEM

The Gate Theatre was bringing *Juno and the Paycock* to Jerusalem. What a cast – John Kavanagh, Donal McCann, Geraldine Plunkett and Maureen Potter. Joe Dowling had directed the production in Dublin and now, Michael Colgan, the Gate's artistic director, led the company.

It was fascinating to watch the production team, lighting designer, floor management, carpenters and electricians presenting this unique theatrical event so far from home. Louis Lentin was making *Juno in Jerusalem,* a documentary about the visit. It was wonderful to spend time with these world-class actors in such an exotic location as Jerusalem, definitely one of the more fascinating cities I have ever worked in.

The production team had a major construction job to do, fitting the sets shipped from Dublin to the theatre in Jerusalem. They worked day and night to ensure it would be ready in time.

During the shoot, we filmed at an opening reception given by our hosts,

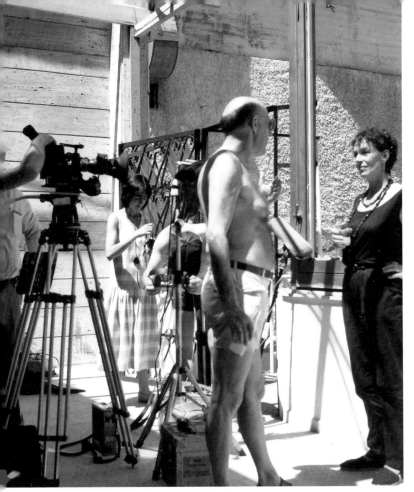

John Hall, Mary O'Riordan, Louis Lentin and Geraldine Plunkett

An arab refugee in a temporary camp since 1948

talking to actors, local critics and Michael Colgan. On a walk through the old city with members of the company, we went into the Church of the Holy Sepulchre. A magical experience. As we walked through the city's narrow streets with some of the cast, I fell into conversation with Maureen Potter, whom I knew only slightly before the visit. When the conversation turned to cricket, I discovered that she was a fanatical fan and a great supporter of Clontarf Cricket Club in Dublin. She knew a lot about the game, particularly English and test match cricket, so we had something in common as we sat in the shade on the steps of a narrow street while Louis decided on the next shot.

President Chaim Herzog attended the opening night. I had met him before on another film with Joe Mulholland and Brian Farrell at his home in Tel Aviv. It was a pleasure to meet him again. Barry McGovern was also presenting a Beckett production at another theatre.

An elaborate translation system was in operation. Members of the audience were using headphones and, as they watched the stage, a group of linguists followed the dialogue, giving simultaneous translations of the action in Hebrew. This was quite unique to observe, and the Israeli audience seemed to identify in a very intimate way with the troubles that the O'Casey characters experienced in the play, and Ireland's struggle to emerge as an independent republic.

Another night, we filmed parts of the play. This is now a unique, albeit brief, record of the performances of Donal McCann, John Kavanagh and Maureen Potter. Fortunately, the lighting designer, Rupert Murray had introduced enough light onto the stage to enable me to shoot without any additional illumination, something that would not have been permitted, of course.

While in Israel, our team got an opportunity to visit the profoundly moving sculpture depicting the Holocaust. That image will remain with me forever. We visited a refugee camp where Arabs had been told way back in 1948 they were going for a temporary period. The tragedy of the displacement of the Arab people is something the Israelis should understand, given the Jewish experience and their long journey to find their homeland. We met one man (his picture is presented on previous page), who had spent most of his life in this 'temporary' refugee camp. He had tremendous dignity and lived in just two very small, bare rooms but, despite his horrible experience, retained a gentleness of spirit that inspired all of us who met him. I often wonder whether he is still alive.

NELSON MANDELA

Cormac Duffy, Dermot O'Grady and I were shooting in Nairobi, Kenya, with Adrian Moynes. We had completed the programme and Adrian took us out for dinner before we flew home to Dublin. My telephone rang in the small hours of the morning. I immediately thought something had happened to Sheila or the children.

It was Andrew Shepard speaking from the RTÉ newsroom. He asked if I could get to Lusaka in Zambia as soon as possible. I told him we were finished our film and that I would speak to the rest of the party to see if they were prepared to travel. Andrew told me that Gerard Collins, our Minister for Foreign Affairs, was on his way to Lusaka to meet Nelson Mandela who had been released from prison some time earlier. He would be meeting him

Gerard Collins and Nelson Mandela

Waiting for Yasser Arafat in Zambia
(Photograph: Cormac Duffy)

two days later. In the morning, I asked my colleagues if they were prepared to travel. Adrian gave us his blessing and a few hundred dollars.

The next problem was to book air tickets to Lusaka and back to Ireland. The travel agent was terrific. He had no idea who we were but, when I told him we had to get to Lusaka urgently to meet Nelson Mandela, he gave us three tickets that were charged to RTÉ.

We had no hotel booking in Lusaka. When we got into the capital, we made enquiries but could not get any reservations or any information with regard to hotels. It was getting dark. A gentleman approached us and said he was an agent for a very nice motel on the outskirts of Lusaka. He could arrange for us to be taken there by taxi. With no alternative, we accepted the offer and loaded our equipment and all our bits and pieces into a really bashed-up taxi that took us down very poor roads to what looked like a motel. Cormac, Dermot and I have travelled a lot and we have been in some very dodgy places but this hotel looked terrible.

We went into the reception but felt uneasy because there were three men standing there. One, a receptionist, approached us but the other two were quite obviously guards. They were armed. They did not want to speak English to us. They gave us three keys and demanded full payment of the bill, in dollars only, before we went any further. The three rooms were side by side and to say that we were unhappy is a bit of an understatement.

We got into our rooms and it was quite obvious that the bathrooms and other parts of the room were not clean. There was a bad smell. A number of large spiders were visible. There were also small reptiles on the wall, four or five inches long, dashing in and out of holes. Dermot, Cormac and I were extremely unsettled by the whole situation and, as I recall, we decided we would all sleep in the same room that night with all our equipment, each of us taking turns to keep watch.

The next morning, we couldn't wait to get out of the place. We went to the Hilton Hotel and checked at reception, to be told rooms had been reserved for us the night before. What a sickener! Our Consul in Lusaka, Frank Whelan, was in an adjoining lounge and when we told him where we had stayed, he was visibly shocked. Frank was very friendly to us. We went out to the Consulate, had a coffee and met the other members of the Irish diplomatic service and Zambian members of staff. A bottle of Jameson appeared very promptly to lace our coffee.

That afternoon, we went out to the airport. Frank Whelan gave us a VW Golf for our stay and great support. Yasser Arafat and other presidents of the non-aligned states were meeting in Lusaka. Finally, Arafat's plane stopped exactly opposite our camera position and we were able to get some very good footage of him. We also shot extensively at government buildings where we met President Karundi.

The next day, Gerard Collins arrived. We found him extremely good company and he really appreciated that we made the journey at short notice to be there to record his meeting with Nelson Mandela. Una O'Hagan from the RTÉ newsroom had also arrived and she was going to carry out the interview.

At Government House, we were given a room in which to photograph Nelson Mandela. Cormac, Dermot and I started to rig the 600 Watt Red Heads and sound gear. An official approached me, saying, 'No lights permitted.' I took a very firm position, as Dermot did. We had travelled a long way for a most important interview with probably the most prominent individual in the world at that time. I was not going to shoot an underlit picture of a black man in a darkened room. We won the day.

When Mandela entered the room, a tremendous calm fell over the place. His presence exuded warmth. President Karundi, Gerard Collins and Mandela talked for a few minutes. Our Minister introduced us to Mandela and explained that we had come at short notice from Nairobi. Una conducted a very interesting interview but had to catch a plane. Gerard Collins presented him with a facsimile of the Book of Kells.

I brought the tape to a television station on the edge of the jungle and participated with the operator in sending our picture and sound to London via satellite and on to Dublin. Before I got back to my hotel, Irish viewers had seen the interview.

THE PEACE PROCESS

Frank Hand, the producer, was researching with Mairead de Buitlear a programme about the individuals who had brought the peace process forward. It was generally accepted that Niall O'Dowd, the editor of *The Irish Voice* newspaper in New York, had played an important role. Frank Hand was at Gormanstown School in County Meath with Niall, so there was a rapport, and memories of football and athletics.

Pat Johns and I were assigned. We started in Drogheda, where we met Niall's mother, a charming person, and other members of the family, before flying to New York, one of the most exciting cities on the planet. It's a joy for a cameraman, pictures everywhere. We have been influenced from childhood by movies set in that city and feel at home there; it's not surprising that so many Irish have got on so well in that wonderful place. There was a great buzz in the offices of *The Irish Voice,* where we spent some time. Bruce Morrison is an interesting guy, seemed to have a great grasp for what needed to be done. Morrison did so much and fought for the visas that were so badly needed by so many young Irish. The visas bore his name. We had a good interview with this very bright man.

In Washington, Ted Kennedy was on the floor of the House when our party arrived. One of his aides brought us to a private room not usually open to visitors. Niall presented Frank Hand's team from Ireland. This seemed to make a difference. It was quite obvious that this was a personal drawing room with its comfortable couches, easy chairs, pictures of all the Kennedy family, a large number of items from Ireland, from J. F. Kennedy's trip in 1963, and a signpost to Ballybunion. We chatted for 15 minutes.

We watched Ted on TV as he finished his speech in which he talked about social conditions for ordinary people, including health. This has been a constant theme over his political career. The Senator joined us. 'Be with you shortly, must freshen up.' He re-joined us after a change in his private quarters. We spent a very pleasant hour in his company after the interview.

Godfrey Graham, Pat Johns, Frank Hand, Senator Edward Kennedy, Mairead de Buitleir and Margaret Costello. (Photograph: Niall O'Dowd)

I got the sense that we were genuinely welcome. I mentioned that I had been in the television press corps when his brother visited Ireland in 1963. He was interested and, of course, Ted's sister Jean was with Jack on that occasion. Jean went on to become US Ambassador to Ireland. I had been in very close proximity to the President for most of that week. A few short months later, he was dead.

We got a long interview with Nancy Soderbergh, the then US representative at the UN She was most revealing about Niall's importance as a go-between for Sinn Féin and the Clinton administration, and that it took some time before enough trust was built up to give Gerry Adams a visa.

Niall O'Dowd had targeted Clinton early on, long before he was running for the Presidency. At an event we met Senator George Mitchell and his wife. Mitchell must have agonised when dealing with the Unionists and the Republicans, wondering if there would ever be a meeting of minds or would they ever trust each other.

O'Dowd and others had lobbied people of goodwill of Irish descent and others, and their achievement will go down in history. This does not mean there is not still a long way to travel. For our team it was fascinating to get

Frank Hand, Pat Johns, Godfrey Graham, Mairead de Buitléir and Margaret Costello in New York

a look at, and to meet some of the major players, such as George Mitchell, Bruce Morrison, Gerry Adams, Garry McMichael and David Irvine.

One Saturday, we went down to Long Island with Niall and his wife. They had extended an invitation to us to visit her family and spend Saturday afternoon with them. They were going to have a barbecue. I can tell you this sounded good to us. We had been filming for about ten days in the sweltering heat.

Long Island is where Jay Gatsby and Nick Caraway drank their way through the summer of 1922 in the classic novel, *The Great Gatsby*. When we visited our friends in Long Island, we noticed that many of the houses are built with clapboard on the outsides. The place has a really English look, reminiscent of that background. Not too far from where we were are the Hamptons, where those with really old money used to live and still do. In more recent decades, the Kennedys, with slightly newer money, settled in the area and still have their place there today.

It didn't take too long to drive down to Long Island, a lovely residential area. The garden was about the size of two tennis courts, with some nice tall green trees. Niall and Pat Johns were playing soccer. Both had been

George Mitchell and Niall O'Dowd

useful soccer players in their youth. A couple of others were pitching short golf shots in the garden. Some others were playing hurling. Conversations started up about all these different sports. I had a cricket ball so I began to bowl in one corner of the garden. Sport is a great uniter, if played in the right spirit. Later, we sat down to a most marvellous American barbecue.

When I picked up my first box brownie camera all those years ago, bought in O'Neill's Pharmacy in Blackrock, I never dreamed it would lead me to so many countries but, best of all, to meet so many fascinating people.

HOME AGAIN...

Peter Canning was making a film about Paddy Carey. Although we had gone to video by then, Peter felt it would be appropriate to shoot the programme on Super 16mm film, in memory of Paddy Carey. I was very pleased to be involved.

Some eight years earlier, I'd had lunch with Paddy Carey in the Shelbourne Hotel two days before he went back to Canada, a disillusioned man. Paddy had spent 20 years in Canada, some of that time with the National Film Board of Canada, and had done very distinguished and award-winning work.

He had shot special sequences in a number of feature films, including the stunning opening sequence of *A Man For All Seasons*, considered a classic. In

Ireland, he had made the films *Yeats Country* for the Department of External Affairs, *Errigal* and *Mists of Time*, but found soon afterwards that there was no more work coming his way, despite enormous recognition for these three films from the public and arts circles in Ireland. I had always been very impressed with Paddy's direction and his cinematography.

Paddy Carey and Maureen Hurley visited my home in Glenageary on one of his last visits home. Sometimes in Ireland the appreciation for the artist is short-lived, despite great achievements. People go in and out of fashion. The memory of the arts establishment, whether in broadcasting or in other disciplines of the arts, is fickle and subject to change. Lasting recognition for the visual artist is far too rare. This is more a reflection on the so-called judges of what is good and of great merit, some of whom have never created anything of artistic merit themselves.

In Ireland, some arts administrators are great street fighters and very ambitious but leave a lot to be desired when dealing with creative people.

THE JAMES JOYCE FILM FESTIVAL

The Board of the James Joyce Centre had agreed to run a film festival and, in 1994, we started with Seán Ó Mordha's *Is There One Who Understands Me?*, produced by RTÉ, which won an Emmy Award. The second year, RTÉ took over the sponsorship of the event. *The Scandal of Ulysses,* directed by Ian Graham, and John Lynch's *A Painful Case* from Joyce's *Dubliners*, starring Sian Phillips, Mick Lally, Ray McAnally and Olwen Foueré, were screened. This film, made by RTÉ and Channel 4, went all over the world.

Our audiences of Joyceans and members of the public who wanted to learn more about Joyce, seemed to love the event. We have always strived to make the Centre a vibrant place, a living tribute to the works of Joyce. A film version of *Exiles,* the only play Joyce wrote, was received well. It was the first drama colour production made by the national broadcaster in collaboration with the Abbey Theatre, directed by Donal Farmer.

What seemed to be happening at our festivals was fascinating. We were screening in the Kenmare Room, one of the most elegant rooms in the house, to an audience of about 90, which created a homely atmosphere. A great mirror hanging over the fireplace picked up reflections from the magnificent ceiling, on which Stapleton and Thorpe had created the Grecian maidens. They seemed to float above our heads in the flickering light from the projector.

1997 was the year we first screened John Houston's *The Dead*. This film stands head and shoulders above all other films based on Joyce's work. Anjelica Houston and Donal McCann, Dan O'Herlihy, Donal Donnelly and Marie Keane were all magnificent. The whole ensemble company gave a unique performance, including Frank Patterson with his lyrical singing of *The Lass of Aughrim*. Joyce's short story is so intimate, the reader and viewer of the film are sucked in and become part of the lives of the characters.

I remember leaving the Kenmare Room at one point. I came out onto the landing and walked down the elegant staircase. Alone, I was suddenly aware of the voices of Joyce's characters that seemed to follow me. It was the dinner scene where Gabriel thanks his hosts. Suddenly, I was aware, as if for the first time, of the living Dublin, then and now. The Dublin characters seemed to be coming up the stairs to meet me. The interior of the house is so evocative of many of the scenes in Joyce's work. I sat on the stairs and listened to the dialogue and to Alex North's score. As a little boy over 60 years ago, I sat on these same stairs, frightened of the dark.

Joe Barry, the Director General of RTÉ, opened the festival for us. Bob Collins continued the support. Jean Kennedy Smith, the US Ambassador, honoured us with many visits and also opened the Film Festival. Veronica Sutherland, the British Ambassador, officiated at another. Both these women played a significant role in the Peace Process. Gregory Peck and Martin Scorsese visited the Joyce Centre in the early 1990s.

Joyce and his friend, Constantine Curran, walked on North Great George's Street on his last visit to Dublin in 1912. I like to think that, if Joyce were to come back now to Dublin in cold, bleak January during our film festival, and wander by his old school, Belvedere College, turning left down North Great George's Street and passing No. 35, he might just hear the voices of some of the characters he created coming from deep behind the great wooden shutters and through the windows which stretch almost from floor to ceiling. These characters still live today in the minds of people who read books all over the world – in Europe, the Americas, China and beyond. These readers continue to be fascinated by the genius of an Irishman, James Joyce, whose spirit still inhabits the pavements of dear old Dublin and will do so 'til the end of time.

FINALE

I heard the sound of my post landing in the hall. There was an envelope with a harp on it, not black, but gold. It was an invitation from President Mary McAleese to join her and others who had been involved in Radio Telefís Éireann over the 40 years to a party on Wednesday 13 November 2002 to celebrate.

The President welcomed us warmly. She is a perfect host. You really feel that Mary McAleese loves to welcome people. It was a strange feeling as I mingled with colleagues with whom I had worked over half a lifetime. There was Myles Merriman who was in the film editing department at the beginning of Irish television in 1961, sitting not far away from where I worked at another editing bench. Myles went on to edit *Strumpet City*. Suddenly, Ken Murphy, the man who photographed *Strumpet City*, was by my side. Both were in great form. Sheamus Smith was in company with the President chatting and on the other side was John Kelleher, ex-Programme Controller at RTÉ who was about to take over the job of Film Censor, following in the footsteps of Smith.

I bumped into Dick Hill, the producer with whom I had worked on the series *Into Europe* in the mid-1960s, and other documentaries. Dick went on to be Programme Controller. The nice thing about Dick is that he was great company and simply had a passion for making good programmes. As he rose to the senior position, his main attribute, I remember, was that he made it possible for other producers who followed in his footsteps to make very fine documentaries. You always felt that, if you went to him with a good idea there was a great chance he would get behind it and support you.

In conversation with the President, I mentioned that I was working on a book of my memories of those 40 years at RTÉ, experiencing the ups and downs of that period. 'Stick at it, Godfrey,' she said, 'we need that record.'

I turned round and bumped into Mike Murphy. Like others, I missed Mike since he left broadcasting. He was always a bundle of laughs to make programmes with and we soldiered together on a number of them. John Bowman was deep in conversation with Cathal Gohan. I felt a touch on my shoulder. It was David Kelly, who played Rashers in Tony Barry's *Strumpet City*. 'When you are going home, dear boy, could I have a lift with you? No hurry, of course.'

As I enjoyed the hospitality, mingled with the company and moved around the beautiful rooms at Áras an Uachtaráin, my thoughts went back to how it all began 40 years ago and how I got into Radio Telefís Éireann two weeks after it went on the air, and the love and support from my young wife Sheila, when we had just bought a house by the skin of our teeth. Where had all the years gone?

I sat on an elegant chair beside a tall window, looking out on the beautiful gardens. It was dusk. As I looked out the window to the darkening gardens, I noticed reflections of the guests as they passed in and out of the panes of glass in the immense window, which stretched from floor to ceiling. There was some distortion. It set my memory reflecting back from those figures of my colleagues. Although blurred, they reminded me of people I had met. One image was of an 80-year-old man in the west of Ireland who was watching us film an interview with a farmer. When we were finished, the ancient one approached us and said with the typical good manners of a country person, 'Sorry to interrupt ye but, would I be right in thinking that you were taking likenesses there?' This was straight out of J.M. Synge or before.

The image changed again. It seemed to be the figure of a man whom I met while filming in jail, who told me that he had been abused in Letterfrack Industrial School by two religious brothers for some minor offence. He was forced to dig his own grave then told to lie down in it. Then they began to shovel soil over his feet and legs, working their evil way up to his face before he had a convulsion and began to tremble all over. The brothers just walked away. This unfortunate man was serving a life sentence for murder when I met him.

Once again, the reflection changed. It seemed to be a group of four people had moved into my vision. Suddenly, it brought me back to the John Field Room in the National Concert Hall, with the Vanburgh String Quartet playing two of E.J. Moeran's string quartets, one metre away from where Jim Plunkett and I were listening with all our concentration. Jim was over 80 by then. He savoured every note. He was so close to the players. I watched Jim's face. He was as happy as I ever saw him.

Outside, the wind was getting up, blowing what remained of the last of the autumn leaves in little circles. Before my eyes were broadcasters I had the privilege of working with, all different, all with their own unique skills in so many diverse areas of television. A voice said, 'Isn't this pleasant, Godfrey?' It was David Kelly again. He sat beside me. He has made such a contribution to theatre, cinema and television.

This special occasion touched me, I suppose because it seemed to telescope 40 years into an instant. All the figures passing in front of me. I wanted to reach out to some of them, to reminisce, to go down memory lane. We had made so many programmes together. It was all passing now; we were almost all retired or nearing retirement age. But what memories we shared!

It was dark now. David and I took our leave of the President and, as we walked to where I had parked the car, the breeze began to increase. We bent over and dipped our heads against the wind. The leaves seemed to follow at our feet.

Those two hours at Áras an Uachtaráin seemed to symbolise the completion of some sort of journey, a journey you are not fully aware of until some event or happening focuses the mind.

REFLECTIONS

PUTTING TOGETHER THIS BOOK has stirred my own curiosity about my family and what they were up to in the 1890s. Like most parents, my father gave me some information about our family, but it was very sketchy. It is only when our parents die that we children develop a thirst for family history. By then, it is often too late.

I owe a great debt of gratitude to Liam O Laoghaire, the cinema historian. We were colleagues at RTÉ in the early 1960s. Liam would stop me in the corridor or in the restaurant and say, 'I have just found out something more about your grandfather's cinemas!' He would have some gem about the title of the films screened in my grandfather's movie-houses. He found articles in the *Bioscope of London,* and an advertisement in the Sinn Féin magazine of the day reporting on Dickie Graham's cinemas in 1911 and 1913. He installed a new Kamm projector from London, following which the first *Buffalo Bill* film was screened in Ireland. Could he have ever imagined that his grandson would be a cameraman working all over the world?

What would he have thought of my meeting someone like Nelson Mandela in Africa, shooting an interview with him, driving to a small TV station on the edge of the bush near Lusaka, inserting a tape of my pictures and Cormac Duffy's sound into a machine which, via a satellite 22,000 miles above the earth, bounced the package back to Dublin where my wife, Sheila, saw it on the news before I even got back to my hotel!

According to Liam O Laoghaire, Dickie Graham was the first person to own and run a cinema in Dublin in 1911. As a lighting cameraman, I would suggest that the attraction to film remained in the family. Ian Graham, my son, has directed four documentaries on Joyce, the definitive film on Swift, a movie about Bram Stoker, and RTÉ's recent tribute to James Plunkett. So

Liam O Laoghaire. Liam is holding the film slicer used by Robert Flaherty while editing *Man of Aran*

the images projected by my grandfather in 1911 in Capel Street were glimpses into the future of a new medium to which his family would continue to make a contribution.

FOR PATRICK KAVANAGH

The poet's eye saw a flash of blue
as he sat there by the stream.
He did not know what he really saw,
or was it a dream.
It moved again it's wounded wing,
his feet were in the brook.
His large hand cupped about the bird, it looked.
The poet felt the beating heart,
as the head moved side to side.
What caused the meeting of these two souls
in the Monaghan countryside?

— G.G.

INDEX